More reactions to *War Plan Iraq*

'Most Iraqis, whether inside Iraq or in exile feel that
and illegal. *War Plan Iraq* proves that opposing the w
ing Saddam's regime. Opposing the war means sup
   'Impressive documentation, clear analysis and con
the US-led war on the Iraqi people: Milan Rai addresses issues facing Iraqis in
relation to the drive for war with rare insight into Iraqi society. Crucially, he
also covers the link between the war on Iraq and the Nekba in Palestine, the
fate of the Kurdish people, and relations with Turkey, Iran and the Arab world.'
   Haifa Zangana, Iraqi writer in exile
   member of Act Together: Women against sanctions and war on Iraq

'It is vitally important to get across to the British people that Trident is being
aimed at what appears to be a non-nuclear country, and that there are nonvio-
lent ways of dealing with Iraq's suspected weapons of mass destruction. *War
Plan Iraq* is a valuable contribution to these efforts.'
   Carol Naughton,
   Chair of the British Campaign for Nuclear Disarmament (CND)

'This excellent book reveals the extent of the injustices perpetrated against the
Iraqi people.'
   Alice Mahon MP

'This book is an excellent weapon for all those opposed to Bush's war. Compul-
sory reading for every centre-left politician.'
   Tariq Ali

'A remarkably thorough account, and required reading for anyone concerned
about the risk of war.'
   Paul Rogers,
   Professor of Peace Studies, Bradford University

'A timely and important book.'
   Hilary Wainwright,
   Red Pepper

Reactions to previous publications by Milan Rai

Gene Genie: Making Choices About Genetic Engineering
The Text Of The Exhibition (Drava Papers, 2001)

'*Gene Genie*'s striking imagery and thoughtful analysis pose important questions and help to promote democratic decision-making about the release of genetically-engineered organisms.'
> Ben Savill, Research and Campaigns Officer,
> National Federation of Women's Institutes

'*Gene Genie* sets out the science behind genetic engineering in a simple and understandable way - a valuable tool.'
> Kathryn Tulip, Genetix Snowball

Tactical Trident: The Rifkind Doctrine and the Third World (Drava Papers, 1995)

'As an example of how rich countries gamble with the security of their own people to maintain influence and control across the globe, this is vital reading'.
> Greg Kent, *Spur*, The World Development Movement magazine

'It is vital that public debate based on knowledge of reality of the British Bomb rather than vague generalities about "defence" and "deterrence" takes place. This pamphlet is an essential contribution to that debate.'
> Janet Bloomfield,
> Chair of the British Campaign for Nuclear Disarmament (CND)

'An effective study of a core part of British defence policy which is all too easily ignored.'
> Paul Rogers, Professor of Peace Studies, Bradford University

'Excellent.'
> Bob Aldridge, former Trident designer

Britain, Maastricht and the Bomb:
The Foreign and Security Policy Implications of the Treaty of European Union
(Drava Papers, 1993)

'Of all the hours of debate on the Maastricht Treaty that dominated the British Parliament, and to a lesser extent other member states' Parliaments, few were spent on the crucial issues of the future foreign and defence policy of a "united" Western Europe. Milan Rai's thoroughly researched pamphlet lifts the lid of this exceptionally murky aspect of the Maastricht process.'
> Jeremy Corbyn MP (from the Preface)

War Plan Iraq

War Plan Iraq

Ten Reasons Against War On Iraq

MILAN RAI

VERSO

London • New York

First published by ARROW Publications on 11 September 2002.
This edition first published by Verso 2002.

Photographs © 2002 Kim Weston-Arnold
Wood engravings and lino cuts © 2002 Emily Johns
Text (apart from Chapters I and II) © 2002 Milan Rai
'Terror and Just Response' © 2002 Noam Chomsky

1 3 5 7 9 10 8 6 4 2

Verso
UK: 6 Meard Street, London W1F 0EG
USA: 180 Varick Street, New York, NY 10014–4606
www.versobooks.com

Verso is the imprint of New Left Books

ISBN 1–85984–501–0

British Library Cataloguing in Publication Data
A CIP catalogue record for this book is available from the British Library.

Library of Congress Cataloging-in-Publication Data
A catalog record for this book is available from the Library of Congress

Typeset in Garamond and Gill Sans extra bold by ARROW Publications.

Printed in Great Britain

Dedication

This book is dedicated to Zahra, an emaciated girl I met in the Al Mansour Teaching Hospital in Baghdad in February 1998. Zahra was suffering from marasmus, a wasting disease of acute malnutrition. She was the first child I met in Iraq. I remember her stillness and her serenity.

Milan Rai,
15 August 2002

'You don't understand.

'Our policy is to get rid of Saddam,
not his regime.'

Richard Haas, director for Middle East Affairs
on the US National Security Council,
March 1991[1]

'The White House's biggest fear is that
UN weapons inspectors will be allowed
to go in.'

Top US Senate foreign policy aide,
May 2002[2]

'This is wrong.

'What are you Brits going to do,
roll over like nice little doggies
just because America says so?'

Scott Ritter, former US Marine,
former UN weapons inspector,
July 2002[3]

CONTENTS

ACKNOWLEDGEMENTS

The author and publishers are grateful to Amber Amundson, Noam Chomsky, David Potorti, and Robin S. Theurkauf for kind permission to use their words. Special thanks to Robin Theurkauf and Amber Amundson for generously contributing the Last Words, specially written for *War Plan Iraq*. We are also extremely grateful to Kim Weston-Arnold and Emily Johns for permission to use their powerful images. Noam Chomsky's 'Terror and Just Response' first appeared in *Terrorism and International Justice: A Collection of Philosophical and Political Reflections,* ed. Jim Sterba (Oxford University Press, 2002). The grammar, punctuation, typographical accuracy and clarity of *War Plan Iraq* have benefited from the careful eye and discriminating judgement of Susan Johns.

Milan Rai wishes to acknowledge years of support from, and stimulating friendship with, ARROW members: David Polden, Andrea Needham, Susan Johns, Emily Johns, Richard Crump, Emily Apple, and especially Gabriel Carlyle, the indomitable co-coordinator and linchpin of **voices in the wilderness uk**. He would also like to thank Glen Rangwala for his rapid and lucid legal advice – not all of which was heeded.

Milan Rai offers heartfelt thanks to Emily Johns, Arkady Johns, and Patrick Nicholson for the support, tolerance, and culinary excellence shown during the labour of producing this book. Without whom, nothing.

PREFACE

The world is standing at a crossroads. Decisions taken in the next few months will cast a shadow for years, perhaps for decades to come. Decisions taken by the Governments of the United States and Britain, certainly, but also decisions taken by us, the peoples of these two warrior states.

The peoples of Britain and the United States have been subjected to an enormous public relations campaign designed to build war fever against Iraq – a nation of 23 million people reduced to a single hated figure. *War Plan Iraq* is intended as a contribution to the task of countering the propaganda, and to setting out some of the realities behind official and media distortions and lies.

President George W. Bush and Prime Minister Tony Blair intend to use the agony suffered on 11 September as a justification for their war drive against Iraq. That is why this book opens and closes with the thoughts of some people highly qualified to comment on the official invocation of pre-emptive violence – the courageous relatives of some of the victims of 11 September who have spoken out for justice instead of vengeance.

Noam Chomsky is a moral beacon for our times, and he has very kindly allowed us to include his most recent reflections on 11 September in this book – followed by a short note on the extraordinary story of the near-extradition of Osama bin Laden.

The heart of this book is an examination of US and British policies towards Iraq over the past twelve years. It is clear from the historical record that Washington has consistently undermined both the democratic Iraqi opposition and UN weapons inspectors throughout this period, while paying lip service to both.

The US helped to destroy the first UN weapons inspection agency, UNSCOM, firstly by infiltrating it with spies, using it to gain intelligence on Iraq's leadership, and coordinating at least one UNSCOM inspection to facilitate a high-level coup attempt in Iraq. Secondly, the US manipulated UNSCOM to create an atmosphere of confrontation, and then instructed UNSCOM to withdraw from Iraq, in November and December 1998. During 2002, Washington has done all that it can to undermine the new inspection agency, UNMOVIC, refusing, for example, to guarantee that it will not bomb Iraq if the inspectors are allowed back in.

The historical record demonstrates clearly that disarmament has not been the priority for Washington or for London – which has slavishly followed US policy. If the disarmament of Iraq had truly been the priority, none of these actions would have been taken, and UNSCOM would almost certainly continue to exist today, maintaining the most effective monitoring system ever devised for detecting weapons of mass destruction.

Following sections of the book dismantle official justifications for launching another war, clarify some aspects of the debate about economic sanctions, and comment briefly on recent British nuclear threats against Iraq. The evidence available at the time of writing demonstrates that there is no hard evidence that Iraq possesses any weapons of mass destruction; that there is no substantiated connection between the Government of Iraq and 11 September, or with the al Qaeda network; that the proposed war carries a very high risk of triggering a humanitarian disaster in Iraq, especially for the Kurds of northern Iraq, and could precipitate a world recession with dire consequences for the world's poor. The President's war is also opposed by Iraq's neighbours, the countries most at risk from Iraq's alleged weapons of mass destruction; denounced by much of world opinion; resisted by top military professionals in Britain and the US; condemned by Labour MPs and Labour Cabinet ministers; and rejected by the great majority of people in Britain (58 per cent opposition compared to 28 per cent support). If carried out, this war would also be in violation of international law, especially if it failed to have the support of a UN Security Council Resolution.

In 1991, Washington called for an uprising, and then betrayed the Iraqi opposition totally. Ever since, the US has been searching for a replacement general to impose on the peoples of Iraq – either an exile who used to serve Saddam Hussein, or someone deep within the regime who is currently still serving Saddam Hussein. A clone of Saddam Hussein who will obey orders. The talk of 'regime change' and the public statements of support for the democratic opposition are confusing and misleading froth. The United States is intent on imposing another Sunni general on Iraq to replace Saddam Hussein – 'leadership change' rather than 'regime change'.

Two of the last chapters deal with the need for intellectual and physical (nonviolent) resistance to lies and war preparation. The final chapter is a reflection on the options facing Washington war planners and their possible consequences, and a summary of the findings of *War Plan Iraq*.

The evocative photographs, wood engravings and lino cuts of Iraqi life by Kim Weston-Arnold and Emily Johns are powerful reminders of the human reality that is at stake. Britain and the United States bear the lion's share of responsibility for the suffering of tens of millions of people in Iraq for the past twelve years. Those who reject the proposed war must avoid falling into the trap of proposing the continuation of 'containment' – the policy of economic strangulation which has cost the lives of hundreds of thousands of children over the past twelve years. The only morally valid way forward must involve the lifting of economic sanctions to spare the innocent peoples of Iraq from yet more despair, decay and death.

We believe firmly that determined popular action in the months after this book is published can help to prevent a massive assault by Britain and the United States. Will we act to rebut official and media lies and defeat war propaganda? Will we use our freedom to help protect the peoples of Iraq? Or will we leave them to their fate?

Milan Rai for ARROW

THE BREADTH OF OPPOSITION

'For the first time in my life, rather to my surprise, I find myself beginning to line up with the doves ... this mooted assault on Iraq strikes me as being in a different category. We are considering acting pre-emptively against a state that has not – has it? – actually sponsored a terrorist threat against us."
  Robert Harris, March 2002.[1]

'Officials in the Ministry of Defence and the Foreign Office are deeply sceptical about the wisdom of military action against Iraq as well as the feasibility. "The whole thing is fraught with danger," said a senior Whitehall official. "The best outcome would be for Saddam Hussein to let in weapons inspectors." ' March 2002.[2]

'Although it is important not to understate the potential threat posed by Iraq, no convincing evidence has been presented to support the argument that Iraq is rebuilding its weapons of mass destruction programme, or that Iraq poses an immediate threat to regional and international security. An attack on another Muslim country – particularly one with no proven link to the September 11 atrocities – would be taken by many as evidence of an inbuilt hostility to the Islamic world.'
  Church of England Board for Social Responsibility, March 2002.[3]

'Apart from the effects of having lived for a generation in states of war of various kinds and under the cruelty of their own government, the terrible toll exacted on Iraq's civilian population by a combination of UN sanctions and US/UK bombing (including the premature deaths of hundreds of thousands of children) has contributed to the devastation of Iraq's infrastructure.

  'It is our considered view that an attack on Iraq would be both immoral and illegal. It is deplorable that the world's most powerful nations continue to regard war and the threat of war as an acceptable instrument of foreign policy, in violation of the ethos of both the United Nations and Christian moral teaching.'
  Archbishop Rowan Williams and 3000 others
  An excerpt from the July 2002 'Christian Declaration' initiated by Pax Christi.[5]

'The last attacks on Iraq killed a lot of innocent civilians and enormously strengthened Saddam Hussein, because a dictator can always blame the death of civilians on the foreign power rather than on himself.'
  Lord (Denis) Healey, former Labour Chancellor, April 2002.[6]

'Does the Right Hon. Gentleman [British Foreign Secretary Jack Straw] understand that many of us are very concerned about the talk of pre-emptive military action against Iraq? Many of us do not believe that it is as yet established that there is a sufficient requirement for that.'

Douglas Hogg MP, former Conservative Cabinet minister, March 2002.[7]

'To invert Boulay de la Meurthe's cynical saying, starting such a war would be worse than a blunder, it would be a crime. A UK government decision to participate in a US-led assault could provoke more severe domestic division than Britain has seen since the Suez crisis. In spite of the Administration's resolve not to be deflected from its policy preferences, it would scarcely be unmoved by a clear signal – whether public or private – from its most solid ally that neither military participation nor political support was to be assumed. Such a signal ought to be given soon.'

Sir Michael Quinlan, August 2002,

former Permanent Under-Secretary of State, Ministry of Defence (1988-1992)[9]

'[Prolonging the 'war against terrorism' in Afghanistan is likely to be disastrous.] Even more disastrous would be its extension, as American opinion seems increasingly to demand, in a "Long March" through other rogue states beginning with Iraq. I can think of no policy more likely not only to indefinitely prolong the war, but to ensure we can never win it.'

Michael Howard, military historian, November 2001.[10]

The invasion and occupation of Iraq would spark 'a civil war [in Iraq] that would make Lebanon's troubles look like a vicarage tea party, and would be a fatal blow to our central policy objective – stability in the region.'

A. F. Green,

former British Ambassador to Syria (1991–94) and Saudi Arabia (1996–2000).[11]

'If the United States were unilaterally to invade Iraq without the political authority and safeguards of 1990, the Kurds and neighbouring states might then follow the American example and move into Iraq to protect their perceived interests and/or to redress historical wrongs, real or imagined. Iraq could implode. The consequent political and military confusion might result in only a "rump" Iraq, for which the United States would become de facto and indefinitely the protecting power, an irritant in the Arab body politic and detrimental to the interests in the region of its friends and allies.'

A. T. Lamb, former British Ambassador to Kuwait (1974–77)[12]

'This is a potentially very dangerous situation in which this country might be swept into a very messy and long-lasting Middle East war. You don't have a licence to attack someone else's country just because you don't like the leadership.'

Field Marshal Lord Bramall, former Chief of Britain's Defence Staff.[13]

'Despite successfully dismantling the Taleban regime, the United States and its supporters failed to eliminate the threat from al-Qaeda. Thousands of fighters are scattered worldwide. Destroying this network is the primary strategic challenge we face. Attacking Iraq will detract from our primary mission against al-Qaeda, supercharging anti-American sentiment in the Arab street, boosting al-Qaeda's recruiting, and causing difficulty for moderate Arab regimes.'

US General Wesley Clark,
former NATO Supreme Allied Commander Europe, August 2002[14]

'Although the US could certainly succeed, we should try our best not to have to go it alone, and the President should reject the advice of those who counsel doing so. The costs will be much greater, as will the political risks, both domestic and international if we end up going it alone or with only one or two countries.'

James Baker,
former US Secretary of State under President George Bush Sr, August 2002[15]

'[A]n attack on Iraq at this time would seriously jeopardise, if not destroy, the global counter-terrorist campaign we have undertaken. There is a virtual consensus in the world against an attack on Iraq at this time.'

Brent Scowcroft,
former US National Security Adviser to President Bush Sr, August 2002[16]

'Unless Saddam has his hand on a trigger for a weapon of mass destruction, and our intelligence is clear, I don't know why we have to do it now, when our allies are opposed to it.' 'If we are so clear in our own minds that this is a real danger, why can't we convince our NATO allies of that fact? There is a disconnect here and I don't understand it.'

Lawrence Eagleburger,
former US Secretary of State under President Bush Sr, August/September 2002[17]

'Before we use military force, we ought to try all of the alternatives: economic sanctions, diplomacy, inspections.'

Arlen Specter, senior Republican Senator, August 2002[18]

'We will continue to work to avoid a military confrontation or a military action because we believe that it will open the gates of hell in the Middle East.'

Amr Moussa, Secretary-General of the Arab League, September 2002[19]

'Under my leadership, Germany will not be part of an intervention [against Iraq]. Friendship should not mean that one does everything that a friend demands. Anything else would just be subordination, and that would be wrong.'

Gerhard Schroeder, Chancellor of Germany, September 2002[20]

'We are really appalled by any country, whether it is a superpower or a poor country, that goes outside the United Nations and attacks independent countries.' 'No country should be allowed to take the law into its own hands. Especially the [US], because they are the only superpower in the world today and they must be exemplary in everything they do. What they are introducing is chaos in international affairs and we condemn that in the strongest terms. '

Nelson Mandela,
Former President of South Africa, September 2002[21]

'As has been emphasized vigorously by foreign allies and responsible leaders of former administrations and incumbent officeholders, there is no current danger to the United States from Baghdad. In the face of intense monitoring and overwhelming American military superiority, and belligerent move by Hussein against a neighbor, even the smallest nuclear test (necessary before weapons construction), a tangible threat to use a weapon of mass destruction, or sharing this technology with terrorist organizations would be suicidal. We cannot ignore the development of chemical, biological or nuclear weapons, but a unilateral war with Iraq is not the answer.'

President Jimmy Carter,
Former President of the United States, September 2002[22]

'We are told a war on Iraq is needed to pre–empt a threat to the region and to free the Iraqi people from Saddam Hussein's tyranny. We, as Iraqis already free from that tyranny, living outside Iraq and in the western democracies, say that both these claims are false.

'As professionals, writers, teachers and other responsible and concerned citizens, many of whom have personally experienced the persecution of the dictatorship in Iraq, we say, "No to war; not in our name, not in the name of the suffering Iraqi people."

'Real change can only be brought about by the Iraqi people themselves within an environment of peace and justice for all the peoples of the Middle East. We call on the UN to put together a timetable for the lifting of the economic sanctions and do all it can to halt the drive for war that will only plunge the region into the abyss.

'We also call on everyone else to challenge the dangerous and irresponsible war plans of the US.'

Mundher Al-Adhami, Researcher, Kings College London
Kamil Mahdi, Lecturer, Exeter University
Tahrir Numan, Teacher
Haifa Zangana, Novelist
and 96 other Iraqi exiles, September 2002[23]

ACHILLES' HEEL

President Bush Needs Prime Minister Blair

In January 2002, US President George W. Bush made clear his intention to extend his "war on terrorism" beyond the destruction of the al Qaeda network to taken on North Korea, Iran, Iraq, and perhaps other official enemies of the United States. While North Korea and Iran were each dismissed in a sentence, the President dwelt on the threat allegedly posed by the third member of the 'axis of evil'. Subsequent speeches by leading figures in the Bush Administration have indicated that Washington is determined to launch a major assault on Iraq – to depose the Iraqi leader, Saddam Hussein.

FATHER AND SON

The looming conflict has sometimes been characterised as an act of filial duty, with President Bush Jr finishing the work of President Bush Sr. A coordinated burst of public interventions in August 2002, however, revealed the deep concerns of close allies of the older President Bush. A large part of the war cabinet of President Bush Sr spoke out against a war on Iraq, signalling a split between the two US Presidents on the burning issue of the day. It was understood that neither James Baker, formerly President George Bush's US Secretary of State, nor Brent Scowcroft, his former National Security Adviser, would have spoken out so publicly without the authorisation of the former President. An anonymous senior Republican with close ties to the current President's inner circle told the *New York Times*, 'This is a clear, direct signal. I think the first President Bush is telling his son: "Be prudent, George." ' The signalling prompted *New York Times* columnist Maureen Dowd to comment, 'Who needs a war plan? We need family therapy.' A closer look revealed some divergences between father and son. President Bush Sr increased taxes after promising not to; his son made tax cuts the centrepiece of his domestic policy. President George Bush felt a barely-concealed contempt for the party's fundamentalist right wing; President George W. Bush 'has made it his job to woo the Christian conservative heartland,' as *Guardian* columnist Julian Borger points out. Lawrence Korb, Assistant Secretary of Defence during President Reagan's first term, observes, 'George Bush Sr was from the North-East. They have always been the internationalist Republicans who want to work with other nations to the extent that they could. The current President is from the old

Robert Taft wing of the party – from the South and Midwest. People call them isolationists, but that really means they're unilateralists. They just want to do what they want to do.' Ivo Daalder, a foreign policy expert at the Brookings Institution in Washington, perceives the division differently: 'What happened is that under Bush II, the Reaganauts came back. They're not only in the ascendancy, they're in control. The real debate is not between Bush I and Bush II but between Bush I and Reagan.' Mr Daalder suggests that George W. Bush may not have been entirely aware of the extent to which he was making a break with his father when he brought the 'Reaganauts' into his Administration: 'It's not clear that the man knows what he was buying.'[1]

While there is no doubt something in these analyses, they may well obscure more than they reveal. In 1981, Michael Klare suggested a useful distinction between 'Prussians' and 'Traders' in the US foreign policy establishment. 'Traders' have called for greater economic collaboration between the major capitalist powers, and support the use of trusted Third World powers as 'surrogate gendarmes' to maintain 'order' in different regions of the world. 'Prussians', on the other hand, favoured direct US military intervention around the world, and a massive expansion of US nuclear capabilities. A particular person might be a Trader on one issue, but a Prussian on another, depending on the perceived costs and benefits.[2] The current debate in the US political mainstream is one between Prussians and Traders. Thus there is conflict between Republicans coming out of the political mainstream, of whom US Secretary of State Colin Powell is the leading example, and those on the fringes, such as Richard Perle of the Pentagon's Defence Advisory Board, former CIA director James Woolsey, and others clustered around Deputy Secretary of Defence Paul Wolfowitz. The debate revolves around the costs – costs to the United States. Thus Republican Senator Chuck Hagel indicated his dissent from the hawks by suggesting, 'Maybe Mr Perle would like to be in the first wave of those who go into Baghdad.'[3] (Those clamouring most loudly for war have the least experience of combat.[4]) Both ends of the spectrum are united in believing that the United States should 'just do what it wants to do', regardless of legality and justice. Differences emerge over perceptions of the relative costs of different courses of actions. The surge of concern about the possible costs to the United States and its 'interests' in the Middle East in late summer 2002 led to some wavering within the Republican Party, forcing the current President to concede, 'I am aware that some very intelligent people are expressing their opinions about Saddam Hussein and Iraq. I listen very carefully to what they have to say'.[5] This is something of a facade. As one Bush policy adviser said in late August 2002, the decision to go to war against Iraq was '95 per cent' taken.[6]

INTERNATIONAL SUPPORT NEEDED

To repeat: the Traders are not men or women of peace. Former US Secretary of State James Baker, for example, is not a dove. He said, in his dissent on the issue of Iraq, 'The issue for policymakers to resolve is not whether to use military force, but how to go about it.' For Mr Baker, a fresh UN Security Council Resolution authorising US military action is an essential pre-condition; it is 'necessary, politically and practically, and will help build international support.' The key is 'international support'. Chuck Hagel, the Republican Senator from Nebraska, commented, 'I don't think it is in the best interests of this country ... or any of our allies for us to act unilaterally. If we would go into Iraq, we certainly would want allies with us, and certainly Arab allies.' Retired US Rear Admiral Stephen Baker, formerly an operations officer in the Gulf War, and once the Navy's chief of staff in Bahrain remarked dryly in August 2002, 'It is a good idea when leading a charge to occasionally stop and look behind to see whether anyone is following.'[7] International support, and particularly Arab support, has been conspicuous by its absence.

The issue of international support appears to be important to domestic US opinion, whose support for unilateral military action has been ebbing since 11 September. The Pew Research Center found that while 83 per cent of the US public thought the military effort in the 'war on terrorism' was going 'very well' or 'fairly well' in October 2001, only 65 per cent felt the same in August 2002. Support for a ground invasion of Iraq fell from 74 per cent in November 2001 to 61 per cent in June 2002, to only 53 per cent in August 2002. Air strikes without the use of troops, and a special forces mission to capture the Iraqi leader, however, continued to command significant US support (63 per cent and 70 per cent of respondents, respectively). A *Newsweek* poll found that there was 70 per cent support for sending an international military force into Iraq. A major poll carried out in August 2002 by the Chicago Council on Foreign Relations and the German Marshall Fund found that only 20 per cent of US citizens supported a unilateral invasion of Iraq. 65 per cent of US respondents believed that an invasion should be carried out only with UN authorisation and the support of allies. The report noted that 'not much concern about Iraq emerges spontaneously when people are asked about big problems facing the country.' Iraq or Saddam Hussein were mentioned by a mere 3 per cent of respondents when asked to name the two or three biggest problems facing the United States. Only 1 per cent named Iraq when asked to identify the two or three biggest problems facing the country today.[8]

THE IMPORTANCE OF TONY BLAIR

It appears then that international support is critical to US public confidence in a major assault on Iraq, particularly one involving significant numbers of ground troops. Admiral Stephen Baker suggested that if President George W. Bush had 'looked behind him' for support in August 2002, he would have found 'some of his staff, a vaguely supportive Congress, a nervous Defence Department and the British Prime Minister, Tony Blair'. 'That's about it,' observed Admiral Baker.[9] Given the reluctance of European and Arab leaders to support the US attack on Iraq, Tony Blair's support becomes an extremely important ingredient in President Bush's war planning. Anatol Lieven, analyst at the Carnegie Endowment for International Peace, suggests that, 'Britain is at least as important as all the other European states put together. If Britain came out publicly and said it was against it, it would really shake them.'[10] Former US Ambassador to the UN, Richard Holbrooke has remarked that, 'If there is one country in the world that might find a way to support us without a UN resolution, it would be the UK.' Unfortunately, according to Mr Holbrooke, while 'Tony Blair has been America's greatest, staunchest, most unstinting friend, ally and supporter since September 11 ... I'm afraid to say that the American Government has not taken account of his own domestic political needs in this process.'[11]

Viewed shortly before the Labour Party Conference in September 2002, Prime Minister Tony Blair appears dangerously exposed, facing intense pressure from within his own party – from grassroots members, from the Parliamentary Labour Party, and even from within his Cabinet. The depth of British hostility to this war does not seem to be entirely appreciated in the United States. There appears to be little sense that the sapping of Mr Blair's support could be the Achilles' heel of the war effort. This is an extraordinary reversal for a Prime Minister who has used foreign policy as a way of stamping his authority on his Cabinet and his party, and as a method of outshining his powerful rival, the Chancellor of the Exchequer, Gordon Brown. In his previous military adventures against Iraq in 1998, over Kosovo in 1999, in Sierra Leone in 2000, again in Iraq in 2001, and finally in Afghanistan in 2001, Tony Blair suffered few political costs, and reaped considerable political benefits. This era is now apparently over. An omen of the rough seas which may lie ahead came with the decision to send British Marines to join a US-led force in Afghanistan, which met with a vociferous response from the Labour Party. The US made clear its concern: 'The criticism of the despatch of 1700 Royal Marines to Afghanistan would pale beside that of participation in an operation against Iraq.'[12] With the intensification of the Israel/Palestine crisis, the pressure has increased still further. Downing Street officials have reportedly been desperate for a Middle East breakthrough to ward off the prospect of a Labour backbench rebellion over Iraq.[13]

FORMER BRITISH MINISTERS REVOLT

Former Labour Defence Minister Peter Kilfoyle is only one of many backbench Members of Parliament to warn of the restlessness within the Labour Party over what he describes as President Bush's 'bellicosity'. Mr Kilfoyle was a Blair loyalist who 'rose to prominence as a party organiser in Liverpool, where he was known as the hammer of the far Left Militant Tendency', and who, in 1994, was 'the political fixer who collected names of MPs prepared to support Tony Blair in the impending election of a new party leader, giving him a huge head start.' Now Mr Kilfoyle says, 'Texan gung-ho will not go down well in the Middle East or in a large section of the Labour Party.' He adds, 'There is no mandate for the UK government to genuflect to the hawks in the American administration over Iraq. My belief is that there would be a great deal of consternation amongst the Parliamentary Labour Party – and, indeed, the British people – about some kind of reflex action that would support an American vendetta against Iraq.' Mr Kilfoyle told Radio 4, 'I have to say that, at the moment, the Government is going through a very, very rocky patch and it's as well that it listens to its backbenchers rather than antagonises them.'[14] Douglas Henderson, formerly a New Labour Defence Minister, and a Minister for Europe, expressed his concerns about going to war with Iraq: 'A lot of us would have severe worries – that the action would not be successful, that Saddam wouldn't be toppled, and we would be left with an invasion force in Iraq; or that we'd alienate too many of the other countries whose support we need to fight terrorism internationally.' From the British perspective, 'Our danger is that the US takes the decisions and we are bound by them; if decisions go wrong, if the campaign goes wrong, we suffer sometimes even more than the Americans do.'[15] Chris Smith, previously Minister for Culture, Media and Sport under Tony Blair, also expressed reservations about Britain's subordinate position: 'I think a lot of my colleagues, including myself, would be worried if there were something being contemplated which was an all-out invasion of Iraq, simply going on the coat tails of an American unilateral decision. I don't think that would be something any of us would be particularly happy about.'[16]

Other former New Labour ministers who have expressed their reservations include Jon Owen Jones, former Welsh Office Minister; George Howarth, former Home Office Minister; Tony Lloyd, a former Foreign Office Minister; and Glenda Jackson, formerly Minister for London.[17] Glenda Jackson said that it was 'very irresponsible to be upping the rhetoric with regard to any possible action on Iraq without the relevant evidence that Saddam is engaged in the creation of weapons of mass destruction and has the ability to deliver them.' Without such evidence, and, 'Until that potential has been verified, the international community should be concentrating on what is already happening in the Middle East.'[18] Former Northern Ireland Minister Mo Mowlam has warned that Britain is drifting into 'offensive, not defensive' war against Iraq: 'Blair seems to be making it clear that he has more sympathy with the wishes of Washington and their reckless attitude to Iraq than he does for his own party and even members of his Cabinet.'[19]

Among the other mainstream Labour figures joining the ranks of the anti-war rebels is Janet Anderson, who spent the first 18 months of the Blair administration enforcing discipline as a party whip before becoming junior Minister for Culture. The right-wing *Daily Telegraph* notes that 'Her decision to join the chorus of critics of Iraq policy is notable because, for years, she was a close ally of Jack Straw, the Foreign Secretary.' Ms Anderson was his personal assistant for six years in the 1980s, and she represents a constituency adjoining his.[20] Other New Labour whips who have signalled their willingness to rebel over a number of issues include Graham Allen, David Clelland, Jim Dowd, George Mudie and John McFall.[21]

It has been noted that there are a large number of embittered former ministers as a result of Tony Blair's policy of creating a Government in his own image 'by regularly reshuffling his team with a ruthlessness not shown by his predecessors, even including

Baroness Thatcher.' Of the 48 ministers who have resigned or been sacked since 1997, only three have been given a second chance so far: Harriet Harman, Nigel Griffiths and Alun Michael. One Minister has admitted that it is becoming 'fashionable' to attack the Government, and that this tendency is hard to control; 'It's not really the whips' fault. How are you supposed to discipline a former member of the Cabinet who knows he [or she] has nothing to lose any more?'[22]

BACKBENCH DISSENT

Donald Anderson, the highly-respected Labour chair of the House of Commons Defence Select Committee, has also expressed concern, saying that the international legal basis for an attack on Iraq is 'pretty shaky'. While supporting the idea of increasing pressure on Baghdad, he has said that, 'If we were to move to support US military action, that would be a different context with a very uncertain outcome.' The MP has added, 'I think that there are fairly reckless elements in the Pentagon who are on a roll because of Afghanistan and I would hope that part of the task of our Government is to influence those who take a contrary view and want to work within the United Nations Security Council and get the weapons inspectors back.'[23]

Ian Gibson, Labour MP for Norwich North and chair of the Commons Science and Technology Committee, seems to have expressed the views of a significant section of the Parliamentary Labour Party: 'People are not happy that we seem to be doing what the Americans want. What is the danger from Iraq? Where is the terrorist threat? Where is the evidence?'[24] A BBC poll of 101 Labour MPs in February 2002 found that 86 said there was insufficient evidence to justify an attack on Iraq.[25]

The threat of war on Iraq led to an extraordinary level of support for a Parliamentary 'Early Day Motion' (EDM) proposed by Labour MP Alice Mahon on 4 March 2002. EDM 927 recognised 'the deep unease among honourable Members on all sides of the House' at the prospect that Britain might support United States military action against Iraq. It 'agree[d] with Kofi Annan that a further military attack on Iraq would be unwise at this time'; warned that war on Iraq 'would disrupt support for the anti-terrorism coalition among the Arab states'; and focused attention instead on the need for diplomacy to secure the return of UN weapons inspectors. 161 MPs signed the motion, including over 125 Labour MPs.[26] Among those who signed were 'serial loyalists Oona King and Jon Trickett' (so labelled by Mark Seddon, left-wing member of the Labour Party National Executive Committee).[27] Tony Blair personally phoned Labour MPs who had signed the EDM, and apparently lobbied them via his close associate, the Minister for Housing and Planning, Lord Falconer. A recipient of Lord Falconer's attentions said, 'At least the Prime Minister is taking us seriously for once.'[28]

The political temperature inside the Labour Party rose when the Prime Minister visited President Bush in Texas at the beginning of April 2002, and endorsed the need for 'regime change' in Iraq. On his return, Tony Blair met considerable hostility, hostility that had been heightened by his description of critics as 'utterly naive'. 'For the first time since he came to power, Labour backbenchers subjected him to hostile questioning during Prime Minister's questions.'[29] 'Many Labour MPs sat with their arms folded, withholding the customary Question Time cheers for the Prime Minister, as one of them after another stood up to raise concerns.' Mr Blair was 'subjected to minor heckling after responding to claims that he had accused MPs of being naive'.[30]

At a private meeting with the Parliamentary Labour Party before Prime Minister's Question Time, the Prime Minister failed to impress his critics. Clive Soley, former chair of the Parliamentary Labour Party, said that the West would be accused of double standards if it allowed Israel to defy UN resolutions but attacked Iraq.[31] One commentator observed, 'rather like the dialogues in Harold Pinter plays in which the two characters are each having half of two separate conversations, Mr Blair and many of his party wanted to speak about different things. They largely wanted to talk about Iraq'– eight of the fifteen questions asked at the meeting concerned Iraq.[32] MPs leaving the 75-minute meeting of the parliamentary Labour party expressed disappointment that their concerns had not been addressed directly.[33] One MP complained, 'That was the shoddiest performance I have ever seen. He seemed to be on another planet.'[34] Another MP described the meeting as 'dysfunctional', as Mr Blair 'talked 80 per cent of the time about domestic policy and 80 per cent of our questions were about Iraq.'[35]

One Westminster correspondent has speculated that, 'Iraq is about to become Labour's Suez – the issue which, before Europe, last caused the biggest split in the Tory Party'. 'Labour will be split asunder,' it has been suggested.[36] Even Ministers speculated that in order to secure Parliamentary approval for a US-led war on Iraq, Tony Blair 'may end up having to rely on the payroll vote [those Labour MPs with positions in the Government] and the Tories against a large proportion of his own backbenches.'[37] 'Those on the Labour backbenches who believe a decision has already been made were reminiscent of another great Rodin sculpture, *The Burghers of Calais*: alternately grim, resigned, and anguished, shackled to a greater force, unsure of where they might be taken.'[38] Hence Mr Blair's decision not to put the invasion of Iraq to a vote of the House of Commons. The Prime Minister is determined to launch what US hawks call a 'war for democracy' in Iraq by undemocratic methods.

THE CABINET REVOLT

The problems are not confined to the backbenches. 'Mr Blair has come to take the support of his government for granted. He was disabused of that in cabinet [on 7 March 2002]. A Cabinet minister said that going to war with Iraq was not what he had gone into politics to do, and he had no enthusiasm for it, a mood shared by those around the table. Mr Blair was apparently surprised by the reaction.' Mr Blair 'listened as one minister after another voiced the caution being increasingly shown on the back benches.' 'Cabinet ministers at their weekly session told Mr Blair that all diplomatic avenues must be explored before military action was even contemplated.' 'During frank exchanges, Mr Blair was warned that any action would have to be justified by detailed, overwhelming evidence of Baghdad's development of weapons of mass destruction, in defiance of international law.' 'The Prime Minister was warned he must not commit British forces without a clear political base and a clear exit plan.' According to one report, the Prime Minister was told that hostility to strikes against Iraq 'was shared at all levels of government'. No decisions were made at the meeting, but 'the clear message was that ministers were alarmed by the US threats'.[39]

The London *Evening Standard* commented, 'the threat of a Cabinet-level mutiny takes the Government into uncharted and dangerous waters'.[40] The *Financial Times* reported, ' "People have talked of low-level resignations, but they could go right up into the cabinet," said a government insider.'[41] The response of the Prime Minister, according to David Blunkett, was rather curious: 'The Prime Minister was able to say, quite rightly, "Look, the management has not lost its marbles." '[42] This did not calm all members of the Cabinet. Robin Cook, Labour Foreign Secretary in the first Blair Government, said candidly and publicly, 'Lots of people have sometimes contradictory instincts on this. Nobody likes military action.' It was reported that Mr Cook was urged (possibly by a former Minister) to resign from the Cabinet, and to 'take on the mantle of the real leader of the opposition'.[43]

Home Secretary David Blunkett struck a very cautious note in a BBC radio interview, hinting that a war on Iraq could trigger riots in British cities: 'There is no point in going to war unless you know what the objective is, that you weighed up what the consequences would be in terms of other major events that affect social cohesion or support.' Mr Blunkett 'did not deny telling colleagues that he had warned the cabinet it could not separate Iraq from Middle East issues, and that to do so would risk "major disturbances".' The Minister 'did nothing to dispel reports of ministerial splits, saying the government faced "genuine dilemmas".' He called for 'intelligent debate' over Iraq's suspected weapons programmes, saying, 'Britain has not only been a good friend [to the United States], but the best friend, and best friends sometimes tell you what you don't want to hear.'[44]

International Development Minister Clare Short, who resigned from the Labour front bench over the 1991 Gulf War, has repeatedly spoken out for restraint: Iraq may be determined to develop weapons of mass destruction, 'But the assumption that some sort of all-out military attack is the answer to that is of course not at all sensible.' 'Blind military action against Iraq doesn't deal with the problem.' With the Middle East in turmoil, and with 'the terrible suffering of both the Israeli and Palestinian people', to 'open up a military flank on Iraq' would be 'very unwise'. 'Of course there are conditions under which I would not be able to support action but I do not expect them to be proposed.' 'Yes, I am the same old Clare Short and I'm proud to be a member of the government but I've got lots of bottom lines. I don't expect the government to breach them but if they did, I would [resign]. That's what you should be like in politics.' 'I would not support any mass attacks on the poor Iraqi people that would not do any harm to Saddam Hussein.' At the same time, the Minister has said,

'I would absolutely support, if it is possible legally, Saddam Hussein's regime being brought down and the people of Iraq being freed from the suffering he has inflicted.'

Clare Short was then punished for her public dissent: 'Mr Blair, bruised from a cabinet meeting on March 7 in which ministers made clear their unhappiness at the prospect of Britain being drawn into military action in Iraq, was extremely annoyed' to hear Ms Short's remarks. No doubt his annoyance was intensified by the fact that they came on the eve of a visit to London by US Vice-President Dick Cheney. The Labour leader therefore met the International Development Minister for a face-to-face dressing-down (which lasted a mere five minutes). 'The incident, rare for Mr Blair who dislikes such confrontation, highlights the prime minister's sensitivity over Iraq and the strain it is placing on his government.' Ms Short was then gagged, being told to express her concerns to the Prime Minister before airing them in public.[45]

Perhaps most dangerously for the Prime Minister, veteran Labour MP Tam Dalyell announced that the second most powerful member of Britain's Labour Government, Chancellor of the Exchequer, Gordon Brown, also believed that Mr Blair was too 'gung ho' over Iraq. Mr Dalyell's claim was denied by a spokesperson for Mr Brown.[46]

THE PARLIAMENTARY TIME BOMB

Tony Blair was warned by a leader column in *The Times* that there was 'real political peril' in delaying a military assault on Iraq to the spring of 2003:

> The first difficulty is that Labour MPs and wider public opinion alike might mistake "not now" for "never" and then be rudely disturbed later. The second is that if there is to be a serious split within the Labour Party over Iraq, then it will be more damaging in the middle of this Parliament than at its outset. The final, intriguing, element is that the Prime Minister might have to make the tough decisions on a military commitment against Saddam at the same time as he must reach a position as to whether or not to call a referendum on the euro.[47]

The euro factor has been blamed by *Guardian* columnist Hugo Young for the sudden unleashing of the national press against Tony Blair and against the Government in mid-2002, as the right-wing press attempt to deter the Prime Minister from calling a referendum in this parliament by damaging him politically on other issues.[48]

Matthew d'Ancona, writing in the *Sunday Telegraph*, has rightly pointed out that the Labour Party supported military action against Iraq in 1998. What has changed, Mr d'Ancona argues, is the way that Mr Blair is perceived by his party: 'In 1998, when cruise missiles rained down on Baghdad, the Prime Minister was still regarded by even the oldest of Old Labour MPs as a sort of intergalactic megabeing who had descended into their midst and, by means which they did not fully understand, transformed a party of losers into an electoral juggernaut.' Dazzled by the Prime Minister's 'strong leadership', if occasionally perplexed by it, the Labour Party went along with an attack of the greatest ferocity against Saddam. Since 1998, things have changed. There has been a string of political disasters, some of them listed by Mr d'Ancona: the Millennium Dome, the petrol mutiny, the 75p pensions debacle, Hinduja, foot and mouth, Railtrack, Jo Moore, MMR, and Mittal. Now, 'In Labour ranks, the plan to oust Saddam has become a metaphor for the Prime Minister's alleged detachment, his disconnection from reality, and his preoccupation with international sideshows when he should be concentrating on the state of the nation and its public services.' The *Telegraph* columnist observes, 'Since September 11, Mr Blair has often been accused of writing a blank cheque to America. But it was the Labour Party itself that wrote a blank cheque to the Prime Minister five years ago; and now it has ripped it up.'[49]

The dissent brewing up over Iraq within the Parliamentary Labour Party is also fed by other concerns. Tory MP for Henley Boris Johnson listed two recent concerns of mainstream Labour MPs: the 'Consignia affair' and the 'treachery' of then Transport Minister Stephen Byers. Labour MPs cheered the 'renationalisation' of the much-despised privatised company Railtrack without compensation. Later, 'Labour MPs were forced to listen not just to the news that 40,000 post office workers were to be sacked, but also that the Railtrack shareholders were to be compensated after all.'[50]

There are also deep concerns about Mr Blair's close alliances with President Bush and with Silvio Berlusconi and other right-wing leaders in the European Union. MPs 'also have deep reservations about the prime minister's enthusiasm for private sector involvement in public services.' Ian Davidson, MP for Glasgow Pollock, said, 'I had thought that our second term would be about keeping the economy on track, delivering on public services and trying to play a progressive role in the world. Instead we seem to be preparing to attack Iraq and cosying up to rightwingers in Europe while espousing free-market solutions for everything.' 'There is a feeling that the government is talking to everyone except the [Labour] party,' said the MP.[51]

As the *Financial Times* pointed out in April 2002, 'Although the anxiety over potential military action in Iraq is genuine – 125 Labour MPs have signed a motion voicing concern – left-of-centre critics admit that it is becoming a vehicle for dissent over other issues.'[52] The prospect of war on Iraq 'is seen by several as a lightning conductor for wider discontent.'[53]

Backbench dissent over Iraq has been a critical ingredient in the re-formation of the Tribune Group, a broad Left grouping of Labour MPs. Michael Connarty, MP for Falkirk East and chair of the Tribune Group, said, 'Tribune is not about damaging the party, it is about getting the party to think again and not continue to damage itself, the damage that is coming from the leadership's approach.' Mr Connarty added, 'We want to be loyal ... but when things are not going down well with their constituents, then I think backbenchers want somewhere they can go, where they can express that view clearly to the government without being accused of being disloyal.' 'There is far too much about loyalty. If you stand up and parrot then you are somehow accepted ... if debate equals disloyalty, then debate stops and we do not think debate does equal disloyalty.' Mr Connarty says, 'I think there is disquiet about the presidential style which has been adopted up to now which makes people feel detached. New Labour was a wheeze and if it is characterised by anything it is characterised by wheezes.' The re-launch of the Tribune group came on the same night that Tony Blair dined with business tycoons and celebrities at a £500-a-head gala fundraising dinner in the Hilton Hotel. 'Labour officials were reluctant to discuss the event.'[54]

Incidentally, Labour does need fundraising. The Party began the year 2002 'facing its worst financial emergency since Tony Blair became leader, after amassing post-election debts of almost £10 million.' Potential donors have been deterred from helping the party after controversies concerning benefactors such as Bernie Ecclestone and Enron, the collapsed US energy firm. The Labour Party also began the year 2002 with party membership 'perilously close to the all-time low of 261,000 in 1991.' Membership fell by 10 per cent over 2001, to 280,000. While donations to the party increased in the first quarter of 2002 compared to the first quarter of 2001 (£3.38 million, compared to £2.42 million), they fell by 88 per cent in the second quarter of 2002 compared to the second quarter of 2001 (just £591,052, compared to £5.3 million). A Labour Party source said hundreds of grassroots activists were refusing to collect money or to make donations themselves: 'This is where the disquiet about Iraq is most obvious.' Additionally, rich donors have been frightened away by scandals, and unions have cut back on their funding in protest against the Government's treatment of public services.[55]

The growth of dissent and dissatisfaction within the ruling party may in part be a reflection of broader changes. Mr d'Ancona fails to register huge wave of sympathy for the ordinary people of Iraq since 1998, affecting attitudes towards both the economic sanctions regime, and the idea of war on Iraq. For example, the third largest political party in Britain, the Liberal Democrats, have, since their party conference in September 2000, called for the lifting of non-military sanctions on Iraq – a policy which did them no noticeable damage at the 2001 general election. This extraordinary change in public attitudes is due to a number of factors, including determined campaigning by a number of groups and individuals, and media initiatives such as the ground-breaking John Pilger documentary, 'Paying The Price'.

58 PER CENT OPPOSE WAR ON IRAQ

For Mr Blair, the most dangerous result of these improvements in the moral climate is that a majority of British people now oppose the idea of launching a war against Iraq. Different opinion polls have put the figure at between 51 and 58 per cent of the population, but either way it is clear that by a significant margin most voters oppose the war which Mr Blair wishes to drive his country into. This revolt has had its effect on the Labour Party, so that an overwhelming majority of Labour constituency chairpersons in the party's most vulnerable parliamentary seats said in August 2002 that they would not support Mr Blair if he committed British forces to war against Iraq.

Only five out of a hundred local party leaders canvassed by *The Times* said unequivocally that they would support the Prime Minister.[56]

It appears that the war may well be scheduled for spring 2003, and 'Labour MPs and wider public opinion' will indeed be outraged by the revival of the threat to Iraq, as the *Times* predicted. The war would be what a *Financial Times* columnist has referred as one of the 'two riskiest ventures of Tony Blair's premiership', the other being the euro referendum, which could also come next year: 'can he have both? And how would the timing of one affect the other?' 'An unsuccessful Iraq campaign would hardly be the best background against which to launch a referendum. A successful one, on the other hand, would strengthen Mr Blair's belief in his ability to dare and win.' Speculation is growing that an announcement will be made before the end of 2002, and that the decision will be deferred until Mr Blair's expected third term. War and European integration: 'the decisions that will define the character of the Blair government for those all-important history books', as Philip Stephens has noted in the *FT*.[57]

Tony Blair is facing his greatest challenge yet as Prime Minister. He can choose either to continue to serve the interests of the United States, and to battle against his Cabinet, his Party, and the British public – and indeed his generals[58] – or he can choose to join the emerging international consensus, to follow British public opinion, to abide by international law, and to withdraw his support from the US invasion of Iraq. Either way, it promises to be the biggest political battle of Mr Blair's career. The consequences for President George W. Bush could be quite as significant. Mr Blair is essential to War Plan Iraq, but he may also prove the weakest link.

THIS WAR IS PREVENTABLE

We can see the challenge facing the Prime Minister from another point of view. If Britain can be forced to withdraw its support for a war against Iraq in the spring of 2003, this could help to terminate, delay or, at the very least, scale down the US war effort. The British Government as a whole appears extremely reluctant to follow Tony Blair into this war. The Cabinet may suffer high-level resignations in the event of war. The Labour backbenches have signalled determined opposition on a scale not seen since Tony Blair came to power. The British military is also an unwilling partner in this enterprise, as we shall see. There is considerable doubt within mainstream political and military circles as to whether to goals of the campaign are achievable without unacceptable cost. For those committed to international law, and with even a minimal concern for the plight of Iraq's 22 million citizens, there is a real window of opportunity to force an isolated British Prime Minister to cease his servile support for an illegal, unpopular and potentially catastrophic US *Blitzkrieg*. What is needed is, in the words of the classic liberal doctrine, the drawn sword of the citizenry – in today's language, a committed campaign of dissent and nonviolent resistance.

PHASE I

AFTER
11 SEPTEMBER

JUSTICE NOT
VENGEANCE

CHAPTER I

Peaceful Tomorrows

Relatives of Victims
of 11 September 2001

11 September 2001 was a devastating, world-changing event. President Bush and Prime Minister Blair have invoked the atrocities suffered on that day in support of their 'war on terrorism'.

However, there is one perspective on 11 September that the President and the Prime Minister seem to have ignored. The perspective of those people who lost loved ones on 11 September, and who have risen above bewilderment and rage to speak out against war and revenge.

ARROW was honoured to bring Ryan Amundson and Kelly Campbell to London in February 2002 to share their thoughts and experiences with us. Ryan's brother, Kelly brother-in-law, Craig Scott Amundson, died in the Pentagon on 11 September.

We are grateful to be able to reprint here some excerpts from the writings and speeches of several relatives, many of whom are members of 'September 11th Families for Peaceful Tomorrows'. ARROW would like to emphasise that the appearance of these quotations by the relatives does not imply an endorsement by them of any of the statements or analyses in *War Plan Iraq*.

GREGORY RODRIGUEZ

We as a nation should not use the same means as the people who attacked us. I know there is anger, I feel it myself. But I don't want my son used as a pawn to justify the killing of others.

Orlando Rodriguez, 19 September 2001

Our son Greg is among the many missing from the World Trade Center attack.

Since we first heard the news, we have shared moments of grief, comfort, hope, despair, fond memories with his wife, the two families, our friends and neighbors, his loving colleagues at Cantor Fitzgerald/ESpeed, and all the grieving families that daily meet at the Pierre Hotel.

We see our hurt and anger reflected among everybody we meet. We cannot pay attention to the daily flow of news about this disaster. But we read enough of the news to sense that our government is heading in the direction of violent revenge, with the prospect of sons, daughters, parents, friends in distant lands dying, suffering, and nursing further grievances against us.

It is not the way to go.

It will not avenge our son's death.

Not in our son's name.

Our son died a victim of an inhuman ideology. Our actions should not serve the same purpose. Let us grieve. Let us reflect and pray. Let us think about a rational response that brings real peace and justice to our world.

But let us not as a nation add to the inhumanity of our times.

> Phyllis and Orlando Rodriguez,
> New York, 15 September 2001

I feel the American public has to join the international community in a meaningful way, and stop being an isolationist nation. One way we can do it is by educating ourselves.

It's not part of our national consciousness - the conditions under which people live in Iraq, Rwanda, Paraguay.

That's the first step: to learn about the sufferings and joys of other people. We have to find out why we are hated in other parts of the world.

> Phyllis Rodriguez, October 2001

ABE ZELMANOWITZ

Rita Lasar lost her brother Abe Zelmanowitz in the World Trade Centre on 11 September. He chose to stay on the 27th floor with a quadriplegic friend who could not descend the stairs. His heroism was later praised publicly by President Bush. Visiting a bereaved family in Afghanistan in January 2002, 70 year-old Rita Lasar said, **There is no heroism in bombing innocent civilians. So many people, especially politicians, seemed so keen to get angry on our behalf. It seemed the only people not in a rage were the families of the victims. We had too much grief to cope with for that.**

TOM THEURKAUF

My husband, Tom Theurkauf, lost his life in the World Trade Center disaster. We all direct our grief in different ways; this is mine.

I offer these thoughts both as a new widow and mother of three fatherless boys as well as a scholar of international law and politics.

We used to know what war was. It was the opposite of peace. Wars took place between states each with armies in uniforms and a hierarchical command structure. States went to war over territory or more recently over ideology. It is a legal status. One must declare it. At war's conclusion, we come to a peace agreement and return to a non-war condition.

This seems different. The enemy stays in the shadows even as they live among us, organised in loosely connected cells. No state has declared war against us, at least in the familiar way. The action was designed to spread fear and hate and so we are not entirely sure what would be required to end this conflict.

As we assemble a military platform in the Persian Gulf it is worth considering the fact that while political scientists know very few things with any confidence, there is substantial consensus on at least one relevant point.

While this attack was intended to provoke, responding in kind will only escalate the violence. Further, if we succumb to the understandable impulse to injure as we have been injured and in the process create even newer widows and fatherless children, perhaps we will deserve what we get.

Some have made the analogy to the attack on Pearl Harbor and in at least one way it is appropriate. In the aftermath of Pearl Harbor, thousands of young men volunteered to join the military. I can only imagine the success of radical Islam's recruiters after our bombs fall on their heads.

If not 'war', what words should we use? I think a better name is 'international crime'. Restating the problems refocuses the solution. In the short term, the first priority should be to hunt down and arrest the criminals with the goal of achieving justice, not revenge.

This is a task left not to the military but to investigative police forces, who can prepare for a trial.

Ordinary Americans also can take steps to fight back against this evil. We can combat fear and hate in part by reaching out to Muslims in our communities and by patronising Arab businesses. This show of solidarity will in part thwart these criminals' purpose of creating division in American communities.

In the long term, eradicating terrorism will require the elimination not of a group of people but rather of a set of ideas. Paradoxically, eliminating the people will reinforce and further legitimise the ideas. Terrorist impulses ferment in cultures of poverty, oppression and ignorance. The elimination of those conditions and the active promotion of a universal respect for human rights must become a national security priority.

Finally, the United States as a matter of policy must recognise and accept our vulnerability. In today's hyper-militarised environment, no state can ensure security within its borders without the cooperation of others.

The Bush administration's unilateralism has been revealed to be hollow. Rather than infringe on our sovereignty, international institutions enhance our ability to perform the functions of national government, including the ability to fight international crime.

Bombing Afghanistan today will not prevent tomorrow's tragedy. We must look beyond military options for long term solutions.

Professor Robin Theurkauf,
September 2001

What we need less of is war rhetoric, and war against Afghanistan in particular ...

The last thing I wanted was for more widows and fatherless children to be created in my name. It would only produce a backlash.

As the victim of violence, I'd never want this to happen to another woman again.

Professor Robin Theurkauf, October 2001

JIM POTORTI

Dad was getting ready to make a ground invasion of Japan the day they dropped the atomic bomb. It was a tradeoff: an estimated one million Americans were expected to lose their lives in that assault. Someone came running into camp saying the war was over, and they thought he was crazy, talking about something out of *Buck Rogers*. You could say the atomic bomb is the only reason I'm here today. You could also say that 200,000 Japanese civilians died to make it possible.

The 20th century was an exceedingly bad time to be a civilian. By one estimate, as the century began, 85 to 90 percent of wartime deaths were military. That dropped to less than 50 percent around World War II. As the century ended, three-quarters of wartime deaths were civilian. But it's soldiers, not civilians, who are seen as heroes - after all, they choose to be put in harm's way.

Maybe that's why I'm reluctant to classify my 52-year-old brother, Jim, as a hero - even though people keep telling me he is. He had the misfortune to be working on the 96th floor of One World Trade Center on the morning of Sept 11. To the best of our knowledge, he took a direct hit from the first airplane.

Jim's wife is a basket case. She can't stop talking, and the reason she can't stop talking, is that when she stops talking, she starts crying. So she keeps talking. Talking to friends on the phone, to family, to neighbors, to her sister, who's been sleeping over. She hugs me and says, "You're the right size. You're the only one who feels like him."

She's got a friend canvassing the hospitals. Jim's company is doing the same. She's filed a missing person's report with the New York City Police Department. It was four pages long and required her to identify her husband's body in intimate detail – down to the metal screws that remained after surgery for a broken leg. That was her trump card: the screws, like fingerprints, would identify him.

We've got more comfort to exchange, so we drive upstate the next day to see my parents. At 76, mom's been around long enough to bury a fair number of her friends. But a son? "This is going to kill my parents," I tell myself. But I know it won't - and the knowing only makes me sadder.

For the past three days, we've had an unspoken mutual agreement: we know Jim's dead, but we pretend he isn't. Word has trickled in: someone on Jim's floor got out. Someone above Jim's floor got out. Survivors have talked about which floor they were on, and how long it took them to run down the stairs before the buildings collapsed.

We've done the math: it would be close, but it's possible – Jim is in a hospital. Jim got ferried to New Jersey. Jim has a head injury and can't say who he is. But Jim is alive, somewhere.

On Friday, I get a call from Jim's wife in Princeton. She's found out exactly where he was sitting. And from an eyewitness, the damage done by the plane. It took out eight floors of the building, each one an acre across, and his floor was one of them.

He's gone, and he probably never knew what hit him. The suffering, she concludes, is all ours.

I reluctantly herd everyone into the living room – mom, dad, my wife, and my thankfully oblivious child – and relate the contents of the call. I have my arm around my mom when I hear a sound I have never heard before. It is a deep, almost mannish series of grunts. It is a heaving that seems to be coming from inside my mother's bones. Doubled over, she is repeating my brother's name: Jim. Jim. Jim.

I watch my parents, with that slight stoop of old age, stand up, shuffle over to each other, embrace, and weep. And I hear my mother say, "I don't want anyone else to ever have to feel this pain."

It's times like these when America becomes two countries, populated by two cultures. For one group, tragedy unites them in fellowship. There's family and friends, saying prayers, lighting candles, donating blood, sending mass cards, food and flowers.

Then there's the other group, the kind for whom an event of this order sharpens the lines of separation and difference. These people want blood – or at least, unquestioning allegiance.

It occurs to me that the only people I hear clamoring for war are people who have never experienced a real one. The president. Talk show hosts. Newspaper columnists. Most of Congress.

But the people who know what war is aren't in a hurry. They're quiet. They approach the topic with a reverence and a respect reserved for something bigger than they are.

Bomb who, bomb what, bomb where? My dad is stone faced. His buddy, Leo, was on Iwo Jima with him until he was wounded by a sniper. Leo earned a Purple Heart. He brings my parents communion every day.

In 1946, the Infantry Journal Press in Washington published *The Fourth Marine Division in World War II*, a hardcover book recounting the progress of the Marines as they island-hopped their way across the South Pacific. Roi-Namur. Saipan. Tinian. Iwo Jima. Dad eventually got three copies, one for each of his sons: Jim, Bill, and David. The book is a product of its time, with references to "Japs" and liberators. But the strategizing and heroics it relates are breathtaking.

The tone, however, is at odds with the note my dad wrote to me on page one: "May you never know the obscenity of war with all its pain and sorrow and destructiveness."

David Potorti
October 2001

This is an excerpt from 'Collateral Damage' by David Potorti.
The full article can be found at
http://www.indyweek.com/durham/2001-10-17/first.html

CRAIG SCOTT AMUNDSON

My husband, Craig Scott Amundson, of the U.S. Army lost his life in the line of duty at the Pentagon on September 11 as the world looked on in horror and disbelief.

Losing my 28-year-old husband and father of our two young children is a terrible and painful experience. His death is also part of an immense national loss and I am comforted by knowing so many share my grief.

But because I have lost Craig as part of this historic tragedy, my anguish is compounded exponentially by fear that his death will be used to justify new violence against other innocent victims.

I have heard angry rhetoric by some Americans, including many of our nation's leaders, who advise a heavy dose of revenge and punishment.

To those leaders, I would like to make clear that my family and I take no comfort in your words of rage. If you choose to respond to this incomprehensible brutality by perpetuating violence against other innocent human beings, you may not do so in the name of justice for my husband.

Your words and imminent acts of revenge only amplify our family's suffering, deny us the dignity of remembering our loved one in a way that would have made him proud, and mock his vision of America as a peacemaker in the world community.

Craig enlisted in the Army and was proud to serve his country. He was a patriotic American and a citizen of the world. Craig believed that by working from within the military system he could help to maintain the military focus on peacekeeping and strategic planning – to prevent violence and war.

For the last two years Craig drove to his job at the Pentagon with a 'visualize world peace' bumper sticker on his car. This was not empty rhetoric or contradictory to him, but part of his dream. He believed his role in the Army could further the cause of peace throughout the world.

Craig would not have wanted a violent response to avenge his death.

And I cannot see how good can come out of it.

I ask our nation's leaders not to take the path that leads to more widespread hatreds – that makes my husband's death just one more in an unending spiral of killing. I call on our national leaders to find the courage to respond to this incomprehensible tragedy by breaking the cycle of violence.

I do not know how to begin making a better world: I do believe it must be done, and I believe it is our leaders' responsibility to find a way.

I urge them to take up this challenge and respond to our nation's and my personal tragedy with a new beginning that gives us hope for a peaceful global community.

Amber Amundson,
25 September 2001

My niece Charlotte, whose father Craig was killed in the Pentagon, was barely two and a half on September 11. We weren't really sure how much Charlotte knew what was going on. One day, we walked this nature trail near their house, and I asked if she had been there before. She looked down at her shoes and said, 'Yes, Daddy used to take me here. A plane crashed into Daddy's work, and Daddy couldn't get out.'

And, in Afghanistan, I met an eight-year-old boy who told us that he had been playing near his house, and his friend had seen something yellow, and picked it up, and he'd watched his friend explode and die.

And now he's in the hospital missing part of his hand. And it is just so horrible that we live in a world where children have these stories.

And it made me think about how I'm going to explain all this to Charlotte some day, and what action has our Government taken to respond to Craig's murder.

As far as I can tell, the main action that they've taken is to kill more innocent people and to give more children horrible stories to tell.

Kelly Campbell
London, February 2002

**SEPTEMBER ELEVENTH FAMILIES
FOR PEACEFUL TOMORROWS**

Peaceful Tomorrows is an advocacy organization
founded by family members of September Eleventh victims.
Its mission is to seek effective nonviolent responses to terrorism,
and identify a commonality with all people similarly affected by violence
throughout the world. By conscientiously exploring peaceful options
in our search for justice, we choose to spare additional innocent families
the suffering that we have already experienced—as well as to break
the endless cycle of violence and retaliation engendered by
war.

www.peacefultomorrows.org

Wars are poor chisels for carving out peaceful tomorrows.

Martin Luther King, Jr.

CHAPTER II

Terror and Just Response
NOAM CHOMSKY

DEFINING TERRORISM

September 11 will surely go down in the annals of terrorism as a defining moment. Throughout the world, the atrocities were condemned as grave crimes against humanity, with near-universal agreement that all states must act to 'rid the world of evildoers,' that 'the evil scourge of terrorism' – particularly state-backed international terrorism – is a plague spread by 'depraved opponents of civilization itself' in a 'return to barbarism' that cannot be tolerated. But beyond the strong support for the words of the US political leadership – respectively, George W. Bush, Ronald Reagan, and his Secretary of State George Shultz[1] – interpretations varied: on the narrow question of the proper response to terrorist crimes, and on the broader problem of determining their nature.

On the latter, an official US definition takes 'terrorism' to be 'the calculated use of violence or threat of violence to attain goals that are political, religious, or ideological in nature ... through intimidation, coercion, or instilling fear.'[2] That formulation leaves many questions open, among them, the legitimacy of actions to realize 'the right to self-determination, freedom, and independence, as derived from the Charter of the United Nations, of people forcibly deprived of that right ... , particularly peoples under colonial and racist regimes and foreign occupation ... ' In its most forceful denunciation of the crime of terrorism, the UN General Assembly endorsed such actions, voting 153 to 2.[3]

Explaining their negative votes, the US and Israel referred to the wording just cited. It was understood to justify resistance against the South African regime, a US ally that was responsible for over 1.5 million dead and $60 billion in damage in neighboring countries in 1980–88 alone, putting aside its practices within. And the resistance was led by Nelson Mandela's African National Congress, one of the 'more notorious terrorist groups' according to a 1988 Pentagon report, in contrast to pro-South African RENAMO, which the same report describes as merely an 'indigenous insurgent group' while observing that it might have killed 100,000 civilians in Mozambique in the preceding two years.[4] The same wording was taken to justify resistance to Israel's military occupation, then in its 20th year, continuing its integration of the occupied territories and harsh practices with decisive US aid and diplomatic support, the latter to block the longstanding international consensus on a peaceful settlement.[5]

Despite such fundamental disagreements, the official US definition seems to me adequate for the purposes at hand,[6] though the disagreements shed some light on the nature of terrorism, as perceived from various perspectives. Let us turn to the question of proper response. Some argue that the evil of terrorism is 'absolute' and merits a 'reciprocally absolute doctrine' in response.[7] That would appear to mean ferocious military assault in accord with the Bush doctrine, cited with apparent approval in the same academic collection on the 'age of terror': '*If you harbor terrorists, you're a terrorist; if you aid and abet terrorists, you're a terrorist – and you will be treated like one.*' The volume reflects articulate opinion in the West in taking the US-UK response to be appropriate and properly 'calibrated,' but the scope of that consensus appears to be limited, judging by the evidence available, to which we return.

More generally, it would be hard to find anyone who accepts the doctrine that massive bombing is the appropriate response to terrorist crimes – whether those of September 11, or even worse ones, which are, unfortunately, not hard to find. That follows if we adopt the principle of universality: if an action is right (or wrong) for others, it is right (or wrong) for us. Those who do not rise to the minimal moral level of applying to themselves the standards they apply to others – more stringent ones, in fact – plainly cannot be taken seriously when they speak of appropriateness of response; or of right and wrong, good and evil.

THE NICARAGUAN EXAMPLE

To illustrate what is at stake, consider a case that is far from the most extreme but is uncontroversial; at least, among those with some respect for international law and treaty obligations. No one would have supported Nicaraguan bombings in Washington when the US rejected the order of the World Court to terminate its 'unlawful use of force' and pay substantial reparations, choosing instead to escalate the international terrorist crimes and to extend them, officially, to attacks on undefended civilian targets, also vetoing a Security Council resolution calling on all states to observe international law and voting alone at the General Assembly (with one or two client states) against similar resolutions. The US dismissed the International Court of Justice on the grounds that other nations do not agree with us, so we must 'reserve to ourselves the power to determine whether the Court has jurisdiction over us in a particular case' and what lies 'essentially within the domestic jurisdiction of the United States' – in this case, terrorist attacks against Nicaragua.[8]

Meanwhile Washington continued to undermine regional efforts to reach a political settlement, following the doctrine formulated by the Administration moderate, George Shultz: the US must 'cut [the Nicaraguan cancer] out,' by force. Shultz dismissed with contempt those who advocate 'utopian, legalistic means like outside mediation, the United Nations, and the World Court, while ignoring the power element of the equation'; 'Negotiations are a euphemism for capitulation if the shadow of power is not cast across the bargaining table,' he declared. Washington continued to adhere to the Shultz doctrine when the Central American Presidents agreed on a peace plan in 1987 over strong US objections: the Esquipulas Accords, which required that all countries of the region move towards democracy and human rights under international supervision, stressing that the 'indispensable element' was the termination of the US attack against Nicaragua. Washington responded by sharply expanding the attack, tripling CIA supply flights for the terrorist forces. Having exempted itself from the Accords, thus effectively undermining them, Washington proceeded to do the same for its client regimes, using the substance – not the shadow – of power to dismantle the International Verification Commission (CIVS) because its conclusions were unacceptable, and demanding, successfully, that the Accords be revised to free US client states to continue their terrorist atrocities. These far surpassed even the devastating US war against Nicaragua that left tens of thousands dead and the country ruined perhaps beyond recovery. Still upholding the Shultz doctrine, the US compelled the government of Nicaragua, under severe threat, to drop the claim for reparations established by the ICJ.[9]

There could hardly be a clearer example of international terrorism as defined officially, or in scholarship: operations aimed at 'demonstrating through apparently indiscriminate violence that the existing regime cannot protect the people nominally under its authority,' thus causing not only 'anxiety, but withdrawal from the relationships making up the established order of society.'[10] State terror elsewhere in Central America in those years also counts as international terrorism, in the light of the decisive US role, and the goals, sometimes frankly articulated; for example, by the Army's School of the Americas, which trains Latin American military officers and takes pride in the fact that 'Liberation Theology ... was defeated with the assistance of the U.S. Army.'[11]

It would seem to follow, clearly enough, that only those who support bombing of Washington in response to these international terrorist crimes – that is, no one – can accept the 'reciprocally absolute doctrine' on response to terrorist atrocities or consider massive bombardment to be an appropriate and properly 'calibrated' response to them.

EXTENDING THE PRINCIPLE

Consider some of the legal arguments that have been presented to justify the US-UK bombing of Afghanistan; I am not concerned here with their soundness, but their implications, if the principle of uniform standards is maintained. Christopher Greenwood argues that the US has the right of 'self-defense' against 'those who caused or threatened ... death and destruction,' appealing to the ICJ ruling in the Nicaragua case. The paragraph he cites applies far more clearly to the US war against Nicaragua than to the Taliban or al-Qaeda, so if it is taken to justify intensive US bombardment and ground attack in Afghanistan, then Nicaragua should have been entitled to carry out much more severe attacks against the US. Another distinguished professor of international law, Thomas Franck, supports the US-UK war on grounds that 'a state is responsible for the consequences of permitting its territory to be used to injure another state'; fair enough, and surely applicable to the US in the case of Nicaragua, Cuba, and many other examples, including some of extreme severity.[12]

Needless to say, in none of these cases would violence in 'self-defense' against continuing acts of 'death and destruction' be considered remotely tolerable; acts, not merely 'threats.'

The same holds of more nuanced proposals about an appropriate response to terrorist atrocities. Military historian Michael Howard proposes 'a police operation conducted under the auspices of the United Nations ... against a criminal conspiracy whose members should be hunted down and brought before an international court, where they would receive a fair trial and, if found guilty, be awarded an appropriate sentence.' Reasonable enough, though the idea that the proposal should be applied universally is unthinkable. The director of the Center for the Politics of Human Rights at Harvard argues that 'The only responsible response to acts of terror is honest police work and judicial prosecution in courts of law, linked to determinate, focused and unrelenting use of military power against those who cannot or will not be brought to justice.'[13] That too seems sensible, if we add Howard's qualification about international supervision, and if the resort to force is undertaken after legal means have been exhausted. The recommendation therefore does not apply to 9–11 (the US refused to provide evidence and rebuffed tentative proposals about transfer of the suspects), but it does apply very clearly to Nicaragua.

It applies to other cases as well. Take Haiti, which has provided ample evidence in its repeated calls for extradition of Emmanuel Constant, who directed the forces responsible for thousands of deaths under the military junta that the US was tacitly supporting (not to speak of earlier history); these requests the US ignores, presumably because of concerns about what Constant would reveal if tried. The most recent request was on 30 September 2001, while the US was demanding that the Taliban hand over Bin Laden.[14] The coincidence was also ignored, in accord with the convention that minimal moral standards must be vigorously rejected.

RESPONDING TO TERROR

Turning to the 'responsible response,' a call for implementation of it where it is clearly applicable would elicit only fury and contempt. Some have formulated more general principles to justify the US war in Afghanistan. Two Oxford scholars propose a principle of 'proportionality': 'The magnitude of response will be determined by the magnitude with which the aggression interfered with key values in the society attacked'; in the US case, 'freedom to pursue self-betterment in a plural society through market economics,' viciously attacked on 9–11 by 'aggressors ... with a moral orthodoxy divergent from the West.' Since 'Afghanistan constitutes a state that sided with the aggressor,' and refused US demands to turn over suspects, 'the United States and its allies, according to the principle of magnitude of interference, could justifiably and morally resort to force against the Taliban government.'[15]

On the assumption of universality, it follows that Haiti and Nicaragua can 'justifiably and morally resort to' far greater force against the US government. The conclusion extends far beyond these two cases, including much more serious ones and even such minor escapades of Western state terror as Clinton's bombing of the al-Shifa pharmaceutical plant in Sudan in 1998, leading to 'several tens of thousands' of deaths according to the German Ambassador and other reputable sources, whose conclusions are consistent with the immediate assessments of knowledgeable observers.[16] The principle of proportionality therefore entails that Sudan had every right to carry out massive terror in retaliation, a conclusion that is strengthened if we go on to adopt the view that this act of 'the empire' had 'appalling consequences for the economy and society' of Sudan so that the atrocity was much worse than the crimes of 9–11, which were appalling enough, but did not have such consequences.[17]

Most commentary on the Sudan bombing keeps to the question of whether the plant was believed to produce chemical weapons; true or false, that has no bearing on 'the magnitude with which the aggression interfered with key values in the society attacked,' such as survival. Others point out that the killings were unintended, as are many of the atrocities we rightly denounce. In this case, we can hardly doubt that the likely human consequences were understood by US planners. The acts can be excused, then, only on the Hegelian assumption that Africans are 'mere things,' whose lives have 'no value,' an attitude that accords with practice in ways that are not overlooked among the victims, who may draw their own conclusions about the 'moral orthodoxy of the West.'

THE FIRST 'WAR ON TERROR'

One participant in the Yale volume (Charles Hill) recognized that 11 September opened the *second* 'war on terror.' The first was declared by the Reagan administration as it came to office 20 years earlier, with the rhetorical accompaniment already illustrated; and 'we won,' Hill reports triumphantly, though the terrorist monster was only wounded, not slain.[18] The first 'age of terror' proved to be a major issue in international affairs through the decade, particularly in Central America, but also in the Middle East, where terrorism was selected by editors as the lead story of the year in 1985 and ranked high in other years.

We can learn a good deal about the current war on terror by inquiring into the first phase, and how it is now portrayed. One leading academic specialist describes the 1980s as the decade of 'state terrorism,' of 'persistent state involvement, or 'sponsorship,' of terrorism, especially by Libya and Iran.' The US merely responded, by adopting 'a "proactive" stance toward terrorism.' Others recommend the methods by which 'we won': the operations for which the US was condemned by the World Court and Security Council (absent the veto) are a model for 'Nicaragua-like support for the Taliban's adversaries (especially the Northern Alliance).' A prominent historian of the subject finds deep roots for the terrorism of Osama Bin Laden: in South Vietnam, where 'the effectiveness of Vietcong terror against the American Goliath armed with modern technology kindled hopes that the Western heartland was vulnerable too.'[19]

Keeping to convention, these analyses portray the US as a benign victim, defending itself from the terror of others: the Vietnamese (in South Vietnam), the Nicaraguans (in Nicaragua), Libyans and Iranians (if they had ever suffered a slight at US hands, it passes unnoticed), and other anti-American forces worldwide.

Not everyone sees the world quite that way. The most obvious place to look is Latin America, which has had considerable experience with international terrorism. The crimes of 9–11 were harshly condemned, but commonly with recollection of their own experiences. One might describe the 9–11 atrocities as 'Armageddon,' the research journal of the Jesuit university in Managua observed, but Nicaragua has 'lived its own Armageddon in excruciating slow motion' under US assault 'and is now submerged in its dismal aftermath,' and others fared far worse under the vast plague of state terror that swept through the continent from the early 1960s, much of it traceable to Washington. A Panamanian journalist joined in the general condemnation of the 9–11 crimes, but recalled the death of perhaps thousands of poor people (Western crimes, therefore unexamined) when the President's father bombed the barrio Chorillo in December 1989 in Operation Just Cause, undertaken to kidnap a disobedient thug who was sentenced to life imprisonment in Florida for crimes mostly committed while he was on the CIA payroll. Uruguayan writer Eduardo Galeano observed that the US claims to oppose terrorism, but actually supports it worldwide, including 'in Indonesia, in Cambodia, in Iran, in South Africa, ... and in the Latin American countries that lived through the dirty war of the Condor Plan,' instituted by South American military dictators who conducted a reign of terror with US backing.[20]

THE MIDDLE EAST

The observations carry over to the second focus of the first 'war on terror': West Asia. The worst single atrocity was the Israeli invasion of Lebanon in 1982, which left some 20,000 people dead and much of the country in ruins, including Beirut. Like the murderous and destructive Rabin-Peres invasions of 1993 and 1996, the 1982 attack had little pretense of self-defense. Chief of Staff Rafael ('Raful') Eitan merely articulated common understanding when he announced that the goal was to 'destroy the PlO as a candidate for negotiations with us about the land of Israel,'[21] a textbook illustration of terror as officially defined. The goal 'was to install a friendly regime and destroy Mr. Arafat's Palestinian Liberation Organization,' Middle East correspondent James Bennet writes: 'That, the theory went, would help persuade Palestinians to accept Israeli rule in the West Bank and Gaza Strip.'[22] This may be the first recognition in the mainstream of facts widely reported in Israel at the time, previously accessible only in dissident literature in the US.

These operations were carried out with the crucial military and diplomatic support of the Reagan and Clinton administrations, and therefore constitute international terrorism. The US was also directly involved in other acts of terror in the region in the 1980s, including the most extreme terrorist atrocities of the peak year of 1985: the CIA car-bombing in Beirut that killed 80 people and wounded 250; Shimon Peres's bombing of Tunis that killed 75 people, expedited by the US and praised by Secretary of State Shultz, unanimously condemned by the UN Security Council as an 'act of armed aggression' (US abstaining); and Peres's 'Iron Fist' operations directed against 'terrorist villagers' in Lebanon, reaching new depths of 'calculated brutality and arbitrary murder,' in the words of a Western diplomat familiar with the area, amply supported by direct coverage.[23] Again, all international terrorism, if not the more severe war crime of aggression.

In journalism and scholarship on terrorism, 1985 is recognized to be the peak year of Middle East terrorism, but not because of these events: rather, because of two terrorist atrocities in which a single person was murdered, in each case an American.[24] But the victims do not so easily forget.

This very recent history takes on added significance because leading figures in the re-declared 'war on terror' played a prominent part in its precursor. The diplomatic component of the current phase is led by John Negroponte, who was Reagan's Ambassador to Honduras, the base for the terrorist atrocities for which his government was condemned by the World Court and for US-backed state terror elsewhere in Central America, activities that 'made the Reagan years the worse decade for Central America since the Spanish conquest,' mostly on Negroponte's watch.[25] The military component of the new phase is led by Donald Rumsfeld, Reagan's special envoy to the Middle East during the years of the worst terrorist atrocities there, initiated or supported by his government.

No less instructive is the fact that such atrocities did not abate in subsequent years. Specifically, Washington's contribution to 'enhancing terror' in the Israel-Arab confrontation continues. The term is President Bush's, intended, according to convention, to apply to the terrorism of others. Departing from convention, we find, again, some rather significant examples. One simple way to enhance terror is to participate in it, for example, by sending helicopters to be used to attack civilian complexes and carry out assassinations, as the US regularly does in full awareness of the consequences. Another is to bar the dispatch of international monitors to reduce violence. The US has insisted on this course, once again vetoing a UN Security Council resolution to this effect on 14 December 2001. Describing Arafat's fall from grace to a position barely above Bin Laden and Saddam Hussein, the press reports that President Bush was 'greatly angered [by] a last-minute hardening of a Palestinian position ... for international monitors in Palestinian areas under a UN Security Council resolution'; that is, by Arafat's joining the rest of the world in calling for means to reduce terror.[26]

Ten days before the veto of monitors, the US boycotted – thus undermined – an international conference in Geneva that reaffirmed the applicability of the Fourth Geneva Convention to the occupied territories, so that most US-Israeli actions there are war crimes – and when 'grave breaches,' as many are, serious war crimes. These include US-funded Israeli settlements and the practice of 'wilful killing, torture, unlawful deportation, wilful depriving of the rights of fair and regular trial, extensive destruction and appropriation of property ... carried out unlawfully and wantonly.'[27] The Convention, instituted to criminalize formally the crimes of the Nazis in occupied Europe, is a core principle of international humanitarian law. Its applicability to the Israeli-occupied territories has repeatedly been affirmed, among other occasions, by UN Ambassador George Bush (September 1971) and by Security Council resolutions: 465 (1980), adopted unanimously, which condemned US-backed Israeli practices as 'flagrant violations' of the Convention; 1322 (Oct. 2000), 14–0, US abstaining, which called on Israel 'to abide scrupulously by its responsibilities under the Fourth Geneva Convention,' which it was again violating flagrantly at that moment. As High Contracting Parties, the US and the European powers are obligated by solemn treaty to apprehend and prosecute those responsible for such crimes, including their own leadership when they are parties to them. By continuing to reject that duty, they are enhancing terror directly and significantly.

TURKEY

Inquiry into the US-Israel-Arab conflicts would carry us too far afield. Let's turn further north, to another region where 'state terror' is being practiced on a massive scale; I borrow the term from the Turkish State Minister for Human Rights, referring to the vast atrocities of 1994; and sociologist Ismail Besikci, returned to prison after publishing his book *State Terror in the Near East*, having already served 15 years for recording Turkish repression of Kurds.[28] I had a chance to see some of the consequences firsthand when visiting the unofficial Kurdish capital of Diyarbakir several months after 9–11. As elsewhere, the crimes of September 11 were harshly condemned, but not without memory of the savage assault the population had suffered at the hands of those who appoint themselves to 'rid the world of evildoers,' and their local agents.

By 1994, the Turkish State Minister and others estimated that 2 million had been driven out of the devastated countryside, many more later, often with barbaric torture and terror described in excruciating detail in international human rights reports, but kept from the eyes of those paying the bills. Tens of thousands were killed. The remnants – whose courage is indescribable – live in a dungeon where radio stations are closed and journalists imprisoned for playing Kurdish music, students are arrested and tortured for submitting requests to take elective courses in their own language, there can be severe penalties if children are found wearing Kurdish national colors by the omnipresent security forces, the respected lawyer who heads the human rights organization was indicted shortly after I was there for using the Kurdish rather than the virtually identical Turkish spelling for the New Year's celebration; and on, and on.

These acts fall under the category of state-sponsored international terrorism. The US provided 80% of the arms, peaking in 1997, when arms transfers exceeded the entire Cold War period combined before the 'counter-terror' campaign began in 1984. Turkey became the leading recipient of US arms worldwide, a position it retained until 1999 when the torch was passed to Colombia, the leading practitioner of state terror in the Western hemisphere.[29]

State terror is also 'enhanced' by silence and evasion. The achievement was particularly notable against the background of an unprecedented chorus of self-congratulation as US foreign policy entered a 'noble phase' with a 'saintly glow,' under the guidance of leaders who for the first time in history were dedicated to 'principles and values' rather than narrow interests.[30] The proof of the new saintliness was their unwillingness to tolerate crimes near the borders of NATO – only within its borders, where even worse crimes, not in reaction to NATO bombs, were not only tolerable but required enthusiastic participation, without comment. US-sponsored Turkish state terror does not pass entirely unnoticed. The State Department's annual report on Washington's 'efforts to combat terrorism' singled out Turkey for its 'positive experiences' in combating terror, along with Algeria and Spain, worthy colleagues.

This was reported without comment in a front-page story in the *New York Times* by its specialist on terrorism. In a leading journal of international affairs, Ambassador Robert Pearson reports that the US 'could have no better friend and ally than Turkey' in its efforts 'to eliminate terrorism' worldwide, thanks to the 'capabilities of its armed forces' demonstrated in its 'anti-terror campaign' in the Kurdish southeast. It thus 'came as no surprise' that Turkey eagerly joined the 'war on terror' declared by George Bush, expressing its thanks to the US for being the only country willing to lend the needed support for the atrocities of the Clinton years – still continuing, though on a lesser scale now that 'we won.'

LAUDING TERROR

As a reward for its achievements, the US is now funding Turkey to provide the ground forces for fighting 'the war on terror' in Kabul, though not beyond.[31] Atrocious state-sponsored international terrorism is thus not overlooked: it is lauded. That also 'comes as no surprise.' After all, in 1995 the Clinton administration welcomed Indonesia's General Suharto, one of the worst killers and torturers of the late 20th century, as 'our kind of guy.' When he came to power 30 years earlier, the 'staggering mass slaughter' of hundreds of thousands of people, mostly landless peasants, was reported fairly accurately and acclaimed with unconstrained euphoria. When Nicaraguans finally succumbed to US terror and voted the right way, the US was 'United in Joy' at this 'Victory for US Fair Play,' headlines proclaimed. It is easy enough to multiply examples. The current episode breaks no new ground in the record of international terrorism and the response it elicits among the perpetrators.

AFTER 11 SEPTEMBER

let's return to the question of the proper response to acts of terror, specifically 9–11.

It is commonly alleged that the US-UK reaction was undertaken with wide international support. That is tenable, however, only if one keeps to elite opinion. An international Gallup poll found only minority support for military attack rather than diplomatic means.[32] In Europe, figures ranged from 8% in Greece to 29% in France. In Latin America, support was even lower: from 2% in Mexico to 16% in Panama. Support for strikes that included civilian targets was very slight. Even in the two countries polled that strongly supported the use of military force, India and Israel (where the reasons were parochial), considerable majorities opposed such attacks. There was, then, overwhelming opposition to the actual policies, which turned major urban concentrations into 'ghost towns' from the first moment, the press reported.

Omitted from the poll, as from most commentary, was the anticipated effect of US policy on Afghans, millions of whom were on the brink of starvation even before 9–11. Unasked, for example, is whether a proper response to 9–11 was to demand that Pakistan eliminate 'truck convoys that provide much of the food and other supplies to Afghanistan's civilian population,' and to cause the withdrawal of aid workers and a severe reduction in food supplies that left 'millions of Afghans … at grave risk of starvation,' eliciting sharp protests from aid organizations and warnings of severe humanitarian crisis, judgments reiterated at the war's end.[33]

It is, of course, the assumptions of planning that are relevant to evaluating the actions taken; that too should be transparent. The actual outcome, a separate matter, is unlikely to be known, even roughly; crimes of others are carefully investigated, but not one's own. Some indication is perhaps suggested by the occasional reports on numbers needing food aid: 5 million before 9–11, 7.5 million at the end of September under the threat of bombing, 9 million six months later, not because of lack of food, which was readily available throughout, but because of distribution problems as the country reverted to warlordism.[34]

There are no reliable studies of Afghan opinion, but information is not entirely lacking. At the outset, President Bush warned Afghans that they would be bombed until they handed over people the US suspected of terrorism. Three weeks later, war aims shifted to overthrow of the regime: the bombing would continue, Admiral Sir Michael Boyce announced, 'until the people of the country themselves recognize that this is going to go on until they get the leadership changed.'[35] Note that the question of whether the overthrow of the miserable Taliban regime justifies the bombing does not arise, because that did not become a war aim until well after the fact. We can, however, ask about the opinions of Afghans within reach of Western observers about these choices – which, in both cases, clearly fall within the official definition of international terrorism.

As war aims shifted to regime replacement in late October, 1000 Afghan leaders gathered in Peshawar, some exiles, some coming from within Afghanistan, all committed to overthrowing the Taliban regime. It was 'a rare display of unity among tribal elders, Islamic scholars, fractious politicians, and former guerrilla commanders,' the press reported. They unanimously 'urged the US to stop the air raids,' appealed to the international media to call for an end to the 'bombing of innocent people,' and 'demanded an end to the US bombing of Afghanistan.' They urged that other means be adopted to overthrow the hated Taliban regime, a goal they believed could be achieved without death and destruction.[36]

A similar message was conveyed by Afghan opposition leader Abdul Haq, who was highly regarded in Washington. Just before he entered Afghanistan, apparently without US support, and was then captured and killed, he condemned the bombing and criticized the US for refusing to support efforts of his and of others 'to create a revolt within the Taliban.' The bombing was 'a big setback for these efforts,' he said. He reported contacts with second-level Taliban commanders and ex-Mujahiddin tribal elders, and discussed how such efforts could proceed, calling on the US to assist them with funding and other support instead of undermining them with bombs. But the US, he said, 'is trying to show its muscle, score a victory and scare everyone in the world. They don't care about the suffering of the Afghans or how many people we will lose.'[37]

The plight of Afghan women elicited some belated concern after 9–11. After the war, there was even some recognition of the courageous women who have been in the forefront of the struggle to defend women's rights for 25 years, RAWA (Revolutionary Association of the Women of Afghanistan). A week after the bombing began, RAWA issued a public statement (Oct. 11) that would have been front-page news wherever concern for Afghan women was real, not a matter of mere expediency. They condemned the resort to 'the monster of a vast war and destruction' as the US 'launched a vast aggression on our country,' that will cause great harm to innocent Afghans. They called instead for 'the eradication of the plague of Taliban and Al Qieda' by 'an overall uprising' of the Afghan people themselves, which alone 'can prevent the repetition and recurrence of the catastrophe that has befallen our country ...'.

All of this was ignored. It is, perhaps, less than obvious that those with the guns are entitled to ignore the judgment of Afghans who have been struggling for freedom and women's rights for many years, and to dismiss with apparent contempt their desire to overthrow the fragile and hated Taliban regime from within without the inevitable crimes of war. In brief, review of global opinion, including what is known about Afghans, lends little support to the consensus among Western intellectuals on the justice of their cause.

One elite reaction, however, is certainly correct: it is necessary to inquire into the reasons for the crimes of 9–11. That much is beyond question, at least among those who hope to reduce the likelihood of further terrorist atrocities.

A narrow question is the motives of the perpetrators. On this matter, there is little disagreement. Serious analysts are in accord that after the US established permanent bases in Saudi Arabia, 'Bin Laden became preoccupied with the need to expel U.S. forces from the sacred soil of Arabia' and to rid the Muslim world of the 'liars and hypocrites' who do not accept his extremist version of Islam.[38]

THE ROOTS OF AL QAEDA

There is also wide, and justified, agreement that 'Unless the social, political, and economic conditions that spawned Al Qaeda and other associated groups are addressed, the United States and its allies in Western Europe and elsewhere will continue to be targeted by Islamist terrorists.'[39] These conditions are doubtless complex, but some factors have long been recognized.

In 1958, a crucial year in postwar history, President Eisenhower advised his staff that in the Arab world, 'the problem is that we have a campaign of hatred against us, not by the governments but by the people,' who are 'on Nasser's side,' supporting independent secular nationalism. The reasons for the 'campaign of hatred' had been outlined by the National Security Council a few months earlier: 'In the eyes of the majority of Arabs the United States appears to be opposed to the realization of the goals of Arab nationalism. They believe that the United States is seeking to protect its interest in Near East oil by supporting the *status quo* and opposing political or economic progress ... '. Furthermore, the perception is accurate: 'our economic and cultural interests in the area have led not unnaturally to close U.S. relations with elements in the Arab world whose primary interest lies in the maintenance of relations with the West and the status quo in their countries ...'[40]

The perceptions persist. Immediately after 9–11, the *Wall Street Journal*, later others, began to investigate opinions of 'moneyed Muslims': bankers, professionals, managers of multinationals, and so on. They strongly support US policies in general, but are bitter about the US role in the region: about US support for corrupt and repressive regimes that undermine democracy and development, and about specific policies, particularly regarding Palestine and Iraq. Though they are not surveyed, attitudes in the slums and villages are probably similar, but harsher; unlike the 'moneyed Muslims,' the mass of the population have never agreed that the wealth of the region should be drained to the West and local collaborators, rather than serving domestic needs. The 'moneyed Muslims' recognize, ruefully, that Bin Laden's angry rhetoric has considerable resonance, in their own circles as well, even though they hate and fear him, if only because they are among his primary targets.[41]

It is doubtless more comforting to believe that the answer to George Bush's plaintive query, 'Why do they hate us?,' lies in their resentment of our freedom and love of democracy, or their cultural failings tracing back many centuries, or their inability to take part in the form of 'globalization' in which they happily participate. Comforting, perhaps, but not wise. Though shocking, the atrocities of 9–11 could not have been entirely unexpected. Related organizations planned very serious terrorist acts through the 1990s, and in 1993 came perilously close to blowing up the World Trade Center, with much more ambitious plans. Their thinking was well understood, certainly by the US intelligence agencies that had helped to recruit, train, and arm them from 1980 and continued to work with them even as they were attacking the US. The Dutch government inquiry into the Srebrenica massacre revealed that while they were attempting to blow up the World Trade Center, radical Islamists from the CIA-formed networks were being flown by the US from Afghanistan to Bosnia, along with Iranian-backed Hizbollah fighters and a huge flow of arms, through Croatia, which took a substantial cut. They were being brought to support the US side in the Balkan wars, while Israel (along with Ukraine and Greece) was arming the Serbs (possibly with US-supplied arms), which explains why 'unexploded mortar bombs landing in Sarajevo sometimes had Hebrew markings,' British political scientist Richard Aldrich observes, reviewing the Dutch government report.[42]

More generally, the atrocities of 9–11 serve as a dramatic reminder of what has long been understood: with contemporary technology, the rich and powerful no longer are assured the near monopoly of violence that has largely prevailed throughout history. Though terrorism is rightly feared everywhere, and is indeed an intolerable 'return to barbarism,' it is not surprising that perceptions about its nature differ rather sharply in the light of sharply differing experiences, facts that will be ignored at their peril by those whom history has accustomed to immunity while they perpetrate terrible crimes.

Noam Chomsky
July 2002

Emily Johns

CHAPTER III

The Smoking Gun

The Taliban Had Agreed To Extradite Bin Laden

The argument for making war on Afghanistan rested on two propositions: firstly, that there was incontrovertible evidence that the atrocities of 11 September were organised by Osama bin Laden; and, secondly, that there was no nonviolent means of apprehending the al Qaeda leader. In fact, these two propositions do not amount to a justification for the use of force, but let us keep to establishment assumptions.

On 4 October 2001, two interesting things happened in Britain. Prime Minister Tony Blair produced a dossier of 'evidence' against Mr bin Laden, which was rubbished throughout the British media – described by the *Independent on Sunday*, for example, as 'conjecture, supposition and assertions of fact'.[1] Hardly incontrovertible evidence.

Also on 4 October 2001, the *Daily Telegraph* carried a story under the heading 'Pakistan halts secret plan for bin Laden trial'.[2] According to this report, leaders of two Pakistani Islamic parties, the Jamaat-i-Islami and the Jamaat Ulema-e-Islam, negotiated Mr bin Laden's extradition to Pakistan to stand trial for the 11 September attacks. The agreement was that Mr bin Laden would be held under house arrest in Peshawar, and tried before an international tribunal under Islamic shar'ia law.

The first stage of the negotiations was apparently carried out in Islamabad on 29 September, when Mullah Abdul Salaam Zaeef, the Taliban Ambassador to Pakistan, met Qazi Hussain Ahmad, leader of the Jamaat-i-Islami, and Hamid Gul, former director of Pakistan's powerful Inter-Service Intelligence agency. The negotiations were concluded in Kandahar on 1 October, when Mr Qazi, and Maaulana Fazlur Rahman, head of the Jamaat Ulema-e-Islam, met the supreme leader of the Taliban, Mullah Omar, who accepted the proposal - 'which had bin Laden's approval'.

One key element of the agreement was that the international tribunal could decide either to try him on the spot or to hand Mr bin Laden over to America. This was a new departure for the Taliban. Up until 1 October, the Taliban had been offering to negotiate bin Laden's extradition to a third country, but had refused to contemplate the possibility of handing him over to Washington.

Why did the extradition break down? It was not blocked by the head of the Taliban, Mullah Omar. According to the *Daily Telegraph*, the extradition was vetoed by Pakistan's military leader, 'President' Musharraf. The ostensible stumbling block 'was that he [Musharraf] could not guarantee bin Laden's safety'. This is rather implausible.

It is intriguing to read that the US Ambassador to Pakistan, Wendy Chamberlain, was notified in advance of the mission to meet Mullah Omar. During the war on Afghanistan, a US official was quoted as saying that 'casting the objectives too narrowly would risk a premature collapse of the international effort if by some lucky chance Mr bin Laden were captured'.[3] It is at least conceivable – in my view it is likely – that it was a US veto that killed the extradition agreement, just as US hostility had rebuffed previous extradition offers from the Taliban (see below).

Far from there having been no nonviolent way to secure the capture or extradition of Osama bin Laden, there was in fact an agreement to extradite the terrorist leader to one of the United States' allies – an extradition agreement that is reported to have had Mr bin Laden's approval. Given Pakistan's new role as a US ally in the so-called 'war on terrorism', the transfer from Afghanistan to Pakistan should have been a welcome step in bringing Mr bin Laden to trial. Furthermore, the *Daily Telegraph* report clearly states that extradition to the United States would be a real possibility under this deal. Nevertheless this agreement failed to receive support or even acknowledgement from either the United States or Britain.

PREVIOUS OFFERS

There were a number of Taliban offers to negotiate the extradition of Mr bin Laden. A week after 11 September, the Taliban Information Minister, Qudrutullah Jamal, said, 'Anyone who is responsible for this act, Osama or not, we will not side with him. We told [a Pakistani delegation to Afghanistan] to give us proof that he did it, because without that how can we give him up?' Days later, Taliban Ambassador to Pakistan, Mullah Zaeef said, 'We are not ready to hand over Osama bin Laden *without evidence*.'[6] On 1 October 2001, the *Independent* asserted that the Taliban 'gave no indication they were prepared to hand him over.' This claim was contradicted by the quotation later in the same story of Mullah Zaeef, Taliban Ambassador: 'We are thinking of negotiation. [If direct evidence of bin Laden's involvement were produced] it might change things.'[9]

President George W. Bush said 'I gave them a fair chance'.[11] The reality is that he rejected negotiations and nonviolent alternatives to war. Rather than publicising and supporting the agreement to extradite bin Laden, the US and Britain ignored and may have helped to destroy the 1 October initiative. For their part, the media effectively suppressed evidence of the Taliban's offers to extradite Mr bin Laden, and distorted the Taliban's position, thereby making war seem natural and inevitable. It was neither.

PHASE II
IRAQ

INSPECTION
IS AN OPTION

This Is Not A War For
UN Weapons Inspectors.

This Is Not A War For
'Regime Change'.

IRAQ
The Background

POPULATION

Total:	23,331,985 (July 2001 estimate)
Population growth rate:	2.84% per annum (2001 estimate)
Infant mortality rate:	60.05 deaths/1,000 live births (2001 estimate)
Life expectancy at birth:	66.95 years (2001 estimate)
Ethnic groups:	Arab 75%-80%, Kurdish 15%-20%, Turkoman, Assyrian or other 5%
Religions:	Muslim 97% (Shi'a 60%-65%, Sunni 32%-37%), Christian or other 3%

ECONOMY

Exports:	$21.8 billion (2000 estimate)
Exports - commodities:	Crude oil
Exports - partners:	Russia, France, Switzerland, China (2000)
Imports:	$13.8 billion (2000 estimate)

Debt - external:	$139 billion (2000 estimate)
Currency:	Iraqi dinar (ID)
Official exchange rate (Iraqi dinars per US$):	0.3109 (fixed since 1982)
Informal market rate (Iraqi dinars per US$):	1,910 (December 1999), 1,815 (December 1998), 1,530 (December 1997), 910 (December 1996), 3,000 (December 1995) note - subject to wide fluctuations

ECONOMIC SUMMARY

Before the invasion of Kuwait, Iraq was a relatively wealthy country, though with large foreign debts. The Iraqi Dinar (ID) was worth roughly £2/$3. Now a monthly salary of 30,000 ID – high by current standards – is worth just £10/$15 a month.

Source: *CIA World Factbook 2001*

IRAQ CRISIS CHRONOLOGY 1980-2002

22 September 1980: Iraq invades Iran, triggering the Iran-Iraq war.

20 August 1988: Iran accepts cease-fire after extensive US military support for Iraq.

2 August 1990: Iraq invades Kuwait.

6 August 1990: UN Security Council Resolution 661 imposes economic sanctions.

17 January 1991: US, Britain, France and others launch war on Iraq.

28 February 1991: Iraq expelled from Kuwait. Cease-fire declared.

March 1991: Uprisings in the south and north of Iraq are crushed. Hundreds of thousands of Kurds flee into Turkey. 'Safe haven' in northern Iraq created by US/UK.

3 April 1991: UN Security Council Resolution 687 continues economic sanctions, demands disarmament of weapons of mass destruction and long-range missiles, and creates the UN Special Commission (UNSCOM) to oversee this process.

7 April 1991: US orders 'no-fly zone' above 36th parallel. Periodic bombings begin.

15 August 1991: UN Security Council Resolution 706 offers Iraq the opportunity to sell oil and purchase essential humanitarian supplies. Iraq refuses. (See Chapter XI.)

26 August 1992: US orders southern 'no-fly zone' below 32nd parallel.

17 January 1993: US launches 40 Tomahawk cruise missiles against a factory alleged to be part of the Iraqi nuclear programme; the al-Rashid Hotel is damaged.

27 June 1993: US missile attack on Baghdad intelligence headquarters kills civilians. It is claimed Iraq had attempted to assassinate former President Bush. (See page 132.)

14 April 1995: UN Security Council Resolution 986 authorises Iraq to sell $2 billion worth of oil every six months to buy humanitarian goods. 30 per cent of this is diverted to compensation for countries, companies and individuals who suffered as a result of the invasion of Kuwait. 13 per cent is channelled to Iraqi Kurdistan in the north. Just over $1 billion is available for relief in the south/centre every six months. All monies from oil sales are held in a UN-controlled bank account in New York - Iraq can apply for them to be spent on humanitarian goods. No money is to reach Baghdad directly.

20 May 1996: As humanitarian conditions deteriorate inside the country, Baghdad reverses its policy, and agrees to the setting up of 'oil-for-food'.

3 September 1996: US cruise missiles fired. Southern no-fly zone raised to 33rd parallel.

20 March 1997: The first shipment of supplies under oil-for-food enters Iraq.

3 September 1997: Mr Denis Halliday now United Nations Humanitarian Coordinator.

War Plan Iraq

20 February 1998: UN Security Council Resolution 1153 more than doubles the amount of oil Iraq is allowed to sell every six months - to $5.52 billion.

23 February 1998: Secretary-General Kofi Annan travels to Baghdad and defuses an international crisis over UN weapons inspections. US and Britain unable to bomb.

28 September 1998: Humanitarian Coordinator Denis Halliday resigns: **'We are in the process of destroying an entire society.'** Replaced by Mr Hans von Sponeck.

30 October 1998: UN Security Council refuses to confirm that economic sanctions would be lifted in the event of verified Iraqi disarmament. (See pages 47–48.)

31 October 1998: Iraq ceases cooperation with UNSCOM.

14 November 1998: Iraq resumes cooperation with UNSCOM.

15 December 1998: UNSCOM inspectors and monitors withdrawn from Iraq on US instruction. (See page 54).

16 December 1998: Operation Desert Fox. Britain and US bomb Iraq for four days, without consulting or warning the United Nations.

7 April 1999: The Security Council's Humanitarian Panel says, **'the humanitarian situation in Iraq will continue to be a dire one in the absence of a sustained revival of the Iraqi economy'.**

12 August 1999: UNICEF surveys reveal that in the south and centre of Iraq - home to 85 per cent of the country's population - the death rate of children under five years of age more than doubled from 56 deaths per 1000 live births (1984–1989) to 131 deaths per 1000 live births (1994–1999). (See page 176.)

17 December 1999: UN Security Council Resolution 1284 offers rolling six-month suspension of sanctions in return for (undefined) co-operation 'in all respects' with UNMOVIC (UNSCOM's successor). Removes ceiling on oil sales for 'oil-for-food'.

12 February 2000: UN Humanitarian Coordinator for Iraq, Mr Hans von Sponeck, also resigns in protest against the sanctions, to be replaced by Mr Tun Myat.

18 September 2000: British Liberal Democrat Party calls for the lifting of 'sanctions other than those directly relevant to military or military related equipment'.

5 December 2000: UN Security Council Resolution 1330 drops the allocation for war compensation to 25 per cent of oil sales; south-central Iraq now gets 59 per cent.

16 February 2001: US and UK bomb radar and command centres outside Baghdad, saying improvements to Iraqi air defences pose an 'unacceptable' risk to their pilots.

14 May 2002: UN Security Council Resolution 1409 allows all civilian imports - except those on a long 'dual-use' list. The head of the Catholic aid agency CAFOD says these 'smart sanctions' are even worse than before. (*Independent*, 12 August 2002, page 4.)

MAP OF IRAQ

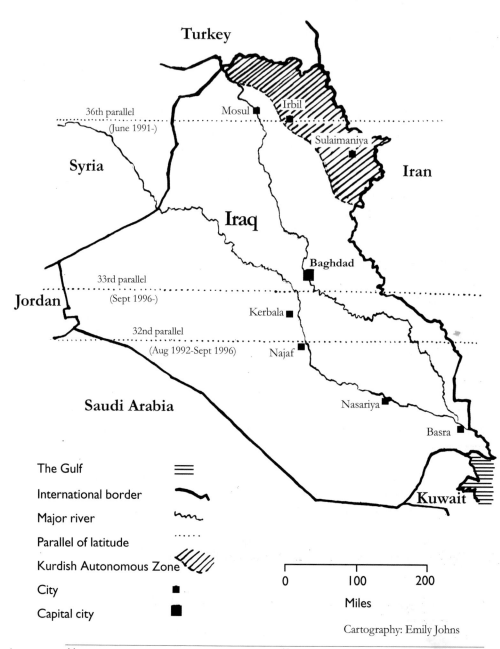

Turkey

36th parallel
(June 1991-)

Mosul

Irbil

Sulaimaniya

Syria

Iran

Iraq

Baghdad

33rd parallel
(Sept 1996-)

Jordan

Kerbala

32nd parallel
(Aug 1992-Sept 1996)

Najaf

Saudi Arabia

Nasariya

Basra

The Gulf

International border

Major river

Parallel of latitude

Kurdish Autonomous Zone

City

Capital city

0   100   200

Miles

Kuwait

Cartography: Emily Johns

CHAPTER IV
Destroying UNSCOM

According to Washington and London, war against Iraq is justified by the (alleged) build-up of Iraq's weapons of mass destruction. Washington and London claim to support the return of UN weapons inspectors to Iraq, and blame Iraq for the failure of negotiations between the UN and Baghdad aimed at re-establishing the inspection system that broke down in December 1998. However, the evidence is that US and British policy has not been focused on the threat from Iraq's suspected weapons, the US in particular has done a great deal to damage the inspection system over the years, and Washington is undermining the current inspection agency at the time of writing.

RESOLUTION 687

Economic sanctions were first imposed on Iraq in August 1990, under UN Security Council Resolution 661, to secure the withdrawal of Iraqi forces from Kuwait. On 3 April 1991, over a month after Iraq had been expelled from Kuwait, economic sanctions were re-imposed on Iraq, in one of the longest and most complex Resolutions ever passed by the Security Council – UN Security Council Resolution 687. Sarah Graham-Brown, author of a major study of the sanctions regime, comments on the long list of requirements imposed by Resolution 687: 'If Resolution 661 had been a coercive measure, the new post-war resolution could also be regarded as punitive.'[1]

The core demands, set out in paragraphs 8 and 12, were that Iraq should 'unconditionally accept the destruction, removal, or rendering harmless, under international supervision', of:

(a) 'All chemical and biological weapons and all stocks of agents and all related subsystems and components and all research, development, support and manufacturing facilities';

(b) 'All ballistic missiles with a range greater than 150 kilometres and related major parts, and repair and production facilities'; and

(c) 'Nuclear weapons or nuclear-weapons-usable material or any subsystems or components or any research, development, support or manufacturing facilities related to the above'.

Note that these items did not have to be destroyed or removed – they could be 'rendered harmless, under international supervision'. Long-term monitoring could ensure that suspect facilities were 'rendered harmless' without physical destruction of equipment that could have civilian uses.

It was Resolution 687 that created the new Iraq-specific weapons inspection agency, the UN Special Commission or 'UNSCOM' – 'largely a British idea', according to British Foreign Policy Adviser Percy Craddock.[2] UNSCOM was created to oversee and verify disarmament of the first three elements of Iraq's weapons of mass destruction (items [a] and [b] above). The nuclear weapons programme was to be inspected and monitored by the International Atomic Energy Agency (IAEA).

PARAGRAPH 22

The Resolution set out different standards of Iraqi behaviour for lifting the import and export sanctions. Paragraph 21 said that restrictions on goods imported into Iraq would be lifted by the Security Council after considering 'the policies and practices of the Government of Iraq, including the implementation of all relevant resolutions of the Security Council'.[3]

The US and Britain seized on the phrase 'all relevant resolutions' to expand the scope of demands to be made on Baghdad. For example, in May 1994, the then US Ambassador to the UN, Madeline Albright demanded among other things an end to Iraqi military action in the southern marshes – an issue that had been addressed in UN Security Council Resolution 688, the resolution immediately after Resolution 687. Historian Dilip Hiro comments, 'Clearly, the phrase "all relevant resolutions" applied to the ones that had been passed on or before April 3, 1991. But what Albright had done was to invoke also the Council resolutions passed *after* that date.'[4]

Whether or not subsequent resolutions were attached, the paragraph was vague in the extreme in its invocation of the 'policies and practices' of the Iraqi Government.

Paragraph 22 of the Resolution, dealing with restrictions on Iraq's exports and the 'financial transactions related thereto', was much clearer. The paragraph said that these sanctions would be lifted once Iraq had complied with internationally supervised disarmament of its weapons of mass destruction, and had accepted a long-term monitoring programme – also under international supervision.

Moscow and Paris strongly defended the significance of Paragraph 22 – the Russian view was that, 'As soon as the chairman of UNSCOM reports favourably, then paragraph 22 is engaged, allowing oil sales without limits.'[5] As the years went by, the US and UK came to a different position. By 1994, the US and UK believed sanctions should remain in place until 'all relevant resolutions' were complied with, 'choosing to ignore or play down the separate requirements of Paragraph 22,' in the words of Ms Graham-Brown.[6] In April 1994, Warren Christopher, US Secretary of State, wrote in the *New York Times*, 'The US does not believe that Iraq's compliance with Paragraph 22 of Resolution 687 is enough to justify lifting the embargo.'[7] In March 1997 this position was reaffirmed by the then US Secretary of State, Madeleine Albright, who said that even if Iraq disarmed, economic sanctions would not be lifted as long as Saddam Hussein remained in power. Former UN weapons inspector Scott Ritter later commented bitterly, 'This violated the provisions of the Security Council resolution governing the sanctions regime and undermined the very framework of UNSCOM's existence.'[8] The effective deletion of this one 'carrot', or staged lifting of the sanctions, was to have fateful consequences for UNSCOM.

THE BREAKDOWN OF COOPERATION

After seven years of inspections, negotiations, monitoring, and confrontation, UNSCOM had achieved a great deal by the beginning of 1998, the final year of its existence. (See Chapter VI.) In February 1998, an inspection crisis was resolved (and air strikes averted) by the personal intervention of UN Secretary-General Kofi Annan. However, relations between Baghdad and UNSCOM continued to be deteriorate, leading to the withdrawal of Iraqi cooperation at the end of October 1998.

One crucial trigger for the breakdown of relations was a letter from the Security Council on 30 October, responding to an Iraqi request for clarification. Several members of the Security Council had been floating the idea of a 'comprehensive review' of Iraq's disarmament efforts in an effort to resuscitate (and wind up) the inspection process. There was an impression that the inspectors were in the last lap. A framework for the 'comprehensive review' proposed by Mr Annan would have shifted the burden of proof from Iraq to Iraq's accusers, who would have had to put up evidence of Iraqi non-compliance. It also would have required a 'reasonable timetable' for the disarmament effort, and therefore set a limit on the life of the export side of the economic sanctions. Britain and the US moved to undermine this constructive suggestion.

The official version of events is purveyed by Ms Graham-Brown: the British Ambassador, serving as President of the Security Council for the month, wrote a letter to Baghdad on 30 October 1998 setting out the Security Council's position on the comprehensive review. The following day, Iraq ordered an end to cooperation with UNSCOM, which led to considerable friction with the agency (which was however allowed to continue with inspections after a time). 'Kofi Annan's offer of a comprehensive review of sanctions was intended to act as a "carrot" which would bring Iraqi compliance,' but it was 'brushed aside' by Baghdad.[9]

In the real world, matters were more complex. The 30 October letter from the British Ambassador had altered the framework considerably from that proposed by Kofi Annan. The then head of UNSCOM, Richard Butler notes in his memoirs that, 'In particular it omitted the guarantee that Iraq would be released from sanctions on a certain date.' Furthermore, the letter 'also restored somewhat the onus of proof on Iraq, which the secretary-general's proposal had sought to shift to UNSCOM.'

Mr Butler's account ignores the most critical aspect of the letter, however. Iraq had asked a number of questions about the new inspection regime, and about the comprehensive review, asking in particular whether the completion of the disarmament tasks would lead to the lifting of economic sanctions. Ms Graham-Brown does not point out, as the *Financial Times* did at the time, that 'Mr Saddam's decision to cripple UNSCOM was triggered by the US refusal explicitly to commit itself to lifting the oil embargo if Iraq complied with disarmament requirements – as stipulated by' Paragraph 22 of Resolution 687.[10] In the letter of 30 October 1998, the *FT* commented, 'the US rejected proposals by Russia, France and China that would have clearly committed the security council to a lifting of the oil embargo if Iraq complied with requirements to eliminate its weapons of mass destruction.'[11] The *Economist* observed, 'Iraq interpreted this as confirmation of its long-held – and plausible – belief that, even if it did come clean on all its weapons, no American administration would lift the oil embargo so long as Mr Hussein remained in power.'[12] The *Independent* commented, 'Saddam had some reason for anger – the integrity of Article 22 is crucial for him.'[13]

Britain and the United States later said that there was no alternative to the use of force in response to Iraqi obstructionism. There was an alternative. It was to reaffirm the provisions of UNSCR 687. Security Council Resolution 687 was subverted in October 1998 not by Baghdad, but by London and Washington. The consequence was a serious blow to the weapons inspection process, the collapse of a promising initiative (the comprehensive review), more loss of life and property destruction and the demise of UNSCOM – as a result of Operation Desert Fox.

THE RESUMPTION OF COOPERATION

Baghdad's 31 October declaration of non-cooperation appeared to set the stage for the military confrontation postponed in February. UNSCOM staff were withdrawn from Iraq on 11 November on instruction from the United States (see below). On 14 November, Iraq resumed cooperation with UNSCOM and IAEA inspectors. The letter from Iraqi Deputy Prime Minister Tariq Aziz announcing this decision had a nine-point 'annexe' attached, with proposals for the conduct of the 'comprehensive review'. Mr Aziz wrote, 'We believe that ... the adoption of the points conveyed to the ambassadors of Russia, France and China, a copy of which I enclose, will render the [comprehensive] review serious, fair and fruitful.' UN Secretary-General Kofi Annan said that the letter met his requirements.[14] The United States reacted to this unexpected and unwanted diplomatic breakthrough by rubbishing the letter and annexe as being 'neither unequivocal nor unconditional' in restoring cooperation with UNSCOM. President Clinton's National Security Adviser, Sandy Berger, said, 'It is unacceptable ... Unfortunately, the letter shows unmistakably that Iraq has no intention of complying with the Security Council resolutions.'[15] Mr Berger misrepresented the annexe as a set of demands; nine conditions which had to be satisfied before Iraq would resume cooperation with UNSCOM. What seems 'unmistakable' is that Washington was intent on a military strike, and was twisting the wording of letter and its appendix to create a confrontation where none existed. It later transpired that US B-52 bombers had left their bases in Louisiana, and were within an hour of unleashing their cruise missiles when Mr Aziz announced the resumption of cooperation on CNN, forcing President Clinton to abort the mission.[16] Iraq's Ambassador to the UN, Nizar Hamdoon, told the Security Council that the annexe had nothing to do with what he called Iraq's unequivocal statement that the UN inspectors were welcome to resume their work unconditionally. The Ambassador said that the new letter from Tariq Aziz rendered void the earlier decision to suspend cooperation with UNSCOM and the IAEA. Richard Butler points out that 'This latter point was important, because Security Council Resolution 1205 had required Iraq to formally rescind those decisions' of 31 October.[17]

Baghdad's 14 November restoration of cooperation with UNSCOM – formally accepted as such by the Security Council on 15 November – has dropped out of the history books, as it is much more comfortable to go immediately from 31 October 1998 'Iraq ends all cooperation with UNSCOM' to 16 December 1998, 'Special commission withdraws staff from Iraq', as happens in the *Guardian*'s chronology of the breakdown of the inspections.[18] Operation Desert Fox makes much more sense if one says simply that Iraq blocked the inspectors, they left in frustration (or were 'expelled' by Iraq, in the more imaginative version of events), and the US and Britain had no option but to use force.

The truth is, however, that on 18 November 1998, UNSCOM inspections resumed, and the great majority of them passed without incident, as we shall see below.

'SENSITIVE SITES'

Another important factor in the breakdown of relations between UNSCOM and Baghdad was a dispute on how to inspect 'sensitive sites' not immediately connected to the manufacture of weapons of mass destruction.

In June 1996, after disputes between the Iraqi Government and UNSCOM over the inspection of such sites, the then head of UNSCOM, Rolf Ekeus, negotiated a set of special procedures with Baghdad for the inspection of sites which the Iraqis considered 'sensitive' in terms of their national security, dignity, and sovereignty. According to former UNSCOM inspector Scott Ritter, sensitive sites included various ministries, Republican Guard and Special Republican Guard facilities, and the offices of four key security and intelligence agencies.[19] The Republican Guard and the Special Republican Guard are elite military units essential to the survival of the Iraq leadership.

The key feature of this agreement was that during the inspection of a 'sensitive site', only four inspectors would be permitted to enter the suspect property.[20] However, given the size of some of the 'presidential/residential' 'sensitive sites', a new additional agreement was negotiated by Richard Butler, Mr Ekeus's successor as head of UNSCOM, in mid-December 1997. More inspectors could be allowed into 'sensitive sites', 'if the size of the site warranted it, as decided on a case-by-case basis'.[21]

Despite the agreement, relations between UNSCOM and Baghdad deteriorated until the international crisis of February 1998, which was resolved by the personal diplomacy of Kofi Annan, the UN Secretary-General, which produced a third element to the 'sensitive sites' formula. Interestingly, in the run-up to the Annan mission, Britain was reportedly prepared to support a French plan that would allow diplomats to accompany the UNSCOM teams if they were allowed to visit all the sensitive sites. This French scheme provoked dismay in Washington, which was concerned that the British might be 'losing their nerve in the face of mounting international opposition to war.'[22]

The French proposal was very much the shape of the eventual agreement. The Memorandum of Agreement of 23 February 1998 re-affirmed the existing 'modalities' for 'sensitive sites', and created a new set of procedures for eight named 'presidential' sites, requiring some form of oversight by senior foreign diplomats.[23]

Far from allowing access to 'anyone, any time, any place', three rounds of negotations between UN officials and Iraq set out a number of rules governing how many weapons inspectors could visit a site, and (in the case of presidential sites) under what conditions: 'sensitive sites' were to be inspected by a maximum of four inspectors; large 'sensitive sites' might have more than four inspectors; and at 'presidential sites' inspection teams were to be accompanied by senior foreign diplomats.

THE BA'ATH PARTY HEADQUARTERS

Dr George Carey, then Archbishop of Canterbury, later said of the December 1998 bombings, 'I do not know what alternative there was when Saddam Hussein refused to allow inspectors in to look at those factories which were capable of producing chemical weapons.'[24] In fact, no one claimed that Iraq had stopped inspections of any weapons factories. One crucial incident – which the Archbishop may have been referring to – came on 9 November 1998, when twelve UNSCOM inspectors sought entry to a Ba'ath Party regional headquarters in Baghdad – an office, not a factory – and were refused. This incident was later described by the *Sunday Times* as 'a decisive moment in the Iraqi leader's war of attrition with the West'.[25] It was rather a 'decisive moment' in Western propaganda, and in the manipulation of the UNSCOM process.

The head of UNSCOM, Richard Butler, later claimed in his memoirs that, 'dismantled missiles were being stored in wooden boxes hidden underground at the Baath party offices on the outskirts of Baghdad... concealed in a cellar below a shed normally used to house uniforms.' According to this account, 'during the last months of 1997' the Iraqis moved the 'sensitive military material by night to a large shed within the compound of the offices of the Aadhamiyya district of the city'.[26]

Scott Ritter, who resigned as UNSCOM chief inspector in August 1998 because he felt the West was trying to rein in UNSCOM, claims, 'Butler wrote that he had solid evidence of "proscribed materials" at the Ba'ath headquarters. I believe from my sources that is not true.'[27]

The *FT* reported that inspectors were turned away 'because modalities for inspections agreed in 1996 stipulated that a limited number of inspectors would enter such sensitive sites'. Mr Butler argued, on the other hand, that 'these modalities had been revised in subsequent discussions with Iraqi officials.'[28] We have already seen that there was an agreement on the modalities for inspecting sensitive sites which had been renegotiated by Mr Butler himself a year earlier.

According to the account in Mr Butler's own memoirs, the December 1997 agreement stated that while normally only four inspectors would be permitted to inspect a sensitive site, more inspectors could be permitted 'if the size of the site warranted it, as decided on a case-by-case basis'.[29] This was to cover the case of large military bases. The Ba'ath Party regional headquarters was not a large military base.

Crucially, the Iraqi authorities did fulfil the 'sensitive sites' agreement: they permitted four inspectors into the yard of the headquarters building – supposedly the hiding place of the dismantled missile components – 'in accordance with the 1996 agreement.'[30] In his account of the incident in his memoirs, Mr Butler leaves out the critical details that, firstly, four inspectors were permitted into the yard where the shed was located, and, secondly, the Iraqis only turned away a group of twelve inspectors – a larger group than permitted by the rules.[31]

On the most generous interpretation, there was a disagreement over which arrangements applied to the inspection of the headquarters complex, a disagreement which ought to have been clarified and negotiated between the Security Council and Baghdad. The *FT* quoted an unnamed 'senior Western diplomat' in Baghdad: 'the revised modalities for inspecting sensitive sites, and allowing more inspectors to enter, had been targeted at large military installations, whereas the Baath party building over which Iraq and inspectors clashed was located in a Baghdad house.'[32]

This crucial incident was portrayed as a straightforward case of Iraqi defiance and noncompliance, when, in fact, it looks like a case of compliance with agreed rules. The crucial fact, obscured by Mr Butler, and by much of the press at the time, is that the Iraqis did permit an UNSCOM inspection of the suspect shed.

It appears, however, that this is too generous an interpretation of UNSCOM/US behaviour. According to an account by former weapons inspector Scott Ritter, after four inspectors were allowed inside the premises, 'the US demanded that 12 more inspectors be allowed in and this time it worked. The demand was denied.'[33]

This view of US manipulation of the inspection process was supported in July 2002 by Rolf Ekeus, who headed UNSCOM between 1991 and 1997. Mr Ekeus told Swedish radio that, 'As time went on, some countries, especially the US, wanted to learn more about other parts of UNSCOM's capacity'. The Swedish diplomat said the US tried to find information about the whereabouts of Saddam Hussein, but he was able to rebuff these pressures. Most damningly, Mr Ekeus said that members of the Security Council 'pressed the inspection leadership to carry out inspections which were controversial from the Iraqis' view, and thereby created a blockage that could be used as a justification for a direct military action.' The former UNSCOM chief added in a newspaper interview that he learned after leaving the inspection agency that the US had placed two of its agents inside the group of inspectors.[34]

The most bizarre aspect of the affair was that the inspection of the Ba'ath Party Headquarters was proposed earlier in the year, and cancelled on US instructions, contributing directly to Mr Ritter's resignation in August 1998. Mr Ritter, as chief inspector, had persuaded Richard Butler to authorise a surprise inspection of the basement of the headquarters building in the Aadhamiyya district of Baghdad, where he believed there were ten crates of missile guidance and control equipment from dismantled Iraqi missiles.

The inspection was cancelled shortly before it was due to take place on 20 July 1998 because of pressure from the US Government to delay until 'a more opportune time'. Rescheduled for 6 August, the inspection was once again delayed and then cancelled after Mr Butler consulted US Secretary of State Madeline Albright. Mr Ritter resigned within weeks in protest at the way that UNSCOM was being subordinated to US foreign policy needs.[35]

The inspection of the headquarters building was not required as a justification for a military strike in mid-1998, and so was dropped on US orders, according to Mr Ritter's inside account. When a confrontation was required, Mr Butler knew which operation to order, and the reworked Ritter plan 'delivered in spades', as Mr Ritter later commented: 'Delays, blockages, evacuated buildings – the classic pattern of Iraqi obstruction – all were provoked and carefully catalogued.'[36]

5 PROBLEMS OUT OF 300 INSPECTIONS

Richard Butler wrote a final UNSCOM report for the Security Council on 14 December 1998. His central conclusion was that Iraq's conduct over the previous month had ensured that 'no progress' was made either in disarmament or in accounting for its prohibited weapons programmes. Therefore, he recorded that UNSCOM 'is not able to conduct the substantive disarmament work mandated to it by the Security Council.'[37] The *Independent* noted that Mr Butler's report 'appeared to have taken all sides by surprise yesterday', and nobody appeared to have been ready for the 'single-mindedness' of his conclusions.[38]

There was a major contradiction between Mr Butler's conclusions, and the evidence in the body of the report. In his conclusions, Mr Butler said that 'no progress' was made. But 'in his report to the UN, Mr Butler conceded, "In statistical terms, the majority of the inspections of facilities and sites under the ongoing monitoring system were carried out with Iraq's cooperation".'[39] Russian ambassador to the UN, Sergei Lavrov, 'said the report's conclusion was biased, and he echoed Iraq's contention that Butler had only cited five incidents in 300 inspection operations' over the previous month.[40]

It was curious that 'all sides' were surprised by the harshness of Mr Butler's December report, as Mr Butler later claimed that he 'signalled' his conclusions on 10

December 'to any ambassador on the Security Council who approached me with the exception of Sergey Lavrov.'[41] Mr Butler may be using this phrasing to disguise the fact that he concealed his conclusions from most Security Council ambassadors. Later, both China and Russia pressed for Mr Butler's dismissal on the basis that his report, which triggered the strikes, 'unfairly characterised Iraqi work with inspectors.'[42] Mr Butler admits in his memoirs that before completing his report he met with US National Security Adviser Sandy Berger on 11 December at the US Mission to the UN in New York. Mr Butler writes, 'The ultimatum President Clinton had laid down on November 15 hung over our conversation, but Berger couldn't or wouldn't say what specific consequences would flow from my report.'[43]

Scott Ritter, the former UN weapons inspector, alleged that 'Clinton's advisers deliberately provoked a showdown with the Iraqis' by manipulating Mr Butler and UNSCOM.[44] Mr Butler is said to have given the first draft of his report to senior US diplomats at the UN on Sunday 13 December. They transmitted it instantly to President Clinton, who apparently found it too 'weak'. According to the *Washington Post*, US officials thereafter played 'a direct role in shaping Butler's text during multiple conversations with him at secure facilities at the US mission to the United Nations.'[45]

When the Butler report was circulated to Security Council members, there was a covering letter from UN Secretary-General Kofi Annan, in which he described the document as presenting a 'mixed picture'.[46] When the US delegation in New York received its copy of Annan's letter on 15 December 1998, a senior US delegate later told reporters, 'We tore it up'.[47]

According to a senior diplomat in Baghdad, Mr Butler's conclusions, 'while pointing to serious problems, should not necessarily have been construed as presenting a fatal blow to the system of inspections or monitoring.' 'The whole diplomatic community, which has been closely monitoring these inspections, was surprised by the report,' said a senior Western diplomat. 'We did not consider that the problems reported during the one month of inspections were major incidents... We are not justifying Iraqi actions, but many of the problems encountered point to the need to establish clearer rules for inspections,' he said. 'UNSCOM's mandate says it should have full access but take into account Iraq's sovereignty, dignity and national security concerns. This leaves room for questions, and will always give rise to problems.'[48]

One of Mr Butler's most famous utterances came in November 1997, when he said, 'Truth in some cultures is kind of what you can get away with saying.'[49] This racist slur could serve as a judgement on his own rendering of events, both in his UNSCOM report, and in his memoirs.

THE WITHDRAWAL OF UNSCOM

It is often said that UNSCOM was thrown out of Iraq in December 1998. In fact, the agency was withdrawn on Washington's orders. If anyone ejected UNSCOM, it was the United States. The first UNSCOM withdrawal in late 1998 came on 11 November

1998, as US military strikes were anticipated. In his memoirs, Richard Butler records that after receiving a telephone call from the acting permanent US representative to the UN, Ambassador Peter Burleigh, he visited Burleigh's office on 10 November 1998. Ambassador Burleigh signalled the US intention to strike Iraq by telling Mr Butler that, 'Considering the crisis Iraq had provoked and its refusal to obey the requirements of the Security Council, the United States had decided to draw down the staff in its embassies throughout the region.' The Ambassador then advised Mr Butler, as executive head of UNSCOM, to consider evacuating UNSCOM staff from Iraq. 'Burleigh emphasized that he was not providing me with advance notice of any decision to take military action against Iraq, merely a suggestion that such an evacuation, given the paramount importance of the safety of staff, would be prudent.' Mr Butler immediately ordered the evacuation of UNSCOM personnel.[50] However, the threat of military action passed on that occasion, and the UNSCOM inspectors and monitors returned and resumed their work in Iraq on 18 November 1998.

It was not until after Mr Butler's December report had been circulated to members of the Security Council on 15 December 1998 that he was called in once again by Ambassador Burleigh. Once again Burleigh urged Mr Butler to be 'prudent' with the safety and security of UNSCOM staff. 'Repeating a familiar script, I told him that I would act on this advice and remove my staff from Iraq,' Mr Butler later wrote.[51] UNSCOM inspectors were withdrawn within hours, never to return. Mr Butler carried out the withdrawal without even informing the Security Council, the body which the inspection agency supposedly reported to.[52]

The planned air strikes were supposed to be provoked by the collapse of the inspection process. It was therefore necessary to withdraw the inspectors to build the political case for military action. So UNSCOM was ejected from Iraq to facilitate a four-day bombing campaign.

The following day, as Mr Butler was making his formal report to the Security Council, and as he was being sternly interrogated by Russian Ambassador Sergey Lavrov, the UN received news that the Anglo-American bombardment of Iraq had begun.[53] After the bombing started, Lavrov said that the crisis had been 'created artificially by the irresponsible acts of Richard Butler', while the Chinese representative at the Security Council said Mr Butler had played a 'dishonourable role' in the confrontation.[54]

THE PENETRATION OF UNSCOM

The final nail in the coffin for UNSCOM was the string of revelations concerning the penetration of the agency by US intelligence, referred to in the July 2002 revelations by former UNSCOM head, Rolf Ekeus. Scott Ritter revealed after his resignation that from the spring of 1992 until November 1993 he worked closely in UNSCOM with a man he called 'Moe Dobbs', a CIA 'Special Activities Staff' covert operations specialist. 'Dobbs and his men provided seasoned personnel who could operate vehicles, organise logistics, run communications – simply put, the kind of people you want around you in a difficult situation. They were not weapons experts, but we had enough of those.'[55]

The Moe Dobbs team was brought back in after the 1995 disclosures regarding Iraq's biological weapons. They were involved in UNSCOM inspection number 143, in March 1996, which was designed to provoke a response from the Iraqi 'concealment organisations', and to collect information regarding their operations. These 'concealment organisations' were security agencies charged both with protecting the Iraqi President, and with hiding materials and documents related to forbidden weapons programmes. 'The plan integrated the work of the inspectors on the ground, surveillance aircraft overhead, and a new element – sensitive communications scanners.' UNSCOM 150 in June 1996 was a similar operation focused on Special Republican Guard facilities believed to house weapons of mass destruction-related material and documentation. There were nine CIA paramilitary covert operators on that inspection team – but they were never involved in UNSCOM communications interceptions. This was the responsibility of a team of 'British operatives'. (Mr Ritter does not describe the nature or background of these 'operatives' in his memoirs.)[56]

Mr Ritter later came to suspect that he had been manipulated, and that UNSCOM 150 had been coordinated with a CIA-backed coup attempt which later came to light. UNSCOM 150 was directed 'almost exclusively' at Special Republican Guard sites; 'the coup plotters were from some of the same units we were trying to inspect'; and 'Dobbs and his Special Activities Staff operators were the CIA's covert operations experts, one of whose specialities was organising coups.' Mr Ritter discovered a document on a later inspection ordering the 'liquidation' of the 3rd Battalion of the Special Republican Guard, which he had been set to inspect, and which it turned out had been involved in organising the coup attempt.[57]

In his book, Mr Ritter reveals that he briefed the US National Security Council with information from UNSCOM operations.[58] According to the *Washington Post*, when Richard Butler sent in a team of seventy-five inspectors in November 1997, 'Following a standard procedure that neither Unscom nor Washington officially acknowledges, Mr Butler's senior staff briefed a liaison officer from the CIA on the target, sources said.'[59] The level of cooperation was extremely high.

US intelligence provided technology for UNSCOM to intercept secret, coded, Iraqi communications from January 1996. Mr Ritter sent the intercepts by satellite relay to Bahrain, the regional headquarters of UNSCOM, where a computer filtered the conversations for relevant key words – 'chemical', 'missile', and so on – and relayed them to the US National Security Agency at Fort Meade, Maryland for decoding and translation.[60] Barton Gellman of the *Washington Post* learned in 1999 that in March 1996 a US military intelligence officer working for UNSCOM had secretly inserted special scanners into UNSCOM cameras, enabling US intelligence to spy on important nodes of Iraqi military communication, quite unknown to UNSCOM.[61] After the NSA failed to produce reports or conclusions based on several major operations, the then head of UNSCOM Rolf Ekeus asked Britain and Israel to carry out the decoding and translation, which they then did.[62]

In his memoirs, Mr Ritter also reveals that an 'UNSCOM-Israeli special relationship' was established in October 1994 – he describes a meeting in September 1997 between Richard Butler, the newly-appointed head of UNSCOM, and three Israeli officials: the Israeli Ambassador to the UN, a colonel of Israeli intelligence, and Major General Ayalon, the director of Israeli military intelligence.[63] His book opens with the frustration he felt when both Britain and Israel withdrew personnel from a major inspection he had organised.[64] In October 1998, Mr Ritter confirmed that he had visited Israel 'many times' for intelligence purposes.[65] Mr Ritter also revealed that some of the all-frequency scanners and digital recorders used to record the coded radio messages of Iraq's innermost security and military forces were supplied by Israel, at his request.[66] These were perhaps the most damaging of the Ritter revelations as far as Middle Eastern opinion was concerned.

Noted US military analyst William Arkin has suggested that the goal of Operation Desert Fox was primarily to target Saddam Hussein's internal security apparatus using the intelligence gathered through UNSCOM. He notes that almost half the targets of Desert Fox were focused on the regime rather than weapons of mass destruction sites. The Pentagon admitted that 'it was inevitable that information supplied by the [UNSCOM] monitors had played a part in the careful selection of targets.'[67]

By using UNSCOM for intelligence purposes, Washington placed its own intelligence and foreign policy goals above the integrity and survival of UNSCOM. Spying on the leader of Iraq – presumably in order to organise his assassination[68] – was more important to the US than securing the disarmament of Iraq.

THE DEATH OF UNSCOM

UNSCOM never returned to Iraq after being withdrawn on US instructions. Baghdad didn't destroy UNSCOM, Washington did. That Operation Desert Fox would terminate the inspection regime was not only predictable, it was predicted. President Clinton himself said in November that one reason for not launching the air assault then was that this would 'mark the end of UNSCOM'.[69]

Former Chair of UNSCOM Richard Butler wrote in his memoirs that it was 'hard not to see Desert Fox as a failure, particularly because of its brevity' – it lasted only four days. 'If one uses the test of looking rationally at outcomes, without ascribing motives,' comments Mr Butler, 'it could be argued that the death of UNSCOM also became US policy because that is what has happened.'[70]

CHAPTER V
Undermining UNMOVIC

THE NEED FOR INSPECTORS

No evidence has been published at the time of writing to prove that Iraq has acquired or developed weapons of mass destruction since December 1998, when UN weapons inspectors were withdrawn on US orders. (See Chapter X, Reason 1.)

Iraqi defectors have made a number of allegations, but it is unclear what weight can be given to their claims.[1] David Albright, a former UN weapons inspector for the International Atomic Energy Agency, who has studied the defector claims in detail, has said, 'The evidence produced so far is worrying. It is an argument for getting the inspectors back in as fast as possible, but not for going to war.'[2]

The ugly truth is that the US has little interest in 'getting the inspectors back in as fast as possible.' Following the disintegration of UNSCOM as a result of US/UK bombing and US penetration of the agency, a new body was formed in December 1999, under UN Security Council Resolution 1284: the 'UN Monitoring, Verification and Inspection Commission' (UNMOVIC). Washington has actually been deliberately restraining and undermining UNMOVIC, and intervening to derail the negotiations that could secure the return of the new inspection agency to Iraq.

THE US OPPOSES INSPECTIONS

World opinion favours a renewal of inspections and the re-entry of UNMOVIC, as a solution to the mystery around Iraq's weapons programmes. The US, on the other hand, has decisively turned against inspections. The *Daily Telegraph* notes, 'Senior German and French politicians argue that negotiations and a resumption of United Nations arms inspections are the way forward – a view that provokes exasperation in Washington.'[3] Seymour Hersh, the noted US investigative reporter, wrote in December 2001: 'Inside the Administration, there is general consensus on one issue, officials told me: there will be no further effort to revive the UN inspection regime withdrawn in late 1998'.[4]

The *Washington Post* reported in January 2002 that 'the United States has yet to begin rallying other countries at the United Nations to force Baghdad to accept inspections': 'UN diplomats said that US officials rarely discuss the president's desire to see weapons inspectors return to Iraq.' John D. Negroponte, the newly-appointed US ambassador to the UN, said in January 2002 that the main focus of US diplomacy towards Iraq 'over the next several months' would be to secure Russia's agreement to a "smart sanctions" resolution. He did not mention the return of the weapons inspectors. Hans Blix, the Swedish executive director of UNMOVIC, said in an interview in the same month that he had seen no sign that the Bush administration had 'accelerated' its efforts.[5]

INSPECTIONS: THE NIGHTMARE SCENARIO

According to the *Guardian*, 'Britain and Russia have been keen for Iraq to accept the weapons inspectors as a way to avoid conflict. But the US has been ambivalent, hinting that even if the inspectors were allowed back it might not be enough to prevent a war.'[6] This is a little misleading. The US position is far stronger than the *Guardian* indicates.

According to one former US official, 'The hawks' nightmare is that inspectors will be admitted, will not be terribly vigorous and not find anything. Economic sanctions would be eased, and the U.S. will be unable to act ... and the closer it comes to the 2004 elections the more difficult it will be to take the military route.' 'The more hawkish members of the US defence department are said to favour direct military action on Iraq, which would be more difficult if weapons inspectors were on the ground.'[7]

It's not just the hawks. US National Security Adviser Condoleeza Rice, who occupies the middle ground in the Administration, close to the President, 'dodged a question on whether the inspections issue provides justification for US military action against Iraq'. She said that Saddam Hussein 'is not likely to ever convince the world, in a reliable way, that he is going to live at peace with his neighbours, that he will not seek weapons of mass destruction, and that he will not repress his own people.'[8]

US Secretary of State Colin Powell made it clear that the US is intent on war, whatever happens with the inspectors: 'US policy is that, regardless of what the inspectors do, the people of Iraq and the people of the region would be better off with a different regime in Baghdad. The United States reserves its option to do whatever it believes might be appropriate to see if there can be a regime change.' The issue of the inspectors is a 'separate and distinct and different' matter from the US position on Saddam Hussein's leadership, said Powell, supposedly an Administration 'dove'.[9] While Powell has expressed a desire to see inspectors to return, the Administration line is that 'regime change' drives on, regardless.

The 'principals' in the Bush Administration 'fear that Saddam is working his own UN angle for the return of weapons inspectors to Iraq, whose presence could make the US look like a bully if it invades.' A 'top Senate foreign policy aide' was quoted by *Time* magazine as saying, 'The White House's biggest fear is that UN weapons inspectors will be allowed to go in.'[10]

Inspectors are not part of the solution; they are part of the problem, as far as the Bush Administration is concerned. Hence the US strategy of leaks and threats detailed below, designed to scupper UN negotiations with Iraq.

THE FUTILITY OF BOMBING

If the primary goal was to secure international verification of the disarmament of Iraq, the focus would be on re-establishing the inspection and monitoring regime. The 1991 Gulf War demonstrated the futility of trying to disarm such weapons facilities by bombing. The US-led coalition launched 970 air and missile strikes against Iraqi chemical, biological and nuclear facilities during the war. 80 per cent of the strikes were carried out with precision-guided weapons.

US strategic bombing severely damaged some chemical weapons production capabilities, but 'did little, however, to destroy Iraq's chemical weapons and scarcely paralyzed its chemical warfare capabilities.' 700 tonnes of mustard gas and nerve agents were recovered by UN weapons inspectors after the war. The harm done to production facilities was less than estimated during the war, because damage to buildings does not necessarily mean damage to key production equipment.[11]

As for biological weapons, US Central Command 'issued reports immediately after the war that implied it had destroyed all known key Iraqi biological research and development facilities and most of Iraq's refrigerated storage facilities.' Two leading US analysts comment, 'It is very difficult, however, to be sure of what really happened.'[12]

On the nuclear weapons front, the US Government's own Gulf War Air Power Survey argued that 'the air campaign no more than "inconvenienced" Iraqi plans to field nuclear weapons'.[13] The definitive study of the military dimensions of the 1991 Gulf War concludes, 'Like the Coalition's failures to attack the Scuds, chemical weapons, and biological weapons, the failure to successfully characterize and attack Iraq's nuclear weapons facilities is a warning about the potential effectiveness of counter-proliferation.'[14]

Without inspectors, Iraq cannot be verifiably disarmed, but, for the US, preventing the development of Iraq's weapons of mass destruction is secondary to overthrowing Saddam Hussein. Inspectors hinder the war effort, so they must be undermined.

UNDERMINING UNMOVIC I
BLOCKING UNMOVIC

This is not the first time the US has tried to stop UN weapons inspectors doing their job in Iraq. In August 1998, the *Washington Post* carried a story entitled, 'US has been blocking UNSCOM searches since last November'.[15] Once UNSCOM disintegrated through US policy decisions, the US calculated that inspections were unnecessary. The *Washington Post* reported in January 2000,

Iraq's Saddam Hussein has no doubt been developing new biological, chemical or nuclear weapons in the year since he finally chased U.N. inspectors from Baghdad. But the Iraqi dictator will use these weapons only in extreme circumstances. He presents no direct challenge to U.S. forces now. He can be outwaited. This is the nature of the calculation that President Clinton and his politically attuned national security adviser, Sandy Berger, have made on Iraq.[16]

UNMOVIC, created by Resolution 1284 in December 1999, was formed gradually, leading to the following sequence of headlines in the *Washington Post* in mid-2000:

'New UN Weapons Inspection Team Is Prepared to Go to Iraq'
(22 August 2000)
'Defiant Iraq Will Not Allow New U.N. Arms Inspectors to Enter'
(24 August 2000)
'Security Council members urge Agency Not to Confront Iraq'
(31 August 2000)

The United States was one of those Security Council members. Dilip Hiro wrote in September 2000 that US Secretary of State Madeleine Albright had 'announced recently that Washington would not use force to compel Iraq to accept inspectors of the newly formed UN Monitoring and Verification and Inspection Commission (UNMOVIC). She then joined the UN ambassadors of Russia, France and China in urging UNMOVIC chief, Hans Blix, not to force the issue.'[17]

UNDERMINING UNMOVIC II
RAISING THE BAR

In April 2002, Tony Blair joined President Bush in demanding that Saddam Hussein grant total freedom for any new inspection regime, saying, 'He has to let the inspectors back in: anyone, any time, any place.'[18]

As we saw in the last chapter, this is not the basis on which UNSCOM operated. UNSCOM had a three-part agreement with Baghdad covering 'sensitive sites', governing the numbers of inspectors that could enter such a site, and, in the case of the presidential sites, dictating that inspectors must be accompanied by senior foreign diplomats.

Given that it is a strikingly harder line than that followed by UNSCOM, the demand by Mr Blair and President Bush for 'anyone, any time, any place' inspections must be a conscious attempt to undermine the diplomatic effort to secure the return of the inspectors, a demand that makes failure inevitable – Baghdad will not tolerate the revocation of the 'sensitive sites' agreements, especially in the light of the evidence concerning US intelligence penetration of UNSCOM.

The *Times* reports, 'Key figures in the White House believe that demands on Saddam to re-admit United Nations weapons inspectors should be set so high that he would fail to meet them unless he provided officials with total freedom.'[19] A US intelligence official said in February 2002 that the White House 'will not take yes for an answer'.[20]

UNDERMINING UNMOVIC III
A STRATEGIC LEAK

The UN Secretary-General Kofi Annan has been attempting to negotiate the return of weapons inspectors to Iraq. When it was leaked in June 2002 that the CIA had been directed to capture or kill Saddam Hussein, Scott Ritter remarked, 'Now that Bush has specifically authorized American covert-operations forces to remove Hussein, however, the Iraqis will never trust an inspection regime that has already shown itself susceptible to infiltration and manipulation by intelligence services hostile to Iraq, regardless of any assurances the U.N. secretary-general might give.'[21] For Ritter, who had revealed the extent of US intelligence penetration of UNSCOM, 'The leaked CIA covert operations plan effectively kills any chance of inspectors returning to Iraq'. It closes 'the last opportunity for shedding light on the true state of affairs regarding any threat in the form of Iraqi weapons of mass destruction.'[22]

UNDERMINING UNMOVIC IV
A WELL-TIMED LEAK

On 4 July, on the first day of Kofi Annan's third round of negotiations with Iraqi diplomats over the return of UNMOVIC, a civilian Pentagon official leaked a detailed Pentagon war planning document to the *New York Times*, spelling out some of the military options under consideration. The US Central Command 'Courses of Action' planning document 'calls for air, land and sea-based forces to attack Iraq from three directions — the north, south and west — in a campaign to topple President Saddam Hussein, according to a person familiar with the document'. While there is no final war plan, 'the concept for such a plan is now highly evolved and is apparently working its way through military channels. Once a consensus is reached on the concept, the steps toward assembling a final war plan and, most importantly, the element of timing for ground deployments and commencement of an air war, represent the final sequencing that Mr. Bush will have to decide.' War was not imminent, but 'there are several signs that the military is preparing for a major air campaign and land invasion.' 'The document envisions tens of thousands of marines and soldiers probably invading from Kuwait. Hundreds of warplanes based in as many as eight countries, possibly including Turkey and Qatar, would unleash a huge air assault against thousands of targets, including airfields, roadways and fiber-optics communications sites.'[23]

The *Independent on Sunday* commented, 'The leak to the *New York Times* – this sort of document never surfaces by accident – seems to be a clear attempt to raise the stakes after a new round of talks in [Vienna] between Iraq and the United Nations failed to produce agreement on the return of UN weapons inspectors'.[24]

True, the leak was no accident, but it did not come *after* the talks failed, it came in the *middle* of the talks. After the first day of talks, both UN officials and Iraqi diplomats declared that progress had been made. UN Secretary General Kofi Annan said he was 'satisfied' with the session. 'Pressed to make a prediction, Annan merely grinned and said "Inshallah", Arabic for "God willing".' Iraqi Foreign Minister Naji Sabri used the same word when he was asked whether he had got what he was seeking from the negotiations.[26] Then the *New York Times* story was published on the morning of the second day of negotiations. Participants in the UN-Iraq talks later said the leaked war plan published in the *New York Times* 'did not help'.[25] There were no grins at the end of the day. 'Most tellingly, Mr Annan and Mr Sabri did not appear together after the talks and no date or place was set for a further high-level meeting.'[27]

The *Daily Telegraph* commented, 'The UN's failure will come as a relief to many in the Pentagon, where senior officials fear that inspections might be granted some form of access, then give Saddam a clean bill of health he did not deserve.'[28] This is revealing. The judgement as to whether Iraq deserves a 'clean bill of health' is not one that can be made in advance of on-the-ground inspections, or against the weight of evidence built up by UN weapons inspectors. The reality is that the war faction fears that the truth about Iraq's weapons may deprive them of the opportunity to attack.

UNDERMINING UNMOVIC V UNANSWERED QUESTIONS

One of the problems bedevilling the UN-Iraq negotiations is a list of nineteen questions that Baghdad submitted to Kofi Annan earlier in the year – rather as they had asked for a re-confirmation of Paragraph 22 of Resolution 687 when trying to negotiate a 'comprehensive review' in 1998. 2002's nineteen questions 'range from technical to political, including queries about what type of weapons [the] inspectors would be looking to find in Iraq, concerns over the UK and US air patrols of northern Iraq, and questions about the creation of a "weapons free zone" in the Middle East.'[29]

'Not in a position to answer the questions, Mr Annan forwarded them to the Security Council.' 'Mr Annan never received any response to the questions from the Security Council.'[30] The central question: 'Iraqi officials have sought assurances that the US would call off its planned military campaign if Baghdad co-operated on weapons inspectors.'[31] The US refused to respond, undermining the inspection effort.

The US/UK position is that, 'Attempting to answer [the 19 questions] would have played into Iraq's hands, weakening Mr Annan's ability to persuade Baghdad to allow the inspectors back into the country, diplomats said' at the UN.[32] The very reverse of the truth. The only way to persuade Iraq to accept a resumption of inspections is to be absolutely clear about the nature of the package, and to offer security from invasion while inspections continue.

UNDERMINING UNMOVIC VI
AN ATTEMPTED SMEAR

Early in 2002, US Deputy Defence Secretary Paul Wolfowitz ordered the CIA to investigate the head of UNMOVIC, Hans Blix, with a particular focus on his record as head of the International Atomic Energy Agency (IAEA) from 1981 to 1997. Mr Wolfowitz and his fellow hawks were hoping to use the failure of the IAEA to detect the Iraqi nuclear weapons programme before 1991 as evidence of Mr Blix's gullibility, and therefore of the pointlessness of UN weapons inspections. Unfortunately for the Wolfowitz faction, the CIA concluded that Mr Blix conducted inspections of Iraqi nuclear facilities 'fully within the parameters he could operate' as head of the IAEA. It was only when the IAEA was permitted more intrusive inspection and monitoring after 1991 that Iraq's nuclear weapons programme was dismantled.

According to the *Washington Post*, Mr Wolfowitz 'hit the ceiling' when the CIA report appeared to support Mr Blix's defence that the IAEA were not permitted intrusive inspections, and were therefore unable to detect the weapons programme. 'The request for a CIA investigation underscored the degree of concern by Wolfowitz and his civilian colleagues in the Pentagon that new inspections could torpedo their plans for military action to remove Hussein from power.'[33]

AN OFFER REJECTED

It's not just the US: Britain has also shown a lack of interest in inspections at times. In March 2002, Baghdad invited Britain to send weapons inspectors. 'Iraq is ready to receive right now any British team sent by Blair and accompanied by the British media to show the world where and how is Iraq developing such weapons,' said an unidentified Iraqi spokesperson in the official *al-Thawra* newspaper. This news wire report was ignored by the Government, and by the British media, apart from a buried note and a fleeting reference in an editorial.[34]

The subsequent offers to the US Congress in August 2002 were impossible to ignore. Iraq offered to allow any member of Congress to come to Iraq with weapons experts to inspect any facility or building they suspected of involvement in prohibited weapons programmes. The offer was rejected out of hand by the US Government.[35] Such offers should be explored, not ignored.

CONCLUSION

Baghdad has blown hot and cold on a resumption of inspection. Sometimes new inspections have been ruled out entirely. Sometimes they have been offered only in return for the lifting of sanctions. Then at other times Baghdad has offered to allow in the new inspection body – for example, if 'the locations to be searched are identified and a timetable is set up and respected.'[36] Analysts consulted by the *Financial Times* 'said Iraq would try to drag out the diplomatic process and would be likely to agree to allow inspectors back only when it felt a US military attack was imminent.'[37] This is a plausible analysis.

Each path carries risks, from the Iraqi perspective. Baghdad has no wish to allow another coordinated inspection-coup attempt, along the lines of UNSCOM 150 in June 1996. On the other hand, a resumption of the inspection and monitoring regime may be the only alternative to a massive invasion.

Washington's role is critical. The evidence at the time of writing is that the US is intent on torpedoing the fragile UN-led efforts to negotiate the return of weapons inspectors to Iraq. Strategic leaks regarding US military plans, a refusal to answer reasonable Iraqi questions or to give reasonable assurances, and maximalist demands for total freedom for weapons inspectors add up to a strategy to stymie UNMOVIC as surely as UNSCOM was destroyed.

To paraphrase Richard Butler, if one uses the test of looking rationally at outcomes, without ascribing motives, it can be argued that the death of UNMOVIC has become US policy – because that is what is happening before our eyes.

What makes this even more poignant is that in December 1998 Richard Butler himself believed that it would only take UNSCOM two months at the most to complete the inspection process. On 4 December 1998, Mr Butler met the Russian Foreign Minister Igor Ivanov in Moscow:

> The foreign minister then asked how long it would take, through a comprehensive review, before we could declare Iraq disarmed. Given the key remaining issues in the missile and chemical areas, I replied, we might have a satisfactory account of Iraq's weapons-of-mass-destruction programme within six to eight weeks.[38]

Instead, the United States demolished the inspection agency, and held back its successor, creating a three year gap before there were serious negotiations between Iraq and the UN over the reintroduction of weapons inspectors. During these negotiations the United States has done its best to demolish the chances of UNMOVIC establishing an inspection and monitoring programme that could ensure Iraq's disarmament.

CHAPTER VI
Inspection Is An Option

THE NEED FOR EARLY ACTION

Speaking at West Point military academy on 1 June 2002, President George W. Bush set out a grim warning of the dangers of weapons of mass destruction. While 'deterrence' and 'containment' had worked during the Cold War, they were not applicable in the new age: 'Containment is not possible when unbalanced dictators with weapons of mass destruction can deliver those weapons on missiles or secretly provide them to terrorist allies.' The US President said, 'We cannot defend America and our friends by hoping for the best. We cannot put our faith in the word of tyrants, who solemnly sign non-proliferation treaties, and then systematically break them. If we wait for threats to fully materialize, we will have waited too long.'[1]

A month later, President Bush warned again of the danger posed by countries developing weapons of mass destruction, saying, 'against such enemies, we cannot sit quietly and hope for the best. To ignore this mounting danger is to invite it.' 'America must act against these terrible threats before they're fully formed.'[2]

British Prime Minister Tony Blair has echoed the President's words, claiming in Parliament that the lesson to be drawn from 11 September is that pre-emptive action should have been taken with regard to al Qaeda: 'What we should learn from that is that, if there is a gathering threat or danger, let us deal with it before it materialises rather than afterwards.'[3]

Utterly sensible truisms, appropriate to all difficult relationships.

In June 2002, President Bush said, 'In this world we have entered, the only path to safety is the path of action.' Earlier, the President had said, 'Inaction is not an option.'[4] This was not strictly speaking true, as inaction not only was available as an option, but as far as Iraq went, it was the option actually chosen by the President for much of 2002. As the Washington correspondent of the *Independent*, Rupert Cornwell, remarked in July 2002, 'The Bush administration appears to be trying to prove that a war can be won by sabre-rattling alone.'[5]

Setting the President's own behaviour to one side, and assuming that 'inaction is not an option' with regard to countries suspected of developing weapons of mass destruction, the question arises, what form of action should one pursue? The answer from Mr Bush and Mr Blair is military action. But military action is not the only option. As Mr Blair said in Parliament in July 2002, 'The issue of weapons of mass destruction and Iraq is an issue we have to deal with. It will not go away. There are many different ways of dealing with it.'[6] Diplomacy is an option. The resolution of the root causes of conflict, and the removal of motives for the proliferation of weapons of mass destruction, are also options. President Bush says the choices are invasion or inaction, but **inspection** is also an option.

INTERNATIONAL CAUTION

Former Soviet President Mikhail Gorbachev has spoken on behalf of much of world opinion, saying, 'We have a full set of political, economic and diplomatic methods that should be used to deal with Iraq. Iraq is an important nation and both that nation and the world should not be put at risk without really trying all the other various measures and approaches available.'[7] Senior German and French politicians argue that negotiations and a resumption of UN weapons inspections is the way forward – 'a view that provokes exasperation in Washington'.[8] There is support for this point of view in London also.[9] It has been suggested that the Foreign Office's preferred option would be 'aggressive containment', whereby air strikes would be intensified if Iraq did not agree to a full inspection agreement.[10] The Father of the House of Commons Tam Dalyell MP has pointed out that, 'George Bush and Tony Blair cannot say they are going to conduct a just war if they have not done everything possible to avoid a war.'[11]

The weight of official opinion across the Atlantic is in the other direction, however. Vice-President Dick Cheney himself has said, 'My concern is that we'll see an agreement to allow inspectors back in, but they'll be constrained. They'll be limited. They won't have the size or the right of penetration that's necessary to be confident that this guy has not developed nuclear weapons or biological or chemical weapons.'[12]

As we have seen, US National Security Adviser Condoleeza Rice has also expressed scepticism. When she 'dodged a question on whether the inspections issue provides justification for US military action against Iraq', Ms Rice has said that Saddam Hussein 'is not likely to ever convince the world, in a reliable way, that he is going to live at peace with his neighbours, that he will not seek weapons of mass destruction, and that he will not repress his own people.'[13] Reflecting such priorities, columnist on *The Times* Tim Haines has suggested that 'There is no other blueprint for dealing with Baghdad that has the remotest shred of credibility,' apart from military action.[14]

As already noted, it has been reported that senior Pentagon officials 'fear that inspectors might be granted some form of access, then give Saddam a clean bill of health he did not deserve.'[15] No evidence is produced that a resumption of the inspection regime would be doomed to ineffectiveness.

As *Time* magazine has pointed out, 'Inspectors discovered and disposed of 38,500 chemical munitions (such as shells, warheads, bombs), 625 tons of chemical weapons agents, 2,700 tons of precursor chemicals, and 426 pieces of chemical production equipment.'[16] These were not destroyed by the bombing campaign of 1991, despite the best efforts of the United States Air Force. They were detected and disposed of by patient inspection on the ground.

WHAT THE INSPECTORS ACHIEVED

Scott Ritter points out that, 'Most of UNSCOM's findings of Iraqi non-compliance concerned either the inability to verify an Iraqi declaration or peripheral matters such as components and documentation, which by and of themselves do not constitute a weapon or a program.' By December 1998, 'Iraq had, in fact, been disarmed to a level unprecedented in modern history, but UNSCOM and the Security Council were unable – and in some instances, unwilling – to acknowledge this accomplishment.'[17]

MISSILE DISARMAMENT

Iraq's long-range missile programme was entirely destroyed by December 1992, according to an UNSCOM report of that time, never contradicted by the years of subsequent investigation.[18]

NUCLEAR DISARMAMENT

As far as nuclear weapons are concerned, according to Mr Ritter, the 'massive infra-structure' Iraq had built up in its nuclear weapons programme 'had been eliminated by 1995' by the International Atomic Energy Agency (IAEA).[19] Even if some components have been retained, 'it would be of no use to Iraq given the extent to which Iraq's nuclear program was dismantled by the IAEA'. Rosemary Hollis, head of the Middle East programme at the Royal Institute of International Affairs, concludes that 'Iraq does not have the capacity to build nuclear weapons': 'She suggests that the emphasis now on Saddam's nuclear ambitions is dictated by Washington's plans for a pre-emptive strike on Iraq.'[20]

CHEMICAL DISARMAMENT

On chemical weapons, Mr Ritter concedes that problems remain regarding VX nerve agent and mustard gas loaded onto 155mm artillery shells. He notes, however, that VX mass-production equipment turned over to UNSCOM in 1996 was never actually used, and argues that the lack of any evidence of VX production found during UNSCOM's numerous inspections of possible storage and production sites 'minimizes the likelihood that Iraq maintains any significant stockpile of VX weapons.' 750 mustard gas artillery shells are unaccounted for. Mr Ritter states that a meaningful chemical weapons attack using artillery requires thousands of rounds, meaning that 'a few hundred 155mm mustard shells have little military value for use on the modern battlefield', and 'cannot be viewed as a serious threat'. Furthermore, an UNSCOM working paper notes, an Iraqi declaration of CW use during the war with Iran is not required for any meaningful verification: 'Taking into consideration the conditions and the quality of CW-agents and munitions produced by Iraq at that time, there is no possibility of weapons remaining from the mid-1980's.'[21]

Chemical weapon production equipment could be easily distributed throughout Iraq's commercial chemical-related facilities but, according to Mr Ritter, the manufacture of chemical weapons 'would require the assembling of production equipment into a single integrated facility, creating an infrastructure readily detectable by the strategic intelligence capabilities of the United States' – not detected to date. An UNSCOM paper notes that, 'Only the proper combination of different pieces of equipment in a particular configuration gives to ... these pieces of equipment the status of a CW production facility.' Mr Ritter comments that 'all of UNSCOM's specu-lative fears concerning reconstitution of an Iraqi CW capability can be laid to rest as long as a viable monitoring inspection regime, one that would detect any specialized configuration of dual-use equipment, is in place – the kind of regime that existed prior to the withdrawal of the inspectors in December 1998.'[22]

BIOLOGICAL DISARMAMENT

For Charles Duelfer, former deputy chair of UNSCOM, 'The biological issue is the biggest issue and least understood.' However, Mr Ritter pointed out in early 2002 that unaccounted-for stocks of chemical and biological weapons 'would no longer be vi-able': 'Weapons built before the Gulf war that slipped through the UNSCOM net would by now have passed their sell-by date.'[23] Iraq has mobile laboratories capable of producing such weapons in large quantities. However, Mr Ritter stated in June 2000 that, 'Contrary to popular belief, BW [biological weaponry] cannot simply be cooked up in the basement; it requires a large and sophisticated infrastructure, especially if the agent is to be filled into munitions. As with CW [chemical weapons], the CIA has not detected any such activity concerning BW since UNSCOM inspectors left Iraq.'

Mr Ritter argues that the reality of the situation in 1998 was that, 'regardless of UNSCOM's ability to verify Iraq's declarations regarding its past BW programs, the major BW production facility at Al Hakum had been destroyed, together with its asso-ciated equipment' by June 1996, and 'extensive monitoring of Iraq's biological infrastructure could find no evidence of continued proscribed activity'. He suggested that 'If weapons inspectors are once again allowed back into Iraq to resume monitor-ing along the lines carried out by UNSCOM, there is no reason to doubt that similar findings would be had, with the same level of confidence.'[24]

CONCLUSION

It is highly unlikely that the weapons programmes so successfully disarmed by UNSCOM could have been reconstituted since weapons inspectors were withdrawn, according to Mr Ritter: 'What took Iraq decades to build through the expenditure of billions of dollars could not, under any rational analysis, have been reconstituted since December 1998.' Despite the attempts by US hawks to downgrade the achievements and potential of UN weapons inspectors – Defence Secretary Rumsfeld has said, 'I just can't picture how intrusive something would have to be that it could offset the ease with which they [the Iraqis] have previously been able to deny and deceive'. The fact is, however, that, as Mr Blair has acknowledged, where inspectors were able to do their job, 'they did have an impact.'[25]

A RATIONAL FEAR

On 18 November 2001, US National Security Adviser Condoleeza Rice said, 'There could be only one reason that he has not wanted UN inspectors in Iraq, and that's so he can build weapons of mass destruction.'[26] Is that the only reason? In March 1993, there were press reports that Israel, using information from UNSCOM/US U-2 overflights, had been planning to assassinate Saddam Hussein the previous year, but had had to cancel the operation when the members of the assassination squad were killed in a training accident.[27] As we have seen, UNSCOM monitoring equipment was used by US intelligence to house a network of covert spying devices monitoring the protection squads around Saddam Hussein – and relaying that information directly and exclusively to the United States.

Recall also that UNSCOM 150, an attempted intrusive inspection of Republican Guard (RG) and Special Republican Guard (SRG) facilities led by Scott Ritter in mid-1996, occurred at the same time as a major attempted coup in Iraq involving the very same units of the super-elite Special Republican Guard. This coup attempt involved the Iraqi National Accord (INA), a group of exiled Iraqi generals, and was initiated at a high-level gathering of intelligence officials from Britain, Jordan, Saudi Arabia, Kuwait and the US in January 1996. The Saudis contributed $6 million, the Kuwaitis $3 million, and the US $6 million, towards the coup attempt.[28] It seems that the CIA paramilitary officers working under Mr Ritter were given the task of contacting the plotting officers in the RG and SRG.[29] The plot was uncovered around the time of UNSCOM 150 in June 1996, and 120 officers from the RG, the SRG, and various top-level intelligence and security agencies were executed. Dilip Hiro comments, 'Once the Iraqi regime had got over its alarm and shock, it stiffened its stance on UNSCOM inspections. It now perceived these exercises as part of communications channels for coordinating a coup to be staged after its attention had been diverted by US military strikes, which would also provide a chance for the Jordan-based INA insurgents to enter Iraq to carry out subversive acts.'[30]

After June 1996, it takes considerable cheek for a US National Security Adviser to say that 'There could be only one reason that Saddam Hussein has not wanted UN inspectors in Iraq, and that's so he can build weapons of mass destruction.'

US BARS INSPECTORS

This is not the only aspect of US policy on weapons inspections in Iraq which requires a certain amount of shamelessness. On 25 July 2001, at a major international conference, Washington announced that it was rejecting a draft Protocol aimed at strengthening the Biological Weapons Convention. US Ambassador Donald Mahley, head of the US delegation, argued that there was an 'inherent flaw' in the Convention's approach to bio-defence because there was not sufficient protection of 'sensitive legitimate acts'. Regular on-site 'transparency visits' risked 'damage' to innocent declared facilities, putting national security and commercial propriety information 'at risk'. The United

States could not agree to subject itself to such risks when there was 'no corresponding benefit in impeding proliferation efforts around the globe'.[31]

On another front, legislation needed to implement the Chemical Weapons Convention (CWC) was passed by the US Senate, but with reservations attached, despite the fact that the treaty explicitly bans the attaching of conditions to the treaty. Human Rights Watch observed that the legislation passed by the Senators 'includes language opposed by the [Clinton] administration that enables the president to refuse a challenge inspection, prohibits samples collected during an inspection from leaving the country for analysis, and limits the number of industrial facilities required to declare their activities with chemicals that could be used to produce chemical warfare agents.'

A violation by the US of key provisions of the CWC would, according to the US Arms Control and Disarmament Agency, make it 'difficult to press the OPCW [Organisation for the Prohibition of Chemical Weapons, the body which oversees the Chemical Weapons Convention] or other State Parties for greater transparency or to work effectively with other Parties to address questions about their implementation of CWC obligations.' Human Rights Watch added, 'Truer words could not have been spoken: in retaliation for the lack of inspections at US commercial plants, several countries promptly threatened to bar future inspection of their factories as well.'

No free access for biological and chemical weapons inspectors, then. Certainly not 'anyone, anywhere, any time'. By Ms Rice's logic, there is only one reason that President Bush could have for blocking weapons inspections. What reason would she give for an attempt to block an inspection regime for the International Convention on Torture – as the US tried to do in July 2002?[32]

THE REGIONAL ARMS RACE

It has been suggested that the real issue in relation to Iraq's weapons of mass destruction programmes 'is not the current production of these weapons *per se* but their existence and the willingness of Iraq to use to them'.[33] The problem with this line of argument is that the drive to possess weapons of mass destruction is, in part, the product of Iraq's strategic position, facing powerful enemies both to the east and to the west. Israel possesses nuclear weapons, and apparently developed a mustard gas and nerve gas production facility in the Sinai as long ago as 1982. According to Anthony Cordesman and Ahmed S. Hashim, on the biological weapons front, Israel is ready to quickly produce biological weapons, but there are 'no reports of active production'. The US analysts suggest that Iran has two major research and production facilities for chemical warfare, and developed cyanide, phosgene, mustard gas, and nerve gas weapons during the Iran-Iraq war.[34] Mr Cordesman and Mr Hashim write,

> It is also dangerous to assume such efforts [to develop weapons of mass destruction] can be linked to the survival of Saddam Hussein and the Ba'ath elite. Most future Iraqi leaders are likely to have somewhat similar fears and ambitions at least in the near term.

No Iraqi leader will be able to ignore the efforts of Iran or Israel, or the potential challenge posed by the US and its allies in the Southern Gulf. Such leaders are likely to be products of the same Sunni elite as Saddam, and to rely on a high degree of authoritarianism and use of the instruments of state power.

Even "pragmatic" or "moderate" replacements for Saddam will not ignore the potential threat posed by Iran and Iran's weapons of mass destruction programs. They are also likely to seek to use weapons of mass destruction as at least covert counters to US power projection capability and ways of intimidating or influencing their Southern Gulf neighbors.[35]

Iraqi Foreign Minister Tariq Aziz told UNSCOM leader Richard Butler in December 1997 that Iraq had developed chemical weapons because of the threat from the 'Persians', and biological weapons because of the 'well-armed Zionist entity'.[36] In short, in the words of Mr Cordesman and Mr Hashim, 'Regardless of what Iraqi leader is in power, it seems likely that Iraq's efforts to develop weapons of mass destruction will be pursued on a target of opportunity basis, and to meet broad political ambitions and the personal goals of Iraq's leaders'.[37]

It seems that the goal of US policy is to achieve the replacement of Saddam Hussein and his inner circle with another set of Sunni military strongmen, essentially continuing the present regime, preferably by means of a military coup (see following chapters). Right-wing advocate of 'regime change', Michael Eisenstadt, a senior fellow at the Washington Institute for Near East Policy, accepts that a military government 'might still be wedded to WMD' – weapons of mass destruction – but suggests hopefully that 'it could be easier to manage the consequences of proliferation in Iraq with a regime less prone to miscalculation and aggression'.[38]

All of which lends weight to the conclusion that the solution to Iraq's weapons of mass destruction programmes lies not in changing the leadership of Iraq, but in mounting an effective inspection and monitoring system. Military attacks were shown in 1991 to be thoroughly ineffective in achieving disarmament. Whoever holds power in Baghdad, they are almost certain to seek weapons of mass destruction. Military action and 'regime change' cannot ensure that Iraq does not develop weapons of mass destruction. A rigorous monitoring programme can. Inspection is not only *an* option, it is *the* option for those who are serious about disarmament.

QUALITATIVE DISARMAMENT

The UNSCOM approach, driven largely by Britain and the United States, was backward-looking and quantitative. It was focused on locating, destroying, removing or 'rendering harmless' all weapons of mass destruction, all long-range missiles, and all the equipment needed to produce them – to establish a 'material balance' for the equipment and weapons in the various programmes. UNSCOM also prioritised the location of all documents relating to the weapons and missiles programmes, to build up a complete history of the various programmes. Many of the most notorious confrontations between UNSCOM and Baghdad actually revolved around documents sought by UNSCOM, not around weapons or components.

An alternative approach was suggested by Scott Ritter in a ground-breaking article in *Arms Control Today* in June 2000.[39] Instead of looking backwards, the international community should look forwards. The aim should be to prevent Iraq being able to develop and use weapons of mass destruction in the future, not to find every single component accumulated in the past. According to Mr Ritter, who was the chief inspector for UNSCOM, and head of the agency's counter-concealment unit, it would be possible to prevent Iraq from assembling missiles and weapons of mass destruction even if it still possessed some of the necessary components and materials.

Instead of concentrating on quantities and 'materials balance' – every nut and every bolt (and even every document) – the UN Security Council should focus on preventing the reconstitution of Iraq's weapons development capabilities – 'qualitative disarmament'. Mr Ritter defines 'qualitative disarmament' as 'the elimination of a meaningful, viable capability to produce or employ weapons of mass destruction'.

The quantitative approach of demanding the verification of 'material balance' is 'a formula for disaster', says Mr Ritter, 'perpetuating the cycle of conflict with Iraq':

> Given the comprehensive nature of the monitoring regime put in place by UNSCOM, which included a strict export-import control regime, it was possible as early as 1997 to determine that, from a qualitative standpoint, Iraq had been disarmed. Iraq no longer possessed any meaningful quantities of chemical or biological agent, if it possessed any at all, and the industrial means to produce these agents had either been eliminated or were subject to stringent monitoring.
>
> The same was true of Iraq's nuclear and ballistic missile capabilities. As long as monitoring inspections remained in place, Iraq presented a WMD-based threat to no one.[40]

That last sentence deserves repetition and emphasis: 'As long as monitoring inspections remained in place, Iraq presented a WMD-based threat to no one.'

INSPECTIONS AND MONITORING

UNSCOM had two very separate tasks in Iraq. One was concerned with inspecting sites to try to discover elements of banned programmes. The other was concerned with monitoring known sites to ensure that weapons programmes could not be restarted at those locations. (Both tasks were initiated by paragraph 12 of Resolution 687.) The monitoring process concentrated on 'choke points' in the weapons production process. The nuclear monitoring team used isotope detectors in rivers to detect the discharge of any radioactive material. The chemical monitoring team used chemical monitors in chemical factories to detect key precursors and chemical agents. The biological weapons monitoring team monitored the pharmaceutical industry.

The system, initiated in 1994, monitored more than 250 sites. Video cameras were installed in 150 locations to ensure that dual-purpose machinery (which could be used for civilian as well as military purposes) was not misused. The cameras were linked by a series of transmitters and repeaters to UNSCOM's Baghdad Monitoring and Verification Centre, and to the UN in New York. Temperature sensors were installed at possible biological weapons sites to check if a factory was operating equipment at a suspicious temperature. Monitoring was also done through weekly U-2 high-altitude reconnaissance flights (the aircraft were owned and operated by the United States, and intelligence went directly to the US) and helicopter photography. This aerial reconnaissance was intended to detect fresh construction, new power lines, or other signs of renewed activity at suspect sites.

Monitoring covered present capacities in terms of building and plant and skilled personnel with previous experience in the research or production of banned weapons and missiles. It also covered any future introduction of new building, equipment or senior scientists and engineers.[41] (As already noted, the monitoring system was riddled with secret US eavesdropping devices.)

The function of the inspection process was distinct and different from the monitoring regime. The inspection process, especially in the aggressive and intrusive form developed by Scott Ritter, was focused on uncovering hidden components, materials and documents related to the weapons programmes, or verifying their destruction. The monitoring process, on the other hand, was designed simply to freeze Iraq's unconventional weapons programmes, and to prevent them from re-starting. Together, the two sides of UNSCOM had successfully disarmed Iraq by 1997, according to Mr Ritter: 'through its extensive investigations, UNSCOM was able to ensure that the vast majority of Iraq's WMD arsenal, along with the means to produce such weaponry, was in fact eliminated. Through monitoring, UNSCOM was able to guarantee that Iraq was not reconstituting that capability in any meaningful way.'[42]

Let us recall that the UNSCOM monitoring effort was terminated by the United States, firstly by penetrating and using UNSCOM for its own spying activities, which discredited the agency fatally, and then by ordering the withdrawal not only of UNSCOM's inspectors, but also of the monitoring team, in December 1998.

A NEW INSPECTION REGIME

Scott Ritter has also warned that the 'no-notice inspections' aspect of a new inspection and monitoring regime 'should focus on facilities that have a legitimate bearing on WMD research, development, and manufacture'. He has urged UNMOVIC head Hans Blix to 'avoid pressure to continue aggressive inspections aimed at Iraqi presidential and security sites': 'Such inspections have historically produced little to do with disarmament, and given the misuse of sensitive information gathered by UNSCOM from such sites in the past, they would be viewed with mistrust not only by Iraq, but also by members of the Security Council.'[43]

THE REGIONAL SOLUTION

UN Security Council Resolution 687, which ordered the disarmament of Iraq, and which set up the ill-fated UN Special Commission, said that the disarmament actions to be taken by Iraq 'represent steps towards the goal of establishing in the Middle East a zone free from weapons of mass destruction and all missiles for their delivery and the objective of a global ban on chemical weapons' (paragraph 14). This has been of critical importance for the Iraqis. Scott Ritter remarks in his *Arms Control Today* essay,

> While monitoring-based inspections in Iraq must be expected to last indefinitely, they cannot be expected to last in a vacuum. Unless arrangements are made to address WMD programs in Iran and Israel, as well as the regional proliferation of advanced conventional weaponry, Iraq will never accept perpetual disarmament.

Disarmament and equally rigorous inspection and monitoring programmes in these and other militarised states in the region are the only long-term solution to the Iraqi weapons issue. It is not simply a matter of principle. As long as there is a threat from Teheran and Tel Aviv, all governments in Baghdad, of whatever complexion, will feel under pressure to seek counter-force.

DON'T WAIT TOO LONG

If the international community is serious about controlling Iraq's weapons of mass destruction, what is needed is the reintroduction and repair of the weapons and missile-centred monitoring system (this time without contamination by US intelligence). Far from there being 'no blueprint for dealing with Iraq's weapons of mass destruction that has the remotest shred of credibility' other than military action (Tim Haines, *The Times*), an inspection and monitoring system is the only blueprint that has any credibility in terms of controlling Iraq's weapons of mass destruction.

President Bush has said that the United States 'cannot put our faith in the word of tyrants, who solemnly sign non-proliferation treaties, and then systemically break them'. This applies to US-imposed Saddam-clones also. Only a monitoring system can prevent Iraqi generals, whether US-favoured or not, from developing weapons of mass destruction. As the President also said, 'If we wait for threats to fully materialize, we will have waited too long.'[44] In the case of Iraq, inspection is an option, and almost certainly the only effective one.

CHAPTER VII
Regime Stabilisation, 1991

The US Helped To Crush The Uprisings

'REGIME CHANGE'

At their historic meeting in Crawford, Texas, in April 2002, British Prime Minister Tony Blair and US President George W. Bush affirmed their joint decision to launch a military assault on Iraq. In a press conference together, President Bush said, 'I explained to the Prime Minister that the policy of my Government is the removal of Saddam Hussein, and that all options are open.'[1] According to one report, Mr Blair – who looked 'uncharacteristically nervous' at the press conference – 'visibly winced' at this rendition of their war aims.[2] Mr Bush was asked what had happened to the long-standing official position of not targeting heads of state personally. The President corrected himself, saying, 'Maybe I should be a little less direct and be a little more nuanced and say we support regime change' – 'Regime change sounds a lot more civil', he conceded.[3] Mr Bush's reference to being 'more nuanced' apparently provoked a roar of laughter from Mr Blair's media adviser, Alistair Campbell.[4]

Mr Blair followed the President to the microphone and, for the first time, used the language of 'regime change' in relation to Iraq. He said that the region, the world, 'and not least the ordinary Iraqi people' would be better off 'without the regime of Saddam Hussein'.[5] He followed this up in a speech the next day at the George Bush Presidential Library, when he said that 'we must be prepared to act where terrorism or weapons of mass destruction threaten us': 'If necessary the action should be military and again, if necessary and justified, it should involve regime change.' Mr Blair boasted that he had been involved as British Prime Minister in three conflicts involving regime change: 'Milosevic. The Taliban. And Sierra Leone, where a country of six million people was saved from a murderous group of gangsters who had hijacked the democratically elected government.'[6]

The *Independent* observed that the British leader's use of the phrase 'regime change' 'mark[ed] an important strengthening of Mr Blair's rhetoric', and signalled a break from traditional Foreign Office caution on the issue.[7]

The hardening of the US/UK position was subjected to some 'spin' by the US Secretary of State, Colin Powell, who said that, 'We *still* believe strongly in regime change in Iraq': 'We have had a policy of regime change, which really has been there all along but was crystallised by President Clinton in 1998 at the time of Desert Fox.'[8]

'LEADERSHIP CHANGE'

A 'regime' is a 'system of government', not simply a leader. The term can extend beyond the dominant political party into the military, the police, the civil service, and even into the centres of economic power. After the Second World War, the 'de-nazification' of Germany extended into all these domains, if very shallowly. In Serbia, Afghanistan and Sierra Leone, the examples chosen by Tony Blair to illustrate 'regime change' operations he had been involved in, the objective was not simply to capture or assassinate President Milosevic or Mullah Omar or any particular military or political leader in Sierra Leone. The actions taken in these countries had a significant impact on the political system.

One can distinguish, then, between a policy of 'regime change', which in Iraq would mean the expulsion of the Ba'ath Party from power, and changes in the make-up and leadership of the security forces and the civil administration, and a policy of 'leadership change', which would require only the replacement of the Leader and his inner circle, leaving the political system essentially unchanged.

The evidence, examined in more detail in the next chapter, suggests that the policy of the United States is to pursue 'leadership change' rather than 'regime change'. This is a long-standing policy, and goes back to 1991.

THE IRAQI UPRISINGS, 1991

On 15 February 1991, a month into the onslaught on Iraq and Kuwait, President George Bush Sr. spoke directly to the ordinary people of Iraq. On two occasions on that day, the President used the same phrase, calling on 'the Iraqi military and the Iraqi people to take matters into their own hands and force Saddam Hussein, the dictator, to step aside'. According to Andrew and Patrick Cockburn, authors of *Out of the Ashes: The Resurrection of Saddam Hussein*, the speech was originally intended to encourage the Iraqi military to stage a coup; the words 'and the Iraqi people' were included 'only as an afterthought.'[9]

Just over a fortnight later, as desperate and angry Iraqi soldiers scrambled to escape from Kuwait, the Iraqi people answered the unintended appeal of the US President.

A spontaneous revolt sprang up that swept away the power of the Ba'ath Party throughout the south, matched by a semi-organised insurrection in Iraqi Kurdistan, in the north. Within days, Saddam Hussein had lost control of fourteen of Iraq's eighteen provinces, and was staring into the abyss.

SPARING THE REPUBLICAN GUARD

The Iraqi regime was saved, barely. It was saved as a matter of Western policy.

One critical decision concerned the decision to terminate the ground war on 28 February 1991, which had the effect of sparing much of the elite Republican Guard, the backbone of the regime, from destruction. The Republican Guard were widely recognised to be the best trained, the most loyal, and the most proficient elements of Iraq's military forces. Percy Craddock, John Major's Foreign Policy Adviser, notes in his memoirs that 'Sizeable portions of the Iraqi forces, including Republican Guard armour, were able to slip out [from US encirclement] to reinforce the reserve held by Saddam around Baghdad'. Mr Craddock notes that, 'Another day of fighting would almost certainly have been enough to eliminate them,' a missed opportunity he greatly regrets. Mr Craddock writes, 'It seemed a curious decision and I was taken aback to learn of it when I came into No. 10 early on the morning of 28 February.' Coalition forces 'had gone to considerable lengths to get into the present position' to be able to destroy the Iraqi divisions that had invaded and held Kuwait: 'To fail to finish the job now would be foolish and perhaps dangerous.'[10]

Mr Craddock was not the only person with something of a fixation with the Republican Guard. The US commander-in-chief of 'coalition' forces in the Gulf, General H. Norman Schwarzkopf designed his pincer movement *blitzkrieg* precisely to be able to enclose and destroy the Republican Guard formations in and near Kuwait. US General Charles Horner, the commander of the 1991 air war against Iraq, later recalled that in a briefing in November 1990 laying out the basic strategy of the coming ground war against Iraq, General Schwarzkopf stressed the significance of the Republican Guard: 'Of course, one of the main goals that Schwarzkopf always had and I think Powell as well was to get the Republican Guard – he considered them more of a political force almost than a military force.' That was the importance of 'the left hook', US tank columns entering deep into Iraq to cut off the Iraqi retreat, and boxing the Republican Guard into a zone of destruction.[11] A major part of the military planning ordered by General Schwarzkopf was not aimed at Kuwait at all, but at the Republican Guard, 'the military cornerstone of Saddam's regime'.[12]

General Schwarzkopf's official biographers describe his final press briefing of the war on 27 February 1991 as 'an extraordinary performance, brisk, articulate, convincing, overpowering.' 'Amid all the bravura at the press conference, however, a key point tended to get obscured. This was that while one part of the mission Schwarzkopf had set himself – the recapture of Kuwait – was completed, the other – the destruction of the Republican Guard was not.'[13]

In his final war press conference, Schwarzkopf had this to say about the Republican Guard:

> If I'm to accomplish the mission that I was given, and that's to make sure that the Republican Guard is rendered incapable of conducting the type of heinous acts that they've conducted so often in the past, what has to be done is these forces continue to attack across here, and put the Republican Guard out of business. We're not in the business of killing them. We have psy ops aircraft up. We're telling them over and over again, all you've got to do is get out of your tanks and move off, and you will not be killed. But they're continuing to fight, and as long as they continue to fight, we're going to continue to fight with them.[14]

It was the tanks and the armoured vehicles of the Republican Guard that were the focus of attention, not the soldiers themselves, according to this rendition.

By the time of Schwarzkopf's 27 February press conference, large elements of the Republican Guard were huddled in a twenty-mile box around Basra. They were spared by the decision by Schwarzkopf's civilian superiors to call a cease-fire at midnight that same night. Major General Barry McCaffrey, leading the US 24th Division, was about to attack the Hammurabi Heavy Division, 'probably the most powerful single force in the Republican Guard', when the cease-fire took effect. McCaffrey said later, 'Going to Basra was easily within our grasp the next day and we had plans to do so. The Republican Guard was crumbling. Any one piece was too much for them. All of our forces together were crushing them.'[15]

Some have alleged that a 'fatal miscalculation' by General Schwarzkopf allowed the Republican Guard to escape.[16] The US commander-in-chief later revealed the truth to David Frost of the BBC,

> Frankly, my recommendation had been, you know, continue the march. I mean, we had them in a rout and we could have continued to wreak great destruction on them. We could have completely closed the doors and made it in fact a battle of annihilation. And the President made the decision that we should stop at a given time, at a given place, that did leave some escape routes open for them to get back out, and I think that was a very humane decision and a very courageous decision on his part also.[17]

Schwarzkopf's biographers refer in the gentlest way possible to the subsequent role of the forces spared so 'humanely' and 'courageously' by President Bush senior: 'It is also difficult to judge the degree to which further destruction of tanks and other military equipment would have hampered Saddam in putting down the subsequent Kurdish and Shiite revolts in the north and south of the country.'[18] The US Defence Intelligence Agency and CIA later estimated that 1,430 armoured personnel carriers, and about 700 tanks (out of 4,550 in southern Iraq), escaped from the trap Schwarzkopf and his forces had laboured to create.[19]

Some doubts have been cast on whether the Republican Guard could have been completely destroyed if the battle had continued.[20] The point, however, is that the decision to spare the strongest element of the Republican Guard was taken deliberately and consciously at the very highest level of the US Administration, against the advice of the commander-in-chief in the field, and against the wishes of the British Government's Foreign Policy Adviser, if not Prime Minister John Major himself. And the consequences of that decision were felt by the people who had answered President Bush's call to 'take matters into their own hands.'

PERMITTING GUNSHIPS TO FLY AGAINST THE REBELS

In the aftermath of the cease-fire, a formal agreement was reached between the Iraqi armed forces and the US-led 'coalition' at Safwan in southern Iraq on 3 March 1991. Until that day, there were standing orders that any Iraqi aircraft detected in flight were to be shot down. At the end of the meeting, General Schwarzkopf agreed to permit Iraqi helicopters to fly, on condition that they did not overfly Western forces in Iraq. He later complained that he had been 'suckered.'[21] Whether or not that is true, the significant issue is not the decision to grant flying rights on 3 March, but the decision to continue to allow Iraqi helicopters to fly after it became clear how they were being used.

Air Forces Monthly recalled in May 2002 the horror of two US Air Force F-15 pilots flying over Iraq in March 1991, as they were forced to watch an Iraqi helicopter gunship swoop down on a column of Kurdish refugees. 'As the gunship worked over the column with bombs and machine guns, the pilots repeatedly radioed the US command post in Saudi Arabia, asking permission to take out the Iraqi machine. When the reply came back from their controller in the negative, the pilots had to back off and allow Saddam Hussein's henchmen to do their worst.'[22]

On 13 March 1991, President Bush Sr. said, 'These helicopters should not be used for combat purposes inside Iraq.' The next day, General Schwarzkopf reiterated the ban on fixed-wing aircraft, but did not mention helicopters. A few days later, Pentagon spokesperson Pete Williams confirmed that Iraq was using 'dozens' of helicopters against the rebellion, and asked, 'Is our policy somewhat ambiguous?' Mr Williams replied to himself, 'Yes.'[23]

Brigadier Ali, an exiled Iraqi officer who joined the rebellion in southern Iraq in 1991, and was later interviewed by the Cockburns, said of the fall of Kerbala to the Republican Guard: 'We had the message that the Americans would support us. But I saw with my own eyes the American planes flying over the helicopters. We were expecting them to help; now we could see them witnessing our demise between Najaf and Kerbala. They were taking pictures and they knew exactly what was happening.'[24]

Incidentally, the United States had sold Bell and Hughes helicopters to Iraq in the 1980s, ostensibly for civilian purposes, though they were widely used for military purposes, either for transportation, or possibly as gunships. The fact that Iraq possessed the Bell 214 helicopters was included in the book *How They Fight: Desert Shield; Order of Battle Handbook*, published by the Pentagon and issued to each US solder in Saudi Arabia during the 1990-91 Gulf Crisis.[25]

DENYING ARMS STORES TO THE REBELS

It has been said that the policy of the US forces towards the uprisings consisted of 'malevolent interference without the use of arms', where US troops even 'stopped the rebels from reaching an arms depot to obtain ammunition.'[26] It appears that there was a systematic policy of denying rebel forces access to Government arms caches under US control.[27] (Some US troops seem to have disobeyed this policy.[28]) Much of the captured stocks were destroyed, but, according to a former US diplomat, an appreciable quantity was seized by the CIA and shipped to fundamentalists in Afghanistan, to support the US-favoured side in the ongoing civil war in that country.[29]

REBUFFING THE OPPOSITION

It was reported many years later that the Bush Administration had 'intercepted a Saudi attempt to help the anti-Saddam rebels'.[30] The cold shoulder given to the Iraqi opposition before, during and after the war made it appear that it was the opposition and not the Iraqi government that was the enemy.

The Kurdish underground inside northern Iraq offered military intelligence to the US during the war, and was refused. The information had to be channelled through Kurdish offices in Iran, Syria, and finally through Detroit to a sympathetic staff director of the Senate Foreign Relations Committee, Peter Galbraith.[31] Kurdish leader Jalal Talabani attempted to enter the State Department on 28 February 1991, to brief US officials on the imminent uprising in northern Iraq. His party was held in the lobby. The following day, Richard Haas, director for Middle East Affairs on the National Security Council telephoned Mr Galbraith of the Senate Foreign Relations Committee to complain about his sponsorship of the unwelcome Kurds. 'You don't understand,' said Mr Haas: 'Our policy is to get rid of Saddam, not his regime.'[32] This statement encapsulates the history of Iraq for the past dozen years.

Inside Iraq, Brigadier Ali, who had defected to the rebels, sought a meeting with US forces outside Nasiriyah on behalf of Grand Ayatollah Abu al-Qassim al-Khoie, the spiritual leader of Iraq's Shia population. The brigadier was told that the US officer he was speaking to had lost touch with headquarters – perhaps he should seek out a nearby French unit? The French were more welcoming, and arranged a meeting with General Schwarzkopf himself in a few days' time. After three days of waiting, the rebel group was told that the meeting had been cancelled.[33]

AN UNDESIRABLE COUP

Asked about the possibility of a coup inside Iraq, a Pentagon official said in April 1991, 'We don't see anything on the horizon'. A large number of oppositionists had been killed. 'The uprisings made it inevitable that there would not be a coup.'[34] This is somewhat misleading. At the height of the rebellions, according to a US Senate Foreign Relations Committee report, a group of Iraqi army officials approached a dissident group of Iraqi exiles with an offer of cooperation. The would-be defectors required 'a sign that the sponsors of the rebellion had the support of the US', said the report.

However, the US State Department refused to meet any section of the opposition, and this public snub 'was read as a clear indication that the US did not want the popular rebellions to succeed.' The defections and the coup attempt did not take place.[35]

It was not that the uprisings destroyed the possibility of a coup. The rebellions made it almost inevitable that there would not be a coup acceptable to Washington.

PRESERVING THE REGIME

White House spokesperson Marlin Fitzwater said in late March 1991,

> I think it's safe to assume that in the kind of warfare being conducted by the rebel forces and the Kurds, as well as by the Government of Iraq, as well as by other groups, that there are all sorts of atrocities and war repercussions taking place – yes. But it is our belief that the best policy is not to involve ourselves in those internal conflicts.[36]

But the United States did involve itself in the internal conflict. President Bush deliberately held back from destroying the key military formations of the regime. President Bush permitted the use of helicopter gunships and transport helicopters against the rebels. President Bush ordered that rebels be blocked from gaining access to Iraqi arms – and that weapons should be destroyed or removed from Iraq. President Bush rebuffed the Iraqi opposition before, during and after the war. Washington intervened decisively to protect the regime and to allow it the means to recover and to survive.

THE BEST OF ALL WORLDS

Why did the United States rebuff the Iraqi opposition, and tip the balance of the civil war against them? Why did a high-ranking US official say that, 'Our policy is to get rid of Saddam, not his regime.'[37] Why did the US pursue a policy of leadership change and not one of regime change in 1991?

In February 2002, the *Financial Times* commented, 'Washington's calculation is that a break-up of Iraq would fundamentally alter the balance of power in the Middle East, especially if it led to the creation of an independent Kurdistan. Turkey, a steadfast US ally with a large Kurd minority, would be destabilised. Iran could exploit the vacuum.'[38]

In March 2002, Whitehall officials were speaking of a potential 'nightmare scenario' with Iraq split into three separate parts, with the Kurds in the north demanding a separate state, 'something which would be fiercely opposed by Turkey, Iran and Syria', which all have substantial Kurdish minorities. In July 2002, Turkish leaders informed US Deputy Defence Secretary Paul Wolfowitz that Ankara would not oppose a US war on Iraq so long as it did not lead to the creation of an independent Iraqi Kurdistan.[39] Echoing these remarks, Sir John Moberly, British ambassador to Iraq between 1982 and 1985, said that after a major war, there would be such instability in the country that 'there would be a great temptation to replace Saddam with another Saddam – another iron-fisted military man.'[40] Whether or not there would be civil unrest, the rise of democratic politics in Iraq would not be looked on with favour by Saudi Arabia, or any of the Gulf's petty kingdoms, and would promote what they regard as 'instability'.

It is just these kinds of concerns that have driven US policy since 1991. Indeed, during the first week of the uprisings in 1991, the Iraqi military intercepted a radio exchange between two rebel groups in southern Iraq confirming that US hostility to the rebellion was based at least in part on Washington's fears concerning the possible extension of Iranian influence into southern Iraq. According to the then head of Iraqi military intelligence, Wafiq al-Sammarai, who subsequently defected to the West, one group informed the other that US forces had refused to support them on the basis that they were from the 'al-Sayed group', the Supreme Council for the Islamic Revolution in Iraq (SCIRI), based in Iran.[41] (The regime seized on this indication that Washington was abandoning the uprising, and 'immediately became more confident', according to al-Samarrai.)

Thomas Friedman, Diplomatic Correspondent of the *New York Times*, explained in mid-1991 that the sanctions regime was designed to provoke a military coup within Iraq to create 'the best of all worlds', 'an iron-fisted Iraqi junta without Saddam Hussein'. This would be a return to the days when Saddam's 'iron fist ... held Iraq together, much to the satisfaction of the American allies Turkey and Saudi Arabia.' In March 1991, this prospect was described by Ahmed Chalabi (now leader of the Iraqi opposition group the Iraqi National Congress) as 'the worst of all possible worlds' for the Iraqi people.[42]

CHAPTER VIII
Regime Stabilisation, 2002

The US Pursues 'Leadership Change', Not 'Regime Change'

ASSASSINATING SADDAM, 2002

In mid-March 2002, President George W. Bush entered a private meeting between US National Security Adviser Condoleeza Rice and Republican and Democratic Senators. The President became very animated while discussing Saddam Hussein. According to one person in the room, President Bush 'used a vulgar epithet to refer to Saddam, and concluded with four words that left no one in doubt about Bush's intentions: "we're taking him out".'[1]

The following month, as we have already seen, President Bush said at a press conference with Mr Blair, 'I explained to the Prime Minister that the policy of my Government is the removal of Saddam Hussein, and that all options are open.'[2] On an earlier occasion, the President said, 'I made up my mind that Saddam needs to go. That's about all I'm willing to share with you.'[3] While he has not used the Wild West phrase 'Dead or Alive' – language used in the case of Osama bin Laden – Mr Bush has made it clear that he is targeting the Iraqi leader personally.

This was made even more obvious in June 2002 when the President let it be known that he had ordered the CIA (some months earlier) to pursue the assassination of Saddam Hussein. The instruction was dressed up in a convoluted formula to avoid a long-standing ban on assassinating foreign heads of state imposed by Congressional legislation. It was said that CIA paramilitary teams or US Special Forces were to attempt to capture the Iraqi President, but were authorised to use deadly force to kill him, if they were acting in self-defence.[4]

ASSASSINATING SADDAM, 1991

This is hardly a new policy. There is little doubt that the United States and Britain systematically attempted to assassinate Saddam Hussein during the 1991 war, despite denials at the time – Douglas Hogg, then Foreign Office minister, said in late February 1991, 'Saddam's removal is in no sense a war aim.'[5] In the aftermath of 11 September, former Prime Minister John Major revealed that the Iraqi President had been personally targeted: 'If you mean in the [Gulf] war, did we try and kill Saddam Hussein by finding out where he was and dropping a bomb on him, of course we did, we were at war then.'[6] The *Sunday Times* reported in 1991, during the war, that the US command had established an elaborate system to try to track the Iraqi president that so he could be targeted in an operation called 'The Yamamoto Option', named after the Japanese admiral assassinated by the US during World War II.[7]

Scott Ritter, a US Marine before he became an UNSCOM inspector, recalls an occasion during the 1991 war when he was summoned to a meeting with General Calvin Waller, deputy commander of US forces, and Prince Turki bin-Faisal, head of Saudi intelligence, to carry out planning for one such attack. Two buildings near Basra were bombed because Saudi agents had reported that Saddam Hussein was to visit a remote location there to meet his commanders.[8]

The US launched a round of bombing just before the ground war began, 'including attacks that became something of a Saddam Hussein hunt, attacking VIP bunkers and the "Winnebago" trailers used at dispersed command facilities'. There was also a last round of leadership attacks on the last night of the war, when the US rushed two special 4,700-pound GBU-28 earth-penetrating bombs that had just arrived in the theatre onto F-111Fs, attacking a leadership bunker at Taji, north of Baghdad.[9]

The Yamamoto Option operation was the fulfilment of a strategic concept first outlined in September 1990 by US Air Force Chief of Staff General Michael Dugan. The General stated, for example, that 'because Saddam is a "one-man show" in Iraq, if and when we choose violence he ought to be at the focus of our efforts'. The *Washington Post* referred to this as 'a military strategy known as decapitation'. General Dugan was sacked immediately for being too open about US plans.[10]

Much the same policy was admitted by the then National Security Adviser, Brent Scowcroft, who said, 'We don't do assassinations, but yes we targeted all the places where Saddam might have been.' His interviewer asked, 'So you deliberately set out to kill him if you possibly could?' Mr Scowcroft answered, 'Yes, that's fair enough.'[11]

It hardly needs to be pointed out that a policy of 'decapitation' is rather different from a policy of 'regime change'. During the 1991 war, it appears, the US and Britain were committed to 'regime stability' and 'leadership decapitation'.

THE PREFERENCE FOR A COUP

This mix of goals is still the ideal, though perhaps out of reach. As *Time* magazine commented revealingly in May 2002, 'The smoothest regime-change scenario – a coup within Saddam's own military ranks – is the least likely.'[12] This comment, which accurately reflects establishment thinking, illustrates the real meaning of 'regime change'.

The longing for a coup goes back to 1991, naturally. National Security Adviser Brent Scowcroft told ABC television later, 'I frankly wish [the uprising] hadn't happened. I envisioned a post-war government being a military government.'[13] The problem was that the uprisings posed a direct threat to the political 'centre', a political and military elite dominated by Sunni Muslims, a minority in Iraq. Andrew and Patrick Cockburn comment that, 'The supreme irony is that Bush and his advisers, in trying to promote a coup [with his call for action], instead encouraged an uprising that may have prevented the very coup they desired.' The Cockburns reveal that a coup being planned by senior generals was derailed by the Iraqi military leaders' fear of the consequences of Shia success.[14]

Mr Scowcroft, who regrets the 1991 uprisings, said: 'It's the colonel with the brigade patrolling his palace that's going to get him [Saddam Hussein] if someone gets him.'[15] Perhaps, but it is interesting that the United States did everything short of firing into the crowds to undermine the uprisings in 1991, when there was a real threat to Saddam Hussein.

There were two kind of coup that could have occurred in March 1991: a regime-stabilising coup from within, such as the one derailed by the uprising; or a possibly regime-changing coup allied with the uprising such as the one mentioned in the last chapter. The first kind of coup was prevented by the rebellion that the United States incited inadvertently. The second kind of coup was prevented by Washington's refusal to support the uprisings, or to give its support to the Iraqi opposition.

Not content with betraying the 1991 uprisings, the US also pulled the plug on another uprising/coup attempt in 1995. This initiative had at its centre the Iraqi National Congress (INC), a coalition of Iraqi opposition groups led by Ahmed Chalabi. According to the plan drawn up by Mr Chalabi and local CIA officer Bob Baer, there would be a joint offensive on two fronts against Iraqi forces around Iraqi Kurdistan by the Patriotic Union of Kurdistan (PUK), the Kurdish Democratic Party (KDP), and the INC's own militants, supported by US air power. Friendly Iraqi forces would mutiny as Saddam was distracted by the troubles in the north, and a coup could take place.

On the morning of the offensive, 3 March 1995, the President's National Security Adviser, Tony Lake, instructed the local CIA officer, Mr Baer, to tell the INC that 'the United States would not support this operation militarily or in any other way'.[16] The offensive, deserted by one of the Kurdish parties, succeeded in capturing hundreds of Iraqi troops, who surrendered, but there were no mutinies anywhere in the country. The PUK withdrew from the few square miles that it captured, and released the prisoners, who the INC could not afford to feed.[17] It was March 1991 all over again. A coup linked to popular forces was anathema to mainstream policymakers.

Incidentally, the five-man CIA team working with the INC was withdrawn from Kurdistan in the aftermath of this fiasco, along with 5,000 INC members, and arrested on their return to the US on charges of attempting to murder Saddam Hussein, in violation of the ban on assassinations of foreign heads of state. The following year, however, the charges were dropped, and the five were actually decorated for their work.[18]

In 2002, it has been made very clear in leaks about Washington's policy towards Iraq that, 'Top of the US wish list would be a coup by an Iraqi officer ... The US might, from its point of view, even get lucky with an air strike on the centre of Baghdad that killed Saddam.'[19] This wish is not confined to the corridors of Mr Bush's White House. A former editor of the British left-liberal newspaper the *Guardian*, Peter Preston wrote in March 2002, 'If some ambitious Iraqi colonel, bank-account-stuffed and ambition-fuelled, put a gun to the old despot's head and pulled the trigger, we could all rejoice.'[20] So, if the present regime were to continue essentially unchanged, but with a fresh face papered on the front of the Party, we would all be overjoyed.

THE IRAQI NATIONAL ACCORD

Rather than working with the INC, the CIA and the State Department have preferred to develop a close relationship with the Iraqi National Accord (INA). This grouping of exiled Iraqi officers, supposedly one of the nineteen constituent bodies of the INC, and therefore formally under the leadership of Mr Chalabi. In fact, the INA has always had a direct link to the US administration, with funding from the CIA. For example, it was the focus for the multi-million-dollar coup attempt in June 1996 (see pages 55 and 69). Indeed, it was to protect this INA scheme (which also ended in abysmal failure) that the White House withdrew its backing for the INC offensive in 1995.[21]

The INA had organised a series of bombings in Baghdad in 1994 and 1995, as part of a CIA-backed programme of preparation for a coup. The bombings – in a cinema, a mosque, outside the offices of the Ba'ath Party newspaper, and other sites – may have killed as many as a hundred civilians. The man who carried out the bombings, Abu Amneh al-Khadami, revealed the role of the INA in a video made in January 1996. Mr Amneh was recruited to the INA's military arm from jail in Iraqi Kurdistan, where he had been imprisoned for the attempted murder of an INC official. Mr Amneh claimed to have been released on the direct intervention of the CIA. Certainly his superior within the INA, Adnan Nuri, a former general in the Iraqi army, had been recruited by the CIA as early as 1992. 'The aim of the bombing campaign, by Amneh's account, was to impress Nuri's sponsors at the CIA with the capabilities of the organisation they were funding.'[22]

Mr Amneh revealed that he was instructed to use a car bomb to assassinate the leader of the INC, Ahmed Chalabi. He refused. In October 1995, however, a massive blast ripped through the INC headquarters in Salahuddin in Kurdistan, killing twenty-eight people, including the security chief of the INC. The KDP arrested three individuals who confessed under severe interrogation that they were members of the

INA, and had planted the bomb on the orders of the INA commander of operations, General Nuri. The results of a CIA investigation into the bombing, based on bomb fragments found at the site, were never released.[23]

The INA was founded by two former high-flying Iraqi insiders: Salih Omar Ali al-Takriti and Iyad Alawi. Mr Omar had enjoyed a glittering career, culminating in the post of Iraq's ambassador to the United Nations – a post he resigned in 1982 under the mistaken impression Saddam Hussein was about to fall as a result of failures in the Iraqi war effort against Iran, creating an opportunity for another Sunni Muslim from Saddam's tribe (the Takritis) to take his place. Reconciled with Saddam after a fashion, Mr Omar was enjoying a lucrative position as head of the London office of Iraqi Freight Services, Ltd, a front company for Baghdad, when Iraq invaded Kuwait in August 1990. He promptly defected once again.

Mr Alawi, on the other hand, was head of the Iraqi Student Union in Europe, carrying out a valuable role for Iraqi intelligence, before launching a successful business career. By 1978, Mr Alawi had reportedly become an agent of MI6, the British equivalent of the CIA. After a dispute over a missing cheque for $40,000 which Saudi intelligence had given the pair to help fund an opposition radio station, Mr Omar withdrew from the INA, and Mr Alawi took complete control. He 'steadily recruited former Ba'athist Sunnis – the type best suited to preserving the regime post Saddam', according to the Cockburns.[24]

IMPOSING SUNNI RULE

Modern Iraq was formed by Britain. In October 1914, the First World War extended into a war between the Ottoman and the British Empires, and Britain landed an expeditionary force near Basra, soon capturing the Ottoman province of that name. By the end of 1918, Britain had conquered the three provinces of Basra, Baghdad and Mosul, a conquest which led directly to the integration of the three territories into the unitary state of Iraq under a British imperial 'Mandate'. At the beginning of the Mandate, there were three millions Iraqis, of whom more than half were Shia Muslims and a fifth were Kurdish, while eight per cent of the population was composed of the Jewish, Christian, Yazidi, Sabaean and Turkoman minorities. 'Yet the government ministers, the senior state officials and the officer corps of the armed forces were drawn almost exclusively from the Sunni Arabs who formed less than 20 per cent of the population.' The Sunni-dominated order of Ottoman times was re-established by the British.[25]

At the Cairo Conference of March 1921, convened by Winston Churchill, the decision was taken to establish a kingdom of Iraq, and to offer the throne to a member of the Hashemite royal family, Amir Faisal, who had fled from Syria after the collapse of a similar British arrangement. Historian Charles Tripp of the School of Oriental and African Studies in London remarks, 'As a public figure he was regarded as having a natural authority in the Arab world, but, equally importantly, he was believed to be amenable to British advice and well aware of the limitations that the reality of British power in the Middle East would place upon his ambitions.'[26]

The key to British decision-making was to choose weak partners who would be reliant on outside power – British power. King Faisal was an outsider with no roots in Iraq, who understood his subordinate position. The Sunni generals and ministers who ran Iraq were equally aware of their minority position within the new state, and the significance of British power in maintaining the unity of the 'nation' – as demonstrated in the role of the RAF in crushing the independent-minded Kurds, and maintaining Baghdad's rule over the northern province of Mosul.[27]

THE SUNNI 'CENTRE'

The Sunni Muslim minority now makes up a third of the population of Iraq, but continues to dominate the centres of power. Iraqis refer to the Sunni Arab heartland as the 'centre', a geographical, political, social and economic term. The key clans within the 'centre' are drawn from the four central provinces of Baghdad, Takrit, Mosul (somewhat smaller than its Ottoman predecessor) and Ramadi. Saddam Hussein himself comes from the Takriti group of clans, and has long had a habit of positioning members of his own Beijat clan in key posts in the political system.[28]

Within the insecurity of Sunni Muslims, outnumbered by the disenfranchised mass of the Shia majority and the large Kurdish minority, lies the even more intense insecurity of the even more privileged Takriti clans. Informed US analysts Anthony H. Cordesman and Ahmed S. Hashim comment,

> In the past, Saddam has been able to count upon the loyalty of these Takritis for a number of reasons: The kinship ties between them, the material benefits and power he has given them, and their role in creating a strong and powerful Iraq – one where they benefit from corruption and a phenomenal growth in wealth.
>
> The Takritis have learned to fear Saddam's personal ruthlessness, and Saddam's actions have shown even his closest associates that they can lose power or die as easily as Hussein Kamel [his son-in-law]. At the same time, they have good reason to fear his fall. They know that if Saddam goes, whether by their hands or the hands of non-Takritis, they may also fall, and do so at the cost of their lives.
>
> As a result, the Takritis face a Hobson's choice: many increasingly fear Saddam and want him out of power because his presence endangers them and their gains, but they also fear what would happen to their gains and their lives if they remove him.[29]

There is a network of perhaps half a million people who are attached to the Iraqi President by ties of blood or tried and tested dedication to his personal service, or who are dependent on networks of patronage and association that extend from his inner circle: 'these are the people whom Saddam Husain needed to convince both that his leadership was better for their interests than any imaginable alternative and that

War Plan Iraq

they would lose everything if he were to be overthrown and a new dispensation of power established itself in Baghdad.' This mass of people is sometimes known as *Umana' Saddam* ('Saddam's faithful').

Beyond his own clan networks, the Iraqi leader has also used the same mechanism of control used by his Ottoman and British predecessors: patronage of tribal sheikhs. In the 1990s Baghdad brought back a form of separate jurisdiction for the 'tribal areas' that recalls the days of the (British-imposed) monarchy.[30] The firing of a rifle or a pistol in the air, an act often used by the Western media to emphasise Mr Saddam's militaristic and aggressive character, is actually 'an act which symbolised a kind of traditional Iraqi tribal celebration (the *hosa*)', according to a rare academic study of the Shia population of Iraq.[31] It is one of the devices used by the Iraqi leadership to emphasise and strengthen the tribal and national identities of Iraq's majority Shia population, and to undermine the political significance of their religious affiliation.

THE MAN ON A WHITE HORSE, 2002

The Iraqi 'centre' is the focus of Washington's attentions. The INA, made up of solid Sunni military officers, is thought to be the key to the 'palace coup' which can achieve the twin goals of 'regime stabilisation' and 'leadership change'. In the words of historian Charles Tripp, the 'favoured method' of the INA has been 'the exploitation of kinship and other informal links within the armed forces to bring about a successful coup d'etat against Saddam Husain.'[32]

According to *Newsweek*, 'At the CIA, State Department and among the uniformed military, specialists are trying to find the proverbial Man on a White Horse, a respected officer who can ride in, take control and unite Iraq's fractious tribes and religious groups': 'the US will need some kind of military strongman to foment a coup, or head a rebel army that could work alongside US forces, or run the Iraqi military after Saddam is gone'.[33] The US magazine then surveyed five generals.

Nizar al-Khazraji, 64, had 'impressive credentials', having held the position of the Iraqi Army chief of staff between 1980 and 1991 – in other words having commanded the Iraqi Army during the Iran-Iraq war, the campaign against the Kurds in the 1980s, and the invasion of Kuwait. Unfortunately for the US, despite these 'impressive credentials', General al-Khazraji, who lives in Copenhagen, is being investigated by the Danish Government for war crimes concerning his role in the gassing of 5000 Kurds in 1988.[34]

The second potential 'Man on a White Horse' surveyed by *Newsweek* was Major General Wafiz al-Samarrai, the former head of Iraqi military intelligence mentioned in the last chapter, who lives in North London, and is presumably similarly 'impressive', having also served at a high level within Saddam Hussein's regime. Unfortunately for the US, General al-Samarrai 'appeared sceptical about an exile-led revolt by the Army', saying, 'This is nonsense, mounting an operation from outside by exiles.' He expressed a preference for a 'quick covert operation' by the CIA.[35]

General Number Three was Lieutenant-General Mahdi al-Dulemi (62), resident in Germany, who favours a rebellion backed by US airpower. Unfortunately for the US, the general commanded the Iraqi 3rd Corps in the Basra area, at a time when Iran accused Iraq of using chemical weapons, which leaves Lt. Gen. al-Dulemi somewhat tainted on the chemicals issue, though he denies any involvement in weapons of mass destruction. This is a little difficult to reconcile with his position at the time as head of the armed forces scientific and technical department.[36]

On to General Fawzi al-Shamari, who commanded nine divisions in the Iran-Iraq war before defecting in 1986 (he now runs a small restaurant in Virginia). The general has 'made no bones about his use of chemical weapons', stating, 'It created a state of chaos'. General al-Shamari mentioned in passing that he knew the effects of the chemical attacks he launched because of US satellite intelligence, a claim verified by *Newsweek* from a former CIA official. The official said that the US supplied information to the Iraqis, and, 'Included in that, I'm sure, would have been some feedback, intended or unintended, on their use of chemical warfare.' (Incidentally, the US also supplied satellite data to the Iranians in 1986, during the Iran-Contra affair, which may have led to a major Iraqi defeat that year in the Fao peninsula.[37])

Presumably such a straight-talking and indiscreet general (who favours a guerrilla warfare strategy) does not quite fit the US mould. Certainly he had yet to be consulted by US officials as of March 2002.[38]

Finally, the fifth and most plausible 'Man on a White Horse', Brigadier-General Najib al-Salhi (50). Having defected in 1995, General al-Salhi heads the 'Free Officers Movement' and claims to be able to raise 30,000 fighters. The general claims to have a plan for a three-pronged rebel assault on Iraq (from Jordan, Kuwait, and Iraqi Kurdistan) that could bring down the regime without the use of US troops.[39] General al-Salhi has been described by 'a senior US official' as 'compelling' person, who 'brings interesting insights based on his previous high-ranking position within the Iraqi military.' The official said that there was an expectation in US policymaking circles that 'he still has some links that are active and can provide some relationships there.' This 'senior official' added, 'We haven't previously dipped into groups that have connections to what you might call mainstream Iraq.'[40]

This is misleading. Recall that the CIA funded the INA, its channel to the Iraqi 'centre', with millions of dollars throughout the INA Baghdad bombing campaign which killed up to a hundred Iraqi civilians, the suspected INA bombing of the INC headquarters, and the miserable coup fiasco of June 1996.

General Salhi was described by the *Guardian* in March 2002 as 'a rising figure in the Iraqi opposition', holding up a vision of a post-Saddam multiparty democracy. Salhi is quoted as saying, 'A democratic system can resolve all problems and give all groups a chance to participate in the next government.'[41] The *Sunday Telegraph* added that the general 'is being actively courted by the State Department as a potential conduit between rival groups,' a man who claimed to be able to get rid of Mr Saddam 'at very low cost'. The Brigadier-General gave an idea of the kind of 'multiparty democratic system' he intended for Iraq by stressing 'the need to encourage Iraqi military leaders to switch sides by promising that no more than 20 of Saddam's closest henchmen would be treated as criminals by an incoming Iraqi government.'[42]

One could not ask for a more clear cut recipe for 'regime stabilisation' and 'leadership change'.

THE KING

There are other candidates for the leadership of Iraq. The last King of Iraq, Faisal's grandson, was killed during a military coup d'etat in 1958, ending the short reign of the Hashemites over Iraq. The current heir to the throne, however, has proven rather reluctant to be involved in 'regime change' of any kind. In July 2002, Prince Adil Mohamed ibn Faisal was being held in Morocco for entering the country on false papers, 'after fleeing "persecution" for his refusal to support Iraqi opposition forces.'[43] It has been reported that Washington favours Prince Hassan bin Talal of Jordan, part of the Jordanian branch of the Hashemite family, over Iraqi members of the royal dynasty. Members of the Hashemite family were imposed on a number of different countries in the Middle East by Winston Churchill. King Faisal was first installed in Syria, then, when ejected by the French, in Iraq. In 1922, his brother, King Abdullah was imposed on 'Transjordan', as it was termed then, in return for his acceptance of a British 'Mandate' over 'his' country.[44]

The *Telegraph* reported in July 2002 that the Hashemite family 'could play a critical unifying role in a post-Saddam Iraq, but officials in the Bush administration are said to favour the prince in particular.'[45] Prince Hassan had been due to succeed his brother as King of Jordan until a few days before King Hussein's death, when the succession was altered in favour of his son, who is now King Abdullah. *The Times* reported that, 'There have been open tensions between the Jordanian King and Prince Hassan' since the coronation.[46]

Prince Hassan came to prominence when he addressed a conference of Iraqi exiles held in London in July 2002, the only foreign dignitary to attend. The prince made a 'theatrical entrance' moments before the meeting began, and left after three-quarters of an hour, reportedly leaving many in the audience 'puzzled' at his intervention.[47] During his visit, Prince Hassan paid tribute to his 'fellow officers' in the Iraqi military, welcomed efforts to 'end the suffering of the Iraqi people', and offered support to his cousin, Sharif Ali bin Hussein, another member of the Iraqi Hashemite family, now leading the Constitutional Monarchy Movement of Iraq.[48] *The Times* observed, 'Until last night the revival of the monarchy in Iraq seemed the least likely option in the event of Saddam's being overthrown', but Prince Hassan's intervention, supposedly in aid of his Iraqi cousin, had changed all of that.[49]

US policymakers may be following the model of Afghanistan, and the double act they developed between King Zahir Shah (whose return had seemed similarly unlikely before 11 September) and Hamid Karzai, a member of the Pashtun ethnic group which formed the social base for the Taliban regime – the Pathan 'centre' of Afghanistan perhaps. Certainly, US officials have been talking increasingly about the search for an 'Iraqi Karzai'.[50] Perhaps they are also seeking an 'Iraqi Zahir Shah'.

THE OUTSIDER

Mr Chalabi of the Iraqi National Congress has ruled himself out of the running: 'I am not a candidate. I don't seek any public office. My job is to manage the overthrow of Saddam,' he said in April 2002. The effect was undermined somewhat by the statement of the Washington director of the INC that, 'He will be Saddam's replacement. And the world, not just Iraq, will be a better place for it.'[51] Given the level of hostility within the US foreign policy establishment towards the INC in general, and Mr Chalabi in particular, this hope can be ruled out entirely.

This hostility is felt almost universally throughout the US foreign policy establishment, consisting of the State Department, the Pentagon, the CIA and the various other intelligence agencies, and mainstream 'think tanks'. One US official said of Mr Chalabi in January 2002, 'Without disputing the merits of taking out Saddam, do you really want to [hand] the keys to American national-security policy to a foreign national who has his own agenda and objectives, to lead us down a path at his time and choosing?'[52]

However, the INC and Mr Chalabi did build support in the US Congress. The Iraq Liberation Act of 1998, in which Congress appropriated $97 million for new efforts to undermine Saddam was written largely with Chalabi and the INC in mind. Very little of this money has been disbursed to the INC, however. The State Department cut off the supply of money for the whole of January 2002, stating that of the $4.3 million that passed through INC accounts, $2,107,093 required 'additional supporting documentation'. Mr Chalabi had gone out 'and insisted on operating a program in contravention of the supervision we provided,' said a State Department official.[53] The opposition coalition requested $25 million, $17 million of which was to be spent on operations inside Iraq. The State Department approved only $8 million in new grant money, 'prompting the opposition group to reject the offer.'[54] The significance of these figures is clear: funding was only being provided for propaganda work outside Iraq, not for operations inside the country.

Mr Chalabi has been shut out of the planning for the war on Iraq, and will almost certainly not be installed as the US choice to replace Mr Saddam.

DEMOCRATIC REVERSAL

In December 2001, a 'senior Administration official' – almost certainly Secretary of State Colin Powell – described Mr Chalabi to a US journalist as 'totally charming', but added that the Administration had no intention of allowing 'a bunch of half-assed people to send foreigners into combat'. The 'half-assed people' included Paul Wolfowitz, Deputy Secretary of Defence, Donald Rumsfeld, the Secretary of Defence, and other extreme right-wing members of the Administration, who are outside the traditional foreign policy establishment, and who have a somewhat hostile attitude to the political mainstream.

Of Chalabi and his supporters inside and outside of government, the 'senior official' said, 'Who among them has ever smelled cordite? These are pissants who can't get the President's ear and have to blame someone else. We're not going to let them lead others down the garden path.'[55] The only notable member of the pro-INC faction who had 'smelt cordite' was ex-Special Forces General Wayne Downing, who drew up a war plan for the INC (see page 157), but who resigned in frustration from his position in the Administration in mid-2002. The other members of the pro-Chalabi faction were civilians.

The peculiar reversal here is that General Powell is on the liberal wing of the Administration, socially and politically, while Mr Wolfowitz and Richard Perle of the Defence Policy Board, and their fellow pro-INC hawks, are on the far right of mainstream US politics. Yet it is Mr Wolfowitz and Mr Perle and other hawks who support the democratic politician Mr Chalabi, and it is General Powell and the more mainstream officials within the Administration who lead the hunt for the 'Man on a White Horse'. Mr Perle, known as the 'Prince of Darkness' during the Reagan Administration twenty years ago, complained in June 2002,

> We need to work together with people who are going to bring a decent regime to Iraq – not substitute one tyranny for another. It seems to me far more preferable to work with a group like the INC than throwing darts at a board with lots of general officers' names on it, and hoping you get one consistent with our values. Various parts of the Government have been trying to propagate a coup for a long time and have failed miserably – and lots of people have died in the process.[56]

It is not easy to be absolutely sure what this commitment to the INC means, apart from its usefulness in inter-factional combat.

The right-wing British newspaper, the *Daily Telegraph,* has reflected some of the thinking of the Perle/Wolfowitz/Rumsfeld grouping, saying in an editorial devoted to the subject 'After Saddam', 'The last thing Iraq needs is another Shah of Iran-type figure, imposed by the CIA and MI6, through covert action.'[57] In an earlier editorial devoted to the topic of 'How Saddam will go', however, the *Telegraph,* which is very closely linked to the British Armed Forces, was more restrained:

> As to the political outcome, it would be gratifying to see in Baghdad a democratic government which respected human rights, rather than a clan-dominated totalitarian state, but the best must not be the enemy to the good. What might follow the collapse of the Takritis is very difficult to predict. The allies need not be committed to a particular successor regime,

although they should certainly encourage popular groups seeking Saddam's replacement, such as the Iraqi National Congress.[58]

To see through this talk of a 'democratic' solution, we need only recall the political solution established in Afghanistan in 2002, in part by Mr Wolfowitz and his pro-INC colleagues. Mr Karzai, the Pathan anti-Taliban activist, became a figurehead President, needing the protection of US bodyguards from his own colleagues, while real power returned to the hands of drug-smuggling warlords.

The Wolfowitz-Rumsfeld faction may be sincerely committed to substantial 're-gime change' in Iraq; they may even have a sincere commitment to the INC and its leader. But 'regime change' flies in the face of US policy over the years – a policy that Wolfowitz, Rumsfeld and company helped to form when they held office in the first Bush Administration in 1991.

SPARING THE REPUBLICAN GUARD?

One critical element in the mix of policy choices is the fate of the Republican Guard, and the super-elite Special Republican Guard. 'Regime change' enthusiast Michael Eisenstadt, of the Washington Institute for Near East Policy, remarks in a right-wing US journal that, 'The bottom line is that as long as the internal security apparatus remains loyal, intact and alert, coup attempts and uprisings are likely to fail.' There are two possible routes here. On the one hand, you can allow these formations to remain intact, but entice them into being disloyal to the supreme leader. On the other hand, one can allow them to remain loyal, but attack them until they are neither intact nor alert. Mr Eisenstadt follows the second path: 'Consequently, US air strikes that land damaging blows to these organizations and thereby disrupt their functioning are a *sine qua non* for a successful coup or uprising ... By forcing the units that form the main pillar of Saddam's rule to disperse and lay low, a US air campaign could create a window of opportunity for a successful coup or uprising.'[59] What is needed, according to Mr Eisenstadt, is a strategy of 'landing crushing blows to the nerve centers of the regime', by 'devastating and decisive American military action'.

Eisenstadt advocates strikes only on these essential targets, 'dealing concentrated blows against the Special Republican Guard, Special Security Organisation and the Republican Guard'. The US 'should avoid the temptation of using the opportunity to hit other target sets (e.g. conventional military units or WMD-related facilities) that could dilute the impact of its effort.' 'The three RG armored divisions around Bagh-dad that would be prime targets of such an effort form the backbone of Iraq's conventional military might.'[60]

From a different point on the US political spectrum, Kenneth Pollack, former Deputy Director of the US National Security Council under President Clinton (1999–2001) makes a similar recommendation: 'A determined air campaign that focused on Saddam's key supporters – the Republican Guard, the Special Republican Guard, the

Ba'ath Party, the Saddam Fedayeen, and the internal security services – might spark a coup.'[61]

Not a great deal is known about the target sets for the US war, but early reports suggested that instead of going for 'crushing blows to the nerve centres' of the regime, the US military was preparing once again to protect the Republican Guard from devastation. The *Sunday Times* reported in February 2002 that the targets initially would be Scud and other missile launch pads inside Iraq, along with sites thought to house weapons of mass destruction. 'The campaign would then be widened to take in communications centres, broadcast outlets, pipelines and supply depots.' With all communications broken and all propaganda channels silenced, western intelligence agents would encourage Iraqi insurgents to gather behind an opposition leader and mount a coup. 'Only Saddam's inner circle would be expected to fight to the death.'[62]

There is no mention of targeting the internal security forces of the regime. The only military targets mentioned specifically are 'Saddam's air force and missiles' – to prevent a retaliatory strike with weapons of mass destruction against Israel.

According to a report in the *Observer*, the INA expects the war to begin with intensive bombing and missile raids launched from the Gulf and Turkey, 'leading to a military rebellion within Saddam Hussein's elite Republican Guard.'[63] The Republican Guard are expected to survive these initial attacks, in other words, and to continue to exist and to seize political power from the Iraqi President and his inner circle.

A US officer in Central Command, which has responsibility for the Persian Gulf region, and would conduct any war against Iraq, told US reporter Seymour Hersh,

> Our question was, 'What about the day after?' For example, do you take the Republican Guard and disarm it? Or is it preferable to turn it from having a capability to protect Saddam to a capability to protect Iraq? You've got Kurds in the north, Arab Shia in the south, and the Baath Party in the middle, with great internal tribal divisions. There's potential for civil war. Layer on external opposition and you've got a potential for great instability. I'm a military planner and plan for the worst case. As bad as this guy is, a stable Iraq is better than instability.[64]

According to one European diplomat, US allies and some people in Washington were asking whether removing Saddam was 'doable in a way that reinforces our security.'[65] For many within the US foreign policy establishment, including the US military, 'our security' now appears to include a continued role for the Republican Guard. This would necessarily involve some form of amnesty, and would indicate that past methods of control, demonstrated in 1991, would be acceptable in the future.

Targeting the Republican Guard can be compatible either with 'regime change' or with 'regime stabilisation, leadership decapitation' (if the US believes other elements of the military can hold Iraq together). A decision not to target the RG and SRG, however, is an unambiguous signal of a 'regime stabilisation' strategy.

NATION-BUILDING

According to one report, Mr Blair and Mr Bush have discussed in detail the political arrangements for Iraq 'once Saddam's Ba'ath regime has been toppled', and the preferred option is to hold a referendum.[66] *The Times* suggested that Washington 'must also make careful provision for his replacement and remain heavily engaged in a country that has the second-largest oil reserves in the Middle East.'[67]

It has been reported that some US generals believe that the US intervention should end after the Iraqi President has been deposed, but the Pentagon is nevertheless considering how US troops could help to stabilise Iraq in the post-Saddam period. One option is to deploy US (and possibly British and Jordanian) troops in the country as peacekeepers after the conflict. This could be portrayed as taking the first step in a US programme of 'Middle East reform'. 'Part of the consideration, though, would be to prevent ethnic rivalries within Iraq, or opportunism by neighbours such as Iran disturbing the country's oil supplies.'[68]

The reference to 'some US generals' being hostile to the idea of a post-conflict deployment seems a little misleading. An earlier report stated that it was the generals' civilian boss, Donald Rumsfeld, the US Defence Secretary, who 'believes strongly that the mission should be focused entirely on Saddam. The toppling of the Iraqi dictator should mark the successful completion of the operation, he believes.' In contrast, General Powell, the Secretary of State, is advocating a broader brief, covering the transitional period: the kind of nation-building that Mr Bush derided in his presidential campaign in 2000.[69]

The Rumsfeld position on limiting war aims is a useful corrective, revealing the depth and sincerity of the hawks' 'pro-democracy' position.

CERTAIN FACTS

At the time of writing (July 2002), there is much that is unclear in US policy and strategy towards Iraq. Perhaps there is much that remains undecided even in the core of the Administration. However, there are some certain facts.

One certain fact is that the United States has since 1991 rigorously pursued the path of 'regime stabilisation, leadership change'. This has meant verbal and financial support for the Iraqi National Congress for public relations purposes, but a real political and military commitment to the Iraqi National Accord – and its indiscriminate no-warning terrorist campaign.

Another certain fact is that the United States is seeking another authoritarian leader, almost certainly another Sunni Muslim general, to replace Saddam Hussein. Sir John Moberly, British ambassador to Iraq (1982 and 1985), has described this as the policy of replacing Mr Saddam 'with another Saddam – another iron-fisted military man.'[70]

What is most uncertain is what would follow the violent destruction of Saddam Hussein. The Arab League's ambassador to London, Ali Muhsin Hamid, prophesies not one, but several civil wars inside Iraq.[71] He is not alone in these fears.

Finally, it is certain, whatever the rhetoric regarding the democratic aspirations or transitional tenure of the new Supreme Leader, if a Sunni general is imposed on Iraq by the Western powers, that general will rule Iraq in the traditional style. US analysts Anthony Cordesman and Ahmed Hashim conclude their analysis with these words:

> A 'centrist' coup or assassination may lead to many initial promises or claims of moderation, liberalization, and political change, but the reality is most likely to be very different. Any efforts to overthrow Saddam within the present ruling Sunni elite are likely be followed by continuing repression of the Shi'ites and Kurds, the arrest and execution of many rivals and supporters of Saddam, and the eventual arrest and execution of other opponents.[72]

It is conceivable that the United States has genuinely broken with its past policies, and intends to accomplish a change of regime, and not merely of political leadership, in Iraq. The available evidence points in a different direction. It points towards the 'Man on a White Horse'.

HERE'S A COUP WE PREPARED EARLIER

The CIA is no stranger to coup plots in Iraq. According to Saddam Hussein's biographer, there was a joint CIA-Ba'ath Party conspiracy against the first Iraqi Ba'athist President General Abdul Karim Kassem: 'The plans to overthrow the Iraqi leader, led by William Lakeland who was stationed at the Baghdad embassy as an attache, represented one of the most elaborate CIA operations in the history of the Middle East.' One element of the preparation for the coup was CIA liaison with minor Ba'athists in Egypt – including a man by the name of Saddam Hussein. In the aftermath of the coup there was an 'elimination' campaign against Communists and leftists (Kassem had been overthrown in part because of his leftward tendencies). Said Aburish has compiled a list of eight hundred names of those killed in the coup – the total is thought to be higher. The new Iraqi regime worked from lists of 'Communists' provided by the CIA – some names were apparently fed to the CIA by Saddam Hussein himself. Ali Saleh Al Sa'adi, who became Minister of the Interior and Deputy Prime Minister, said, 'We came to power on a CIA train'.[73]

Another element of the CIA-Ba'athist coup was the withdrawal of CIA support to a Kurdish rebellion that had been going on for two years. After the 1963 coup, the US flew in arms from Turkey and Iran (then under the Shah) to enable the new Government to crush the Kurds. All this despite the fact that the Kurds had been consulted about the coup in advance, and had given their tacit cooperation.[74] The foreshadowing of the present US project is eerie, and a grim portent for Iraq's Kurds.

Emily Johns

CHAPTER IX
The Control of Oil

THE IMPORTANCE OF OIL

In September 1945, Lord Altrincham, the British Minister Resident in the Middle East, explained the importance of the Middle East to Britain in an internal memo. His opening sentence focuses on the economic factor:

> As a funnel of communication between the western, eastern and southern peoples of the British Commonwealth, as their richest reservoir of lubricant and motive oil, and furthermore as an area in which, without desiring to dominate ourselves, we cannot allow any other Power to dominate and must preserve for ourselves the maximum of friendship and goodwill, the Middle East is no less vital to Britain than Central and South America to the United States, or than the eastern and western glacis of the Russian landmass to the Soviet Union.

This was the lesson of the Second World War: 'It was not for nothing that we sent to Egypt in 1940, when this island was in imminent jeopardy of invasion, the only armoured division of which we stood possessed. It was no mere accident that the whole face of the war began to change after our victory, two years later, at Alamein.' In 1949, Labour's first Foreign Secretary re-affirmed that, 'In peace and war, the Middle Easts is an area of cardinal importance to the United Kingdom itself': 'It is essential that we should maintain our special position, and carry out our special responsibilities.'[1] The 'maximum of friendship and goodwill' translate in reality into the servility of quislings, to be obtained by demonstrations of 'credibility' – of the kind that Mafia dons must maintain, as Noam Chomsky points out.

The State Department, considering the matter at about the same time, saw the Middle East in a similar light, viewing the Saudi oil reserves for example as 'a stupendous source of strategic power, and one of the great material prizes in world history.'[2] Unfortunately for Lord Altrincham and his colleagues in the Foreign Office, the waning of British power meant that domination of the Middle East passed largely to the United States – though Britain was permitted a junior role in the region it had ruled unquestioningly.

IRAN

One telling example came after the nationalisation of the oil industry in Iran in May 1951. The Anglo-Indian Oil Company (AIOC, now known as British Petroleum) was an enormously powerful force in Iran, taking £170 million in profit in 1950 alone. The Labour Government in Britain, which had just carried out a number of nationalisations of its own, was furious at the Iranian nationalisation decree. Britain demanded a new oil concession for the AIOC, or compensation for all profits that the AIOC might have made over the next forty years. This demand was rejected by the democratically-elected Government of Iran (which had offered a normal level of compensation). The Foreign Office declared (privately) in January 1952 that 'the only hope of getting rid of Mr Mussadiq [the Iranian Prime Minister] lies in a coup d'etat, provided always that a strong man can be found equal to the task.' 'Such a dictator,' observed the Foreign Office, 'would carry out the necessary administrative and economic reforms and settle the oil question on reasonable terms.'[3]

The US poured in $1 million, and Britain $1.5 million, organising among other things what then CIA agent Richard Cottam described as a 'mercenary mob' which was organised to appear to be a violent, Communist, pro-Mussadiq gang on the verge of making revolution. The purpose was to lay the basis for a military coup by a Man on a White Horse who could portray himself as rescuing the country from a Communist take-over by deposing the Prime Minister.[4] The MI6-CIA coup was successful in August 1953: General Zahidi took a firm grip on the country, and the re-invigorated Shah of Iran quickly agreed new oil concession arrangements with the West.

Britain's interest was reduced to 40 per cent, while US oil companies were allowed to hold an interest in Iran for the first time – they also received 40 per cent of the concession. Thus the CIA's first major covert operation, carried out in cooperation with MI6, enabled US oil companies to penetrate a country which had previously been closed to them by British power, a matter of some bitterness in Whitehall. The US share of total Middle East oil rose from 44 per cent to 58 per cent as a result of the coup, while Britain's share dropped from 53 per cent to 24 per cent, leading the British ambassador to the US, Sir Roger Makins to ask, 'Are the Americans consciously trying to substitute their influence for ours in the Middle East?'[5] The Shah's regime set new standards for the systematic use of torture as a means of political control.

RUTHLESSLY TO INTERVENE

Another illuminating example comes from July 1958, when a military coup by nationalist officers in Iraq threatened US-British control of the oil-producing regions for the first time. Immediately after the Iraqi coup, British Foreign Secretary Selwyn Lloyd sent a secret telegram to the Prime Minister in which he considered two options with regard to Kuwait, which it was thought might be occupied by the new Iraqi regime. The first option was 'immediate British occupation'. This was unwise, wrote the Foreign Secretary, though 'The advantage of this action would be that we would get our hands firmly on the Kuwait oil' – precisely what the Iraqis were being accused of wanting. The move was unwise because the cost was too high; 'The effect on international opinion and the rest of the Arab world would not be good.'

The second option was some move towards nominal independence, setting up 'a kind of Kuwait Switzerland where the British do not exercise physical control.' 'If this alternative is accepted,' wrote the Minister, 'we must also accept the need, if things go wrong, ruthlessly to intervene, whoever it is has caused the trouble.'[6]

Mr Selwyn Lloyd had earlier summarised British interests in the Gulf thus:

> (a) to ensure free access for Britain and other Western countries to oil products produced in States bordering the Gulf; (b) to ensure the continued availability of that oil on favourable terms and for sterling; and to maintain suitable arrangements for the investment of the surplus revenues of Kuwait; (c) to bar the spread of Communism and pseudo-Communism in the area and subsequently beyond; and, as a pre-condition of this, to defend the area against the brand of Arab nationalism under cover of which the Soviet Government at present prefers to advance.[7]

'Ruthless intervention', whether covert or overt, is sometimes needed to establish or re-establish Western control of the Middle East oil, to ensure that Western oil companies can derive a 'favourable' level of profit, and to guarantee that profits are fed back to the weakening economies of Britain and – since the 1970s – the US.

RAPID DEPLOYMENT FORCES

Britain's ability 'ruthlessly to intervene' in the Gulf declined abruptly in 1971, when the British military presence in the region was withdrawn, a milestone in the process of Britain's imperial contraction. The United States complained, as the British garrison had been playing a useful role as what one historian has described as 'an integral element of US power in the region.'[8] Because of the popular revulsion against military aggression aroused by the Vietnam War, the US was forced to adopt an indirect strategy known as the 'Nixon Doctrine', relying on Iran, Saudi Arabia and Israel to maintain the preferred social and economic order in the Gulf.

Once the dreaded 'Vietnam Syndrome' was perceived to have abated, however, President Jimmy Carter secretly ordered the establishment of a Rapid Deployment Force (RDF) aimed at the Persian/Arabian Gulf. The RDF was publicly announced in 1979 – long before the Iranian hostage crisis or the Soviet invasion of Afghanistan, two events later used to justify the strike force's existence.[9] The RDF was later upgraded into a separate military 'Command' – Central Command (CENTCOM) – covering the region from Kenya to Pakistan, and given nuclear weapons. The Carter Doctrine stated, 'Any attempt by any outside force to gain control of the Persian Gulf region will be regarded as an assault on the vital interests of the United States' to be 'repelled by any means necessary, including military force.' (This is tantamount to a nuclear guarantee to US-friendly regimes.) The US itself is not considered 'an outside force', of course. Under Secretary of Defence for Policy Robert Komer admitted in 1980 that 'the most immediate threat in the Indian Ocean area is not an overt Russian attack, but rather internal instability, coups, subversion.' President Reagan was still more explicit about the 'outside forces': 'Saudi Arabia we will not permit to be an Iran.'[10] Arab nationalism, the strange doctrine that the oil resources of Arab lands should be used for national development rather than the profits of foreign corporations and the stability of British and US financial markets, is an 'outside force'.

One way in which a CENTCOM rapid deployment force could succeed against numerically superior forces was spelled out in the US Army's 'how to fight' manual, the *AirLand Battle Field Manual FM 100–5 (Operations)* in 1982: 'A relatively small rapidly deployable force with nuclear weapons may be assigned a contingency mission. This force might succeed as a deterrent while a larger force might deploy too late.'[11]

THE SOUTH WEST ASIA IMPACT STUDY

Washington pushed its NATO allies to become involved in the RDF, presenting a 'South West Asia Impact Study' in 1982, requiring NATO allies to provide replacements for US forces diverted from Europe and the Mediterranean to the Gulf, and logistical support for US intervention forces.[12] This support was codified in a series of secret 'Wartime Host Nation Support' (WHNS) treaties between the US and various European allies. In the case of Britain, the 1983 'US-UK Lines of Communication' agreement was far-reaching, requiring British civil airports, sea ports, army camps, civil transport, and up to thirty large civilian hospitals to be turned over to the US. Emergency powers bills drawn up but not passed in 1985 would enable the establishment of 'Ground Defence Areas' around military installations – eventually covering half of Britain – within which military commanders would have the power to commandeer property and move residents. Successive bills would empower the military to commandeer transport, arrest protesters, requisition private property, and conscript civilians, both adults and children, into forced labour gangs. Censorship, internment without trial, the banning of strikes, and finally, ministerial powers of life and death over the entire population, would be in place by the passing of the third and final bill.[13]

The other British contribution to CENTCOM was the direct provision of troops in the form of a junior RDF. Beginning life as the 'Joint Force Headquarters' in 1983, this body evolved into the Joint Rapid Deployment Force (JRDF) commanded by the 'Permanent Joint Headquarters' based in Northwood, the military base near London used to command the Falklands War. The JRDF was formed to 'strengthen our existing capability to project power quickly and potentially worldwide in support of British interests', according to the Defence White Paper of 1995. As with CENTCOM forces, there is a (somewhat more subtle) nuclear dimension to the JRDF. According to one report in the *Independent*, chemical weapons were deployed during the 1991 Gulf War to provide British forces with a retaliatory capability.[14]

ON THE STREETS OF IRAQ

Photographs by
Kim Weston-Arnold

May 2002

Kim Weston-Arnold

Kim Weston-Arnold

Kim Weston-Arnold

Kim Weston-Arnold

Kim Weston-Arnold

TEN REASONS

AGAINST

WAR ON IRAQ

Reason 1 *The Phantom Menace*
There is no evidence Iraq has developed or acquired weapons of mass destruction.
Reason 2 *Prague No Show*
There is no link between Iraq and the terrorist attacks of 11 September.
Reason 3 *Cloning Saddam*
This is not a war for democracy.
Reason 4 *Catastrophe*
A war on Iraq could trigger a humanitarian disaster.
Reason 5 *Unsafe Haven*
A war on Iraq could demolish Iraqi Kurdistan.
Reason 6 *Crime Time*
A war on Iraq would be illegal
Reason 7 *Ring Of Anger*
Iraq's neighbours oppose the war, and fear its consequences.
Reason 8 *GI Joe Says No*
Generals on both sides of the Atlantic oppose the war.
Reason 9 *No Mandate*
A majority of people in Britain oppose the war.
Reason 10 *It's The Economy, Stupid*
A war on Iraq could trigger a world recession.

Emily Johns

REASON I

The Phantom Menace

There Is No Evidence Iraq Has These Weapons

MR BLAIR'S CERTAINTY

In March 2002, Tony Blair told the House of Commons, 'Iraq is plainly in breach of the United Nations Security Council resolutions in relation to the accumulation of weapons of mass destruction, and we have to deal with it.'[1] This can be interpreted in one of two ways. Either Iraq is in breach because it has acquired or developed weapons of mass destruction which it is banned from possessing, or, on the other hand, Baghdad is in breach because it is blocking the weapons inspections that the Resolutions require.

The Prime Minister soon made clear which of these meanings he intended. Interviewed by US television news in early April 2002, Tony Blair said, 'We know that he has stockpiles of major amounts of chemical and biological weapons', he is 'trying to acquire nuclear capability' and 'ballistic missile capability of a greater range'.[2] At a press conference with George Bush a few days later, Blair said, 'We know he has been developing these weapons. We know that those weapons constitute a threat.'[3] The Prime Minister says bluntly, 'Let's be in no doubt whatever, Saddam Hussein has acquired weapons of mass destruction over a long period of time.'[4]

On 11 March 2002, as President Bush was making an important speech to mark the six month anniversary of 11 September, Mr Blair had a joint press conference with US Vice-President Dick Cheney. The *Guardian* noted that during this press conference, 'Mr Blair was more hawkish than Mr Bush, declaring emphatically that Iraq had weapons of mass destruction.' The Prime Minister said, 'There is a threat from Saddam and the weapons of mass destruction he has acquired. It is not in doubt.'[5]

Mr Bush was more circumspect, saying, for example, 'Every nation in our coalition must take seriously the growing threat of terror on a catastrophic scale – terror armed with biological, chemical or nuclear weapons.'[6] The US President went on to say, 'men with no respect for life must never be allowed to control the ultimate instruments of death.' The *Times* seized on this statement, commenting, 'That sentence and sentiment have become the absolute essence of American foreign policy.'[7] Vice-President Dick Cheney provided an alternative formulation when he said, 'The United States will not permit the forces of terror to gain the tools of genocide.'[8] Neither US leader stated categorically that Iraq possessed weapons of mass destruction in the way that the British Prime Minister did.

It was not for some weeks that President Bush allowed himself the kind of certainty that Mr Blair had shown in March. According to *Time* magazine in May, Mr Bush said of Saddam Hussein, 'He is a dangerous man possessing the world's most dangerous weapons. It is incumbent upon freedom-loving nations to hold him accountable, which is precisely what the United States of America will do.'[9] This looks like a momentary Presidential aberration from a policy decision not to make strong claims regarding Iraq's weapons. In the same issue of *Time*, a US intelligence official is quoted as saying only that, 'The Iraqis have been putting themselves in a position to rejuvenate their weapons-of-mass-destruction programs.'[10] This is a much weaker claim than the line that Tony Blair has been taking, and consistent with the script US leaders have been following. For example, US Secretary of State Colin Powell's warning on 7 November 2001, during the war in Afghanistan, that, 'Nations such as Iraq, which have tried to possess weapons of mass destruction, should not think that we will not be concerned about those activities and will not turn our attention to them.'[11] Mr Powell placed Iraq's weapons development in the past, Mr Cheney and Mr Bush placed it in the future, only Mr Blair claims it exists in the present.

Why the divergence between Mr Blair and Mr Bush? One reason may be that Mr Blair is under much greater political pressure at home, and an overwhelming Iraqi threat is the only kind of justification that will 'sell' President Bush's war on Iraq to, for example, the Labour Party. Hence the need for bolder and more terrifying claims.

THE NEED FOR EVIDENCE

The only problem with making bold claims is that at some point they must be backed up with evidence. As the *Financial Times* has observed, 'MPs are uneasy about the lack of evidence supporting statements that Iraq threatens the security of the west.'[12] The *Guardian* and its sister newspaper the *Observer*, on the liberal wing of mainstream politics, have cautioned that the United States has 'failed to show why yet another American war should be supported', stating, 'Any action against Saddam Hussein must be justified by evidence.'[13]

In March 2002, Russian Foreign Minister Igor Ivanov spoke for much of the world when he said there was 'still no evidence that Iraq has, or may have, weapons of mass destruction'.[14] Canadian Foreign Minister Bill Graham observed, 'Nobody is supporting Saddam Hussein, but everyone recognises in international politics you have to have a process where, before you invade a sovereign country, there has to be a reason for it, or we are going to lead to international chaos.'[15]

The Church of England's Board for Social Responsibility reiterates the point that, while no one should understate the 'potential threat' posed by Iraq, 'no convincing evidence has been presented to support the argument that Iraq is rebuilding its weapons of mass destruction programme or that Iraq poses an immediate threat to regional and international security.'[16] This brought an angry response from former Conservative Minister Ann Widdecombe: 'I don't know where the Church gets its information that he isn't stockpiling such weapons. Perhaps they get secret intelligence reports every day.'[17] Ms Widdecombe stands the problem on its head. The challenge is not to prove that Iraq does not have weapons of mass destruction. It is Mr Blair who claims that Iraq does possess chemical, biological or nuclear weapons, and it is Mr Blair who is seeking to justify a massive assault on Iraq on this basis. The burden of proof lies on those who claim that there is an imminent threat, not on those who seek substantiation of the claim. Up to the moment of writing, Mr Blair has failed the test.

THE MISSING DOSSIER

This is not to say that the Prime Minister has been unaware of the task ahead of him. At the time of his press conference with Dick Cheney on 11 March 2002, Mr Blair had already set in motion an intelligence gathering operation to provide precisely the 'killer facts' which would establish the case for going to war with Iraq. The first notification of this effort came in the *Daily Telegraph* on 7 March: 'The Government is understood to be preparing a dossier on Iraq's terrorist links and attempts to produce nuclear, chemical and biological weapons. This is likely to be published before any military action.'[18] The *Financial Times* sharpened up the timetable: 'Tony Blair is expected to publish a dossier of evidence of Iraq's weapons programmes before the prime minister visits President George W. Bush in Texas on April 5.'[19]

As the council of war approached, Dick Cheney made it clear 'the administration would rely on Tony Blair to lay out evidence against the Iraqi leader, as he did in the aftermath of September 11, when Mr Blair detailed evidence against Osama bin Laden and al Qaeda.'[20] A White House spokesperson was more offhand during the summit with Bush: 'It's a British government matter and it's really up to them to decide when and what to do.'[21] By then, it had become clear that the dossier would not be published before, during or immediately after the meeting at the President's ranch in Crawford, Texas. 'Mr Blair's spokesman said the information will be released in the public domain "at the appropriate time".'[22]

Downing Street put a brave face on the delay: 'We will put it out when we feel the time is right. You shouldn't read any significance into the fact that we haven't done so yet. We have to keep security under consideration too, in terms of what we can release.'[23] A few days after the Crawford conference, the *Financial Times* reported, 'Mr Blair has deferred publication of a dossier of evidence against Mr Saddam, fearing that it would inflame matters while not presenting a convincing case.'[24] There were 'fears that the evidence is not as strong as Mr Blair would like.'[25]

The *FT* reported on 1 April, 'The Foreign Office had been due to publish the document, prepared by Cabinet Office intelligence chiefs, last week, until Mr Blair intervened.' Apparently the dossier was to have been launched by British Foreign Secretary Jack Straw on 25 March, 'but No 10 told him the weekend before that it was no longer "politically useful" to continue with the plans.' The explanation given for the delay was that, 'The government feared that publishing the dossier before the summit would feed the mood of frenzy at a time when no clear plan of action had been fashioned, and exacerbate fears among Arab states that attacks were imminent.'[26] The *Guardian* provided a more plausible insiders' explanation: 'Whitehall sources claimed that the promised dossier on Saddam Hussein's nuclear, chemical and biological weapons was being kept under wraps precisely because of a lack of hard evidence, that would only serve to deepen concern.'[27]

The editor of the right-wing *Spectator* magazine, Peter Osborne, commented, 'Downing Street's incompetence over the Saddam Hussein dossier beggared belief.' Two accounts of the dossier's non-appearance were in circulation. 'According to one, the foreign and security services have been unable to rustle up the necessary material. That sounds less plausible than the alternative explanation, namely that Tony Blair did not want to put the wind up his own supporters by issuing such a belligerent document.'[28] In view of the Prime Minister's bold accusations against Iraq, and the pressure on him both in Parliament and abroad to support these allegations, Mr Osborne's analysis seems somewhat flawed, and in fact the first explanation is the correct one.

The *Sunday Times* had reported in early March, 'Blair has encouraged expectations among MPs and cabinet colleagues that an intelligence dossier would provide fresh support for action to overthrow the Iraqi dictator. But there is little new information worth sharing or publishing, according to insiders.'[29] Apparently, the Prime Minister had given the task of compiling the dossier to the Joint Intelligence Committee (JIC), which lies at the apex of British intelligence, and receives reports from every agency within the security services. 'The JIC report will focus on Saddam's attempts to acquire weapons of mass destruction, but there is said to be little new or surprising evidence in this area,' reported the *Sunday Times*.[30] A senior Foreign Office official commented, 'It will say what you would expect it to say: this is a man who is politically unpredictable, capable of doing bad things to his neighbours and to his own people. We have known that for a long time.'[31]

On 31 March, the *Observer* reported that, 'Officials have been told to look again at declassifying more documents to make a more powerful case against the Iraqi dictator.' Backbench MPs with expertise in military matters had been consulted by Jack Straw around 10 March and 'shown two pages of a report due to form the backbone of the Government's evidence.' 'The document, seen by *The Observer*, was said by one MP to be "pretty unconvincing".' The MP added, 'They will have to do a lot better if they are going to get the widespread support they need for a move against Iraq.'[32]

The *Sunday Times* stated flatly, 'Tony Blair has been forced to abandon plans to release an intelligence dossier on Iraq because it did not contain enough evidence to support a military campaign against the country. The six-page document, prepared by Cabinet Office intelligence chiefs, was withdrawn before it was due to be published last week because it failed to established that Saddam Hussein was a growing threat.' According to the newspaper,

> The dossier, circulated in Whitehall last week by John Scarlett, chairman of the joint intelligence committee (JIC), confirmed that Saddam had made fresh attempts in the past six to nine months to upgrade his arsenal, including biological weapons of mass destruction and long-range missiles. But it contained no evidence that the threat from Iraq had increased significantly since the end of the Gulf war in 1991.
>
> Jack Straw, the foreign secretary, was said by Whitehall sources to be furious that the intelligence document did not contain a more detailed or compelling case against Saddam ...
>
> The prime minister had wanted a dossier on Saddam similar to the evidence sheet published last year by the government linking Osama bin Laden and Al-Qaeda to the September 11 attacks. But Whitehall sources said that was impossible on the strength of the intelligence available.[33]

Given the weakness of the bin Laden dossier (see page 37), this is quite an admission. The reference to Jack Straw's 'fury' is interesting, and suggests that the initiative to delay the release of the dossier may have come from this quarter rather than from the Prime Minister.

The *Guardian* had some more details:

> A dossier on Iraq's nuclear, biological and chemical warfare capabilities was drawn up earlier this month by the Cabinet Office's joint intelligence committee chaired by John Scarlett, a former MI6 officer, after intense discussions within the intelligence community about what should be published and how much speculation it should contain. In the end it was agreed that the dossier should be "factual" and not contain speculation ...
>
> However, many of the new allegations about Iraq's programme for weapons of mass destruction are based on assumption and speculation. Though the dossier contains evidence about Baghdad's development of biological weapons – including anthrax and botulinum toxin – it is largely based on what was discovered by UN weapons inspectors back in 1998.
>
> Even the CIA admits that intelligence gathered after that date, when the weapons inspectors were expelled from Iraq, is far from reliable.[34]

(Recall that the inspectors were in fact withdrawn on US orders – see page 54.)

According to a later report by the *Financial Times*, the delay in publishing the dossier is the result of 'an unresolved dispute at the highest levels of government':

> Number 10 is thought to have encountered resistance to the plan among senior Whitehall officials, some ministers, and the secret intelligence service MI6 ... British officials believe Mr Saddam has managed to protect his plans from intrusion by signals and satellite intelligence, forcing US and British intelligence to draw assumptions rather than certainties about his true capability.
>
> In contrast to previous intelligence dossiers on al-Qaeda and the Diamonds-for-Arms trade deliberately used over the last two years by the Blair government to justify policy initiatives, the information on Iraq was judged by some Whitehall officials as insufficient to convince critics within the Labour party that the full-scale offensive against Iraq was justified.[35]

Either Saddam Hussein has protected his weapons of mass destruction programmes from signals or satellite intelligence, or signals and satellite intelligence cannot detect these programmes because they do not exist. A diplomat 'familiar with the British findings' gave them a gentle critique: 'they would be persuasive to someone familiar with the underlying intelligence but that they might not "convince the more doubtful".' In other words, the open-minded would find in it no hard evidence to substantiate British and US claims. The unnamed diplomat said of the dossier, 'It's nonspecific.'[36]

On 1 April 2002, the *Financial Times* said of the dossier, 'Publication could now be weeks away.'[37] At the time of writing, the dossier still has not been published, and no date has been set for its publication. Despite this, senior Ministry of Defence officials still claim with a straight face that Britain has 'ample classified evidence' of Iraqi manufacture and stockpiling of weapons of mass destruction. 'It will not be made public yet because it would compromise the means by which it was acquired,' according to the official.[38] We shall see. The accounts available suggest that the Government is actually hiding the shallowness of its evidence behind the claim that secret intelligence must be protected.

US CLAIMS

Despite the apocalyptic language used by US leaders about the threat from Iraq, very few specific accusations have been made. In the Security Council, much was made of photographs which the US claimed proved the diversion of trucks bought through the oil-for-food programme into the Iraqi military. Washington accused Iraq of having converted the trucks into missile launchers. Mr Tun Myat, then UN Humanitarian Coordinator for Iraq, asked the United States for evidence that the truck-launchers in US photographs are diverted from the humanitarian programme he oversees. Before leaving office – as of June 2002 – he did not receive a reply.[39]

War Plan Iraq

The crucial question as far as Iraqi disarmament obligations go is whether the missiles carried by these launchers are long-range or short range. Iraq is permitted missiles with a range of 150 kilometres or less under paragraph 7 of UN Security Council Resolution 687.[40] The Iraqi National Congress, a major opposition group, has claimed that the missiles, displayed in Baghdad in 2001, 'appeared to violate the UN ban on long-range missiles that is meant to prevent Iraq from threatening Europe.'.[41] According to Scott Ritter, though, 'What we are talking about is the conversion of lorries to take rocket artillery systems, [which are] short-range and inaccurate.' Ritter scoffs at the idea that the hydraulic fluid from the lorries could be used in missile guidance systems, as some US officials have suggested.[42]

CIA director George Tenet told Congress in February, 'Baghdad is expanding its civilian chemical industry in ways that could be diverted quickly to chemical weapons production.' *Time* magazine comments, 'Procedurally, there is not much difference between making pesticides and making chemical weapons.'[43] That is not the view of Scott Ritter, former UNSCOM weapons inspector in Iraq. In an article for *Arms Control Today* in June 2000, Mr Ritter wrote that 'manufacturing CW [chemical weapons] would require the assembling of production equipment into a single, integrated facility, creating an infrastructure readily detectable by the strategic intelligence capabilities of the United States.'[44] No such finding has been made to date.

Hans Blix, head of UNMOVIC, the new UN weapons inspection agency which has replaced UNSCOM, has said he 'does not accept as fact the US and UK's repeated assertions that Baghdad has used the time to rebuild its weapons of mass destruction': 'It would be inappropriate for me to accept and adopt this position, but it would also be naïve of me to conclude that there may be no veracity – of course it is possible, I won't go as far as saying probable,' said Mr Blix.[45]

The United States tried to impress Mr Blix with satellite photography supposedly demonstrating the reconstruction of Iraq's weapons capacities. Some of the sites were weapons facilities in the past, according to Washington. US intelligence officials interpret the building work as showing that 'The Iraqis have been putting themselves in a position to rejuvenate their weapons of mass destruction programs.' The head of the UN's inspection agency dissents somewhat: 'You can see hundreds of new roofs in these photos. But you don't know what's under them.'[46]

A number of unsupported claims have been made. The chief of the German intelligence agency, the BND, said in the autumn of 2001, 'It is our estimate that Iraq will have an atomic bomb in three years.'[47] *The Times* reported in June 2002 that Iraq had smuggled military items from Syria under cover of a humanitarian aid mission to victims of a dam collapse. Among the items were supposedly spare parts for so-called 'flow-forming machines' used to produce components for uranium-enrichment systems'; tank spare parts; and spares for the Iraqi air force.[48] A *Times* correspondent claimed in late 2001 that six specialist devices bought from Switzerland ('a couple of years ago') for breaking up kidney stones with high-powered shock waves could actually be adapted to trigger a nuclear bomb.[49] Charles Duelfer, previously deputy director of UNSCOM, and Anthony Cordesman, a military analyst at the Center for Strategic and International Studies in Washington DC, claim that 'Saddam has the sophisticated triggers, weapon housings and everything else he needs to build a nuclear device – except for a sufficient supply of weapons-grade enriched uranium.' Enriching uranium inside Iraq could take three to six years, according to these experts.[50] No evidence is provided to substantiate these 'expert' speculations. Such claims swirl around without substantiation and then wash away unresolved and unproven, leaving a threatening impression on the public mind.

US Vice-President Cheney has focused attention on the 'potential marriage' between terrorist groups and those states with weapons of mass destruction.[51] 'Mr Blair pointed out that as early as September 14 he had spoken of the threat of countries "trading" in such weapons'.[52] President Bush warned that every nation in 'our coalition' should take seriously the 'growing threat' of 'terror on a catastrophic scale – terror armed with biological, chemical or nuclear weapons.' He stated, 'Terrorist groups are hungry for these weapons and would use them without a hint of conscience.'[53] On the other hand, no evidence has been produced that Iraq has 'married' its weapons with any terrorist groups, or 'traded' in weapons of mass destruction with anyone.

DEFECTIVE EVIDENCE

A number of Iraqi defectors have made very serious allegations about the Iraqi weapons of mass destruction programme. 'In the increasingly bitter debate about the level of the threat, it is the evidence of these INC-sponsored defectors that has become the source of the greatest controversy. Even those who support an American hard line on Iraq, such as the British former UN weapons inspector Terry Taylor, urge caution about what they say.' Taylor and other former inspectors, who also handled Iraqi defectors and checked their evidence in Iraq, 'claims that many of them have a tendency to exaggerate their personal knowledge and importance to guarantee pensions, protection and employment in their new host countries, particularly the US.'[54]

Perhaps the most notorious weapons-related defector is Dr Khidir Hamza, the self-described former head of Iraq's nuclear weapons programme, who defected in 1994. Until 1990, when he retired from the Iraqi nuclear programme, the US-educated theoretical nuclear physicist was a senior managerial administrator in Saddam's secret bombmaking programme, which included six months in 1987 spent in charge of the programme. That much is certain. 'What troubles his former supporters – now his fiercest critics – is not the valuable information he was able to give. Rather, it is about claims he has subsequently made about programmes and technical issues of which, they believe, he has no direct knowledge. These, they say, are claims driven by a desire to persuade the US that military intervention is the best course.'[55]

It is Hamza who insists Iraq was close to assembling a viable nuclear bomb. It is Hamza who has claimed Iraq was near to building a viable 'radiation weapon'. It is Hamza who was prominent on US television speculating that Iraq had assisted Osama bin Laden and al Qaeda in their attacks on 11 September and the later anthrax attacks on the US.[56]

David Albright, 'Hamza's former mentor in the US,' according to the *Observer*, and himself a former nuclear inspector involved in assessing the scope of Iraq's nuclear ambitions, is now wary of his former protege. 'If Hamza has become a monster, I partly blame myself,' says Albright: 'He had good information on what he knew about, but where we fell out was that I was concerned he was telling me stuff he had read elsewhere, including stuff he could have read in *Time* magazine.'

According to Albright, once outside Iraq and while being debriefed by US intelligence, Hamza was given access to evidence provided by another high-level defector. 'Hamza, says Albright, was recycling this as his own first-hand knowledge':

'His book is full of technical inaccuracies and there is no doubt he exaggerated his importance. For instance he has a section about the biological weapons programme which he had no knowledge of or access to,' comments Albright.[57]

According to Albright, Hamza's unreliability began in 1998 when the Clinton administration published its Iraq Liberation Bill, voting funds to depose Saddam. 'From that point on he felt US military action was the only course. He told me he wanted to get a gun himself and go back and fight with his sons. These days he travels with people with a very heavy agenda.'[58]

Former UN weapons inspector Scott Ritter describes Hamza simply as a 'fraud' who has consistently lied about his importance in Iraq's nuclear programme and his own knowledge of it. 'In over seven years as a weapons inspector I chased down countless so-called intelligence sources and defector stories saying what Iraq was doing. Most were completely baseless. It is in the nature of the intelligence business that there is an awful lot of crap,' Ritter says. 'The biggest problem you get with defectors is that they often have legitimate tit-bits that are squeezed out in their debriefings. They feel under pressure to say more. So they read up what others have claimed and develop it, saying a cousin or a friend visited such and such a plant and saw such and such a thing, and you end up with a circle of falsehood.'[59]

One of the more recent defectors is Adnan Saeed al-Haideri, an influential Iraqi civil engineer who had close contacts with Saddam Hussein's regime, who fled Iraq in the summer of 2001 after a spell in jail on what he said were trumped-up charges for corruption. Through the offices of the opposition umbrella group the Iraqi National Congress (INC), al-Haideri contacted US intelligence with his story of having helped to construct and maintain hidden bunkers in which Baghdad intended to design and manufacture chemical, biological and nuclear weapons. According to al-Haideri, the walls of these special bunkers were lined with epoxy resin for easy decontamination, and there were lead-lined rooms and concrete mixed with chemicals to guard against radiation. Mr al-Haideri says he created "clean rooms" under buildings including the Saddam Hussein hospital in Baghdad. He claims to have made a mustard gas unit between two factories in the Al Taji compound north of Baghdad, and a biological weapons laboratory beneath the Adwaniya presidential palace, ten miles south of Baghdad.[60] Bronwen Maddox, the Foreign Editor of the *Times*, appears to have been the only British journalist to have pointed out that Mr al-Haideri 'does not claim to have direct evidence that the facilities he saw had the functions he suspected. No one told him explicitly that the plants were engaged in banned weapons production, nor did he see anything personally, as he was cementing and sealing various rooms and laboratories, which appeared to prove it.'[61]

Another anonymous defector claims to have worked in a concealment unit to foil UN inspectors, moving seven mobile germ laboratories disguised as milk lorries and yoghurt vans, between Hilla and Kut.[62]

The evidence of defectors and refugees, of course, must always be taken with a pinch of salt. The unbalanced relationship between a defector and her or his new host is prone to generate distortions, exaggerations and fabrications. David Albright, formerly a nuclear inspector in Iraq for the International Atomic Energy Agency, remarked in March 2002, 'The evidence produced so far is worrying. It is an argument for getting the inspectors back in as fast as possible, but not for going to war.'[63]

CONCLUSION

There appears to be no hard evidence that Iraq has acquired or developed weapons of mass destruction since December 1998, when inspectors were withdrawn on US instructions. No evidence has been provided that Iraq has supplied weapons of mass destruction to terrorist groups or to other nations. There is a growing mass of claims by Iraqi defectors, unverifiable without a reconstruction of the inspection and monitoring system. Finally, the best efforts of British intelligence to construct a case against Baghdad over its weapons programmes seems to have turned up nothing worth publishing or sharing with others. It is expected that Mr Blair's famous dossier will be published within months, perhaps weeks, of the publication of this book. We shall discover then what the Prime Minister has based his confident claims on. Not on the evidence, it would appear.

Updated information on this and other chapters
will be available weekly from www.justicenotvengeance.org

REASON 2
Prague No Show

There Is No Link Between Iraq and 11 September

WOOLSEY'S QUEST

Washington hawks have made strenuous efforts to link Iraq to the terrorist attacks on 11 September. A leading figure in this effort has been former CIA director James Woolsey, who said within days of the atrocities that there had been 'state sponsorship' of the attacks, and mentioned Iraq as a suspect. Launching his own personal search for corroboration, Mr Woolsey flew to London to seek out the Iraqi opposition, unearthing a rumour that Osama bin Laden had sent an al Qaeda delegation to Baghdad on 25 April 1988, to celebrate Saddam Hussein's birthday. The delegation was said to have secured a promise of training for al Qaeda recruits and established a joint force of al Qaeda elite fighters and Iraqi intelligence agents.[1] While on his visit to London, Mr Woolsey said, 'Evidentiary standards are the wrong standards. I would talk about indications, information' as all that should be necessary to identify Osama bin Laden as the perpetrator.[2] It was natural then that his own search for evidence of Iraqi complicity followed the same approach. No evidence was ever produced to support the '25 April 1988' allegation. Expert opinion rules out such a partnership, as we shall see.

Mr Woolsey's sponsor within the US Administration, Donald Rumsfeld, the Defence Secretary, was 'so determined to find a rationale' for an attack on Iraq that 'on ten separate occasions he asked the CIA to find evidence linking Iraq to the terrorist attacks of September 11.' Unfortunately for Mr Woolsey and Mr Rumsfeld, 'The intelligence agencies repeatedly came back empty handed.'[3] But not for want of trying – and when evidence turned out to be scarce, there was always rumour and speculation dressed up as intelligence: 'American intelligence sources claim Iraq's secret banking networks may have been used to finance [al Qaeda] operations.'[4] According to 'US sources', Osama bin Laden 'did meet Iraqi intelligence agents in 1998 and may have accepted their offer of money.'[5] Director of the CIA George Tenet was supposed to have traced a series of contacts and linkages between Iraq and al-Qaeda within days of the attacks. But the evidence to support these claims was never produced.

The intellectual level was indicated by President Bush's argument, 'I see linkage between someone who is willing to murder his own people. I hold Saddam Hussein to account and we are going to do that.'[6] Weakening his stance, on 19 September 2001 Mr Woolsey said, 'There's never been anything inconsistent with the idea that bin Laden would be providing most of the people in this and Iraqi intelligence helping logistically and otherwise being behind it.'[7] Mr Woolsey was contradicted in the very same article by another (unnamed) ex-CIA officer: 'The reality is that Osama bin Laden doesn't like Saddam Hussein. Saddam is a secularist who has killed more Islamic clergy than he has Americans. They share almost nothing in common except a hatred of the US. Saddam is the ultimate control freak, and for him terrorists are the ultimate loose cannon.'[8]

EXPERT DISSENT

'A senior [US] defence official told the *FT* last week that the contacts between Iraq and al-Qaeda had been more extensive than the US previously thought, shattering the conventional wisdom in Washington about connections between the secular Iraqi state and an extremist Islamic group.'[9] Is the conventional wisdom shattered? Not according to Peter L. Bergen, author of *Holy War Inc.*, a study of bin Laden and his fundamentalist supporters, who said in March 2002, 'scant evidence exists that any state actors – except the Taliban – actively supported bin Laden.'[10]

President Vladimir Putin of Russia said, 'We know which nations' representatives and citizens were fighting alongside the Taliban, and where their activities were financed from. Iraq is not on the list.'[11] Michael Griffin, author of *Reaping the Whirlwind*, a study of the Taliban, pointed out that when you study lists of suspects in previous al Qaeda operations, you find Syrians, Jordanians, Yemenis, Egyptians, Saudis, but no Iraqis, Iranians, Afghans, or Libyans.[12]

The conventional wisdom seems rather solid. Major General Amos Malka, head of Israeli intelligence, said in late September 2001, 'I don't see a direct link between Iraq and the hijackings ... there is no Iraqi angle or infrastructure that we can point to at this stage.'[13] Veteran Middle East journalist, Robert Fisk points out, 'Mr bin Laden hates Saddam Hussein, regarding the Iraqi leader as a Western-created dictator – a not entirely inaccurate description'.[14]

BRITISH SCEPTICISM

Since the first days of the crisis, the British Government have held unwaveringly to the line that there is no link between Iraq and 11 September. Earlier, we discussed an intelligence dossier that Mr Blair promised to release to the public in April 2002 (see Reason 1). This same Joint Intelligence Committee dossier also addressed the question of a 'link' between 11 September and Baghdad: 'British intelligence sources say that despite attempts by the CIA and FBI to find links between Osama bin Laden's al Qaeda network and Iraq, the British dossier does not refer to them because there is no evidence to back up the US claims.' While the CIA had suggested a link, 'British intelligence officials are sceptical.' 'Tony Blair is to be told by Britain's most senior intelligence officer that there is no evidence linking Iraq to the September 11 attacks or to Osama bin Laden's terror networks'. The *Sunday Times* described the dossier as 'a blow to attempts by Downing Street to rally public and political support behind a military campaign against Iraq.'[15]

It is true that at the time of the 11 September atrocities, headlines read, 'Iraq stands alone as Arab world offers sympathy and regrets.' The Iraqi response to the disasters inflicted in New York and Washington DC was interpreted as gloating. An official Iraqi statement said that the US was reaping the fruits of its 'crimes against humanity': 'The collapse of US centres of power is a collapse of the US policy, which deviates from human values, and stands by world Zionism'.[16] However, a week after the atrocities, Iraqi Deputy Prime Minister Tariq Aziz sent a letter to be forwarded to the families of the victims, which offered 'sincere condolences for the American victims who fell in the events last Tuesday'. This message was recorded in the *Daily Telegraph*.[17] Curiously, on the very same page, the British newspaper suggested that, 'Significantly, Saddam has been the only Arab leader to praise the hijackers who wreaked such devastation in New York and Washington.'[18] No such 'praise' is on record, to my knowledge. Gloating at someone else's suffering, however reprehensible, is scarcely the same as praising the architects of that suffering.

MR ATTA DOES NOT GO TO PRAGUE

The key piece of 'evidence' used to link Baghdad to 11 September was the supposed meeting of the ringleader of the suicide hijackers, Mohamed Atta, with an Iraqi intelligence agent in the Czech republic in 2001. The first rumblings of this allegation were somewhat confused. Atta 'held a meeting with a "low-level" Iraqi agent in Europe last year, said the source.'[19] By the next day, the Iraqi agent(s) had been promoted, though there were three versions of the rank. In different British newspapers, US intelligence claimed that Mr Atta had met 'mid-ranking' Iraqi intelligence officers, 'senior' Iraqi intelligence officials, or, alternatively, 'the head of Baghdad's intelligence services' earlier in 2001.[20] The *FT* was the only paper to ask whether there was any evidence that this alleged 'meeting' had anything to do with the destruction of the World Trade Centre, a key issue and therefore largely ignored in the media.

While most reports agreed the 'meeting' occurred in 2001, the first reports varied on exactly when during the year. One edition of the *Guardian* managed to place the 'meeting' both 'in the months preceding the attack' (page 8), and 'last year' (page 2).[21] The 'story' finally settled down, placing Atta in Prague in April 2001, a 'fact' confirmed by Czech interior minister Stanislav Gross in October 2001, though 'Mr Gross said he had no details of what was discussed between Atta and Ahmad Khalil Ibrahim Samir al-Ani, an Iraqi diplomat who was expelled several weeks after the meeting for "activities incompatible with his status".[22] Among the many wild stories that then circulated, a German magazine floated the theory that Atta had been given his instructions regarding 11 September on an earlier occasion, then returned to Prague to collect a flask of anthrax in April 2001.[23]

When the Czech police completed their inquiry into the Atta/al-Ani 'meeting' in mid-December 2001, however, 'Jiri Kolar, the police chief, said there were no documents showing that Atta visited Prague at any time this year, although he had visited twice in 2000'. Atta could have visited under false papers, 'but Mr Gross questioned why Atta would do so when he was not a wanted man: "I don't see any reason for him to visit under a false name", he said.'

It turned out that another man by the name of Mohammed Atta *did* visit Prague in 2001, but according to a Czech interior ministry source, 'He didn't have the same identity card number, there was a great difference in their ages, their nationalities didn't match, basically nothing. It was someone else.' And a man who looked very much like Mohammed Atta *did* meet Mr al-Ani, but he was an Iraqi called 'Saleh', a used car dealer from Nuremburg in Germany. The story had started because Czech intelligence had an informer following the Iraqi diplomat, who after 11 September recollected Mr al-Ani meeting someone looking identical to Mohammed Atta.[24]

The story had disintegrated. However, the collapse of this important US propaganda weapon was reported only in the *Daily Telegraph*. No other British newspaper carried the story. The BBC News Online service has no report of Jiri Kolar's statement in its archive.

In fact, there continued to be references to the 'Atta/al-Ani meeting' after the mid-December revelations, until the US Administration finally appeared to give up in May 2002. *Time* magazine reported, 'The best hope for Iraqi ties to the attack – a report that lead hijacker Mohammed Atta met with an Iraqi intelligence officer in the Czech Republic – was discredited last week.'[25] The BBC reported, 'Atta is known to have been in Prague in June 2000, but investigations indicate that at the time of the alleged meeting with the Iraqi agent, Ahmed Chalil Ibrahim Samir Ani, in April 2001, he was in Virginia Beach and Florida.'[26] Presumably this had been discovered by the FBI. However, useful lies are often revived, so the famous Prague meeting may yet be resuscitated.

A WAR ON TERRORISM?

This was supposed to be a 'war on terrorism'. Why then the focus on Iraq? Richard Perle, a Reagan-era official now heading the Pentagon's Defence Advisory Board, believes that the US should attempt to bring down Saddam Hussein 'even if Iraq was not involved [in 11 September] because no war against terrorism could be successful without his removal.'[27] Unfortunately for Mr Perle, there is a distinct lack of evidence that Iraq has played any significant role in international terrorism recently.

Despite the best efforts by the US intelligence services, no link between Iraq and international terrorism has been discovered. The famously 'delayed' British intelligence dossier on Iraq dissented sharply from the CIA rumour mill. The *Sunday Times* reported in March 2002, 'Tony Blair is to be told by Britain's most senior intelligence official that there is no evidence linking Iraq to the September 11 attacks or to Osama bin Laden's network.' The report, compiled by John Scarlett, chair of the Joint Intelligence Committee, 'disputes claims that Saddam Hussein financed or gave refuge to Al-Qaeda fighters', according to the *Sunday Times*.[28] 'British intelligence sources say that despite attempts by the CIA and FBI to find links between Osama bin Laden's al Qaeda network and Iraq, the British dossier does not refer to them because there is no evidence to back up the US claims – such as the meeting between Mohammed Atta, the September 11 hijacker, and an Iraqi intelligence officer.'[29]

Sunday Telegraph columnist Con Coughlin demonstrated the desperate levels that anti-Saddam propagandists are willing to go to. He wrote, 'I am surprised that there are still those who have reason to doubt that Iraq is a legitimate target' in the 'war on terrorism.' 'While there is no hard evidence of direct Iraqi involvement in the events of September 11… there is more than enough evidence to link Saddam with a galaxy of infamous terrorists from Abu Nidal to Carlos the Jackal.' The only claims Mr Coughlin could deploy, however, dated to 1978 (when the former Iraqi Prime Minister was shot dead in London), and 1982 (when the former Israeli ambassador to London suffered severe brain damage during an assassination attempt).[30] This list would suggest that Baghdad has been rather quiet on the international terrorism front lately.

Lieutenant General Brent Scowcroft, former National Security Adviser to President Bush Sr. during the 1991 Gulf War, argues that Iraq should not be part of the new war on terrorism at all. General Scowcroft says, 'It's not a terrorist state. The only thing that Saddam Hussein and Osama bin Laden have in common is hatred of the United States.' Saddam Hussein 'is primarily a problem of hostile military power. He may get weapons of mass destruction or he may not. But it's a pretty traditional enemy.'[31] An editorial in the *Independent* observes, 'If Saddam wants to sponsor anti-American terrorism he has had plenty of opportunity; he has either been uninterested or unsuccessful.'[32]

The *New York Times* carried an article on Baghdad's record: 'The Central Intelligence Agency has no evidence that Iraq has engaged in terrorist operations against the United States in nearly a decade, and the agency is also convinced that President Saddam Hussein has not provided chemical or biological weapons to Al Qaeda or related terrorist groups, according to several American intelligence officials.'[33] There were revelations about Baghdad's sinister links with 'infamous terrorist' Abu Nidal:

> In 1998, American and Middle Eastern intelligence agencies discovered that Abu Nidal, the Palestinian who had been one of the most feared terrorists of the 1970's and early 80's, had moved to Baghdad. Abu Nidal had been ousted from his previous haven in Libya, after Col. Muammar el-Qaddafi

decided he wanted to end Libya's ties to terrorists in order to get out from under international sanctions. But Abu Nidal does not appear to have engaged in any anti-American operations since his arrival in Iraq, and he may have ended his terrorism activities, officials said.

Not exactly a smoking gun there, then.

THE FAKE BOMB PLOT

The CIA officials said they believed that 'the last terrorist operation tried by Iraq against the United States was the assassination attempt against the first President Bush during his visit to Kuwait in 1993' – an alleged plot that was supposedly disrupted before it could be carried out.[34] This fabricated 'plot' to assassinate former President George Bush Sr. was comprehensively demolished by Seymour Hersh in a forensic article in the *New Yorker* many years later. One of the key claims linking the alleged plot to the Iraqi Government was that the remote-control firing device found in the Kuwaiti car bomb supposedly intended for George Bush had a uniquely identifying 'signature' used in previously recovered Iraqi bombs.

The US Administration released colour photographs of the firing devices to substantiate its case. Mr Hersh asked seven independent experts in electrical engineering and bomb forensics to look at the photographs. They all told him 'essentially the same thing': the remote-controlled devices shown in the White House photographs were mass-produced items, commonly used for walkie-talkies and model airplanes and cars, and had not been modified in any significant way. The experts, who included former police officers, government contract employees and professors of electrical engineering, agreed, too, that the two devices had no 'signatures': 'They said that there was no conceivable way that the Clinton Administration, given the materials made public at the United Nations, could assert that the remote-controlled devices had been put together by the same Iraqi technician.'[35]

The US retaliation for the alleged Iraqi bomb plot was to launch 23 Tomahawk cruise missiles, 20 of which hit their targets, three of which landed on houses in the surrounding residential area. Eight civilians were killed.[36] Even if the car bomb plot had been proven to be the work of the Iraqis, there was no legal basis for this assault, which must therefore count as an act of international terrorism.

BREAKING THE LINK

Richard Butler, former head of the UNSCOM weapons inspectorate, testified to the US Senate Foreign Relations Committee in July 2002: 'I have seen no evidence of Iraq providing [weapons of mass destruction] to non-Iraqi terrorist groups. I suspect that, especially given his psychology and aspirations, Saddam would be reluctant to share with others what he believes to be an indelible source of his own power.'[37] This refutes precisely the central terrorist scare that US hawks wish to use to ignite war fever.

REASON 3
Cloning Saddam

This Is Not About 'Regime Change'

There are probably millions of people in Britain and the United States who support the idea of launching an invasion of Iraq because they hate the present system in Iraq, and they believe that Washington and London genuinely intend to create 'regime change' in that country, and establish a decent social order.

The evidence is, however, that the men leading us towards war are intent on replacing the current President with a member of his military elite, maintaining the structures of power and ways of operating much as they are. The 'Man on a White Horse' will continue to buttress domination by the Sunni minority, and will continue to hold the country together in a fashion approved in Riyadh and Ankara.

Those who are hoping for real change should realise that the options being sought by the United States amount to 'Saddam the lesser', 'Saddamism without Saddam', or 'authoritarian moderation'. These terms are used by Anthony H. Cordesman and Ahmed S. Hashim to describe the possible consequences of a coup or assassination. 'Saddam the lesser' would be another Ba'athist leader with similar beliefs and ambitions, but without Mr Saddam's charisma and authority. 'Saddamism without Saddam' would describe the rule of one of the Iraqi President's closest associates. The two Centre for Strategic and International Studies analysts use the term 'authoritarian moderate' to describe an undemocratic leader who was willing to concentrate on internal economic development, the need to reach an accommodation with the Shia and Kurdish populations, and the rebuilding of links with neighbouring countries.[1]

A number of different sources have suggested that (in the absence of an agreed plan) for deposing Mr Saddam, the US is pursuing a strategy of psychological warfare. In February 2002, *Guardian* columnist Martin Woollacott mused that 'there is always the possibility that the threat iself will induce a change in Iraq'.[2] A rather euphemistic description of this scenario. The *Independent*, in a July 2002 editorial worrying about the 'dangerous pitch' of US anti-Iraq rhetoric, suggested the most positive interpretation might be that 'Washington is merely trying to scare Baghdad, in the hope of triggering a revolt among the top brass, or scaring Saddam Hussein into complying with the UN weapons inspection team.'[3] The latter is hardly a realistic suggestion, for reasons we have already surveyed (see Chapter V).

After interviewing widely within the Bush Administration, US journalist Nicholas Lemann predicted in April 2002 that there would be an enormous troop deployment to the Gulf in the late summer or early autumn. The US hoped that these and other moves 'will destabilize Iraq enough to cause the Republican Guard, the military key to the country, to turn against Saddam and topple him on its own.'[4] Christopher Langton of the London International Institute of Strategic Studies said in July 2002, 'We're in the phase of psychological pressure on the Iraqi regime by a steady build-up of forces and meetings of the opposition.'[5]

Mr Langton was referring to a gathering of military exiles in London in mid-July 2002. At the time of that conference, there was a characteristically indiscreet revelation by an Iraqi dissident with contacts inside the US administration – undoubtedly a member of the INA. This Iraqi 'dissident' said that covert operations inside Iraq were 'part of a larger plan aimed primarily at unnerving the regime and gradually seizing power from it.'[6]

The US is committed to fostering a military coup of some kind, bolstering the Sunni 'centre' of Iraq, and keeping Iraq in the 'best of all possible worlds'. The words of Mr Cordesman and Mr Hashim quoted in Chapter VIII bear repetition:

> A "centrist" coup or assassination may lead to many initial promises or claims of moderation, liberalization, and political change, but the reality is most likely to be very different. Any efforts to overthrow Saddam within the present ruling Sunni elite are likely to be followed by continuing repression of the Shi'ites and Kurds, the arrest and execution of many rivals and supporters of Saddam, and the eventual arrest and execution of other opponents.[7]

Perhaps there are some individuals who are willing to break international law, see millions of ordinary families put at risk of starvation and disease, cause waves of revolt and terrorism throughout the Middle East, and risk triggering the destruction of the small gains Iraqi Kurds have made over the past decade, all to replace the Iraqi President with 'Saddam the lesser'. It is hard not to believe that the huge majority of war supporters feel quite differently.

REASON 4

Catastrophe

War Could Trigger
A Humanitarian Disaster

NEAR-APOCALYPSE, 1991

In the immediate aftermath of the Gulf War of 1991, the UN Secretary-General, Javier Perez de Cuellar sent a humanitarian assessment mission to Iraq, led by UN diplomat Martti Ahtisaari. Mr Ahtisaari wrote these famous words on his return:

> I and the members of my mission were fully conversant with media reports regarding the situation in Iraq and, of course, with the recent WHO/UNICEF report on water, sanitary and health conditions in the Greater Baghdad area. It should, however, be said at once that nothing that we had seen or read had quite prepared us for the particular form of devastation which has now befallen the country.
>
> The recent conflict has wrought near-apocalyptic results upon the economic infrastructure of what had been, until January 1991, a rather highly urbanized and mechanized society. Now, most means of modern life support have been destroyed or rendered tenuous. Iraq has, for some time to come, been relegated to a pre-industrial age, but with all the disabilities of post-industrial dependency on an intensive use of energy and technology.[1]

Mr Ahtisaari warned of the possibility of 'a further imminent catastrophe'.

INFRASTRUCTURE

The problem in Iraq was that the US-led forces had deliberately destroyed the civilian infrastructure which supported public health. The Arab Monetary Fund estimated the value of destroyed infrastructure and economic assets during the 1991 war at $232 billion.[2] (By comparison, the eight-year Iran-Iraq war caused only $67bn worth of economic damage.[3]) Dr Eric Hoskins, a UNICEF adviser, observes that,

> Eighteen of Iraq's twenty power-generating plants were rendered inoperable [during the 1991 war], reducing [immediate] postwar electricity to just 4 per cent of prewar levels. Food storage facilities, industrial complexes, oil refineries, sewage pumping stations, telecommunications facilities, roads, railroads, and dozens of bridges were destroyed during the war.

Dr Hoskins comments, 'It took Iraq many decades, vast amounts of foreign currency, and considerable foreign expertise to build the estimated $232 billion worth of assets destroyed in the forty-three-day bombing campaign.'[4]

POWER VACUUM

The damage was deliberate. One target was the critical electricity sector. A draft congressional report of February 1992 noted that 'senior commanders made deliberate exceptions to the policy of limiting damage to certain power installations.'[5] That's one way of putting it. US-led forces carried out 890 strikes on electrical and oil facilities during the war. According to one authoritative source, US targeting 'did not deliberately attempt to destroy Iraq's economic infrastructure or inflict long-term damage', with bombers instructed to focus on transformers and switching yards and control buildings rather than turbines, generator halls, and boilers.[6] In February, guidance was passed down the chain of command (backdated to January). 'Electrical targets will be targeted to minimize recuperation time. At electrical production/transformer stations the objective will be transformer/switching yards and the central buildings in these yards,' the memo said. 'Boilers and generators will not be aimpoints.'[7] However, 'This guidance was often ignored in the heat of combat': 'Many generator buildings were hit ... partly because they were the largest buildings in the 25 major power stations in Iraq and the most obvious targets and partly because the attacking units were sometimes given inadequate briefings on the need to try to exercise restraint.' One generator building was hit repeatedly because it was a secondary target for aircraft that did not strike their primary target.[8]

In 'an exception' to the general policy, US General Buster Glosson directed that the electrical generators at the Al Hartha plant near Basra and several substations be levelled. The US feared that the plant might be used by the Iraqi military to provide power to the pumping stations in Kuwait to fill 'fire trenches' along the border with crude oil. The plant was bombed more than a dozen times. The US Navy, in particular, used it as a 'dump' target to dispose of any bombs its planes might still have on their way back to the carriers.[9]

General Schwarzkopf, commander-in-chief of the US-led forces, claimed during the 1991 war that 'we never had any intention of destroying all of Iraqi electrical power.' Yet US-led attacks on power generation facilities continued after he made this statement – including the destruction of two of Iraq's critical hydroelectric facilities, not hit by 'coalition' bombers until early February.[10]

US human rights group Middle East Watch demolished the official justification for the targeting of civilian electrical installations:

> The apparent justification for attacking almost the entire electrical system in Iraq was that the system functioned as an integrated grid, meaning that power could be shifted countrywide, including to military functions such as command-and-control centres and weapons-manufacturing facilities. But these key military targets were attacked in the opening days of the war. The direct attacks by the allies on these military targets should have obviated the need simultaneously to destroy the fixed power sources thought to have formerly supplied them. If these and other purely military targets could be attacked at will, then arguably the principle of humanity would make the wholesale destruction of Iraq's electrical-generating capability superfluous to the accomplishment of legitimate military objectives.[11]

And, in fact, the military effects were limited as Iraqi forces in Kuwait and in Iraq had their own generating plants. Military analysts Anthony Cordesman and Abraham Wagner comment, 'The loss of electrical power almost certainly had some impact on the attitudes of the Iraqi leadership, and the perceptions of the Iraqi public, but it is difficult to translate them into a significant impact on direct Iraqi warfighting capability.'[12]

The loss of electrical power may not have had much impact on the Iraqi military, but it certainly had a tremendous impact on the civilian population. Mr Ahtisaari placed a special emphasis on the needs of the electricity sector in his March 1991 report. While the Secretary-General's envoy was convinced that there needed to be 'a major mobilization and movement of resources to deal with aspects of this deep crisis in the fields of agriculture and food, water, sanitation and health', he cautioned that 'it will be difficult, if not impossible, to remedy these immediate humanitarian needs without dealing with the underlying need for energy, on an equally urgent basis.'

As the Harvard Study Team wrote in their report, 'There is a link in Iraq between electrical power and public health. Without electricity, water cannot be purified, sewage cannot be treated, water-borne diseases flourish and hospitals cannot cure treatable diseases.'[13] Seasoned Middle East observer Robert Fisk, reported on the impact of failing electricity supply on drinking water in early 1998. Fisk was told by Philippe Heffinck, UNICEF Representative in Baghdad, that to provide clean drinking water, both water-treatment plants and water pipes needed repair – 'Then you have the lack of electricity that contributes to the deterioration in health.' Fisk noted,

I already understood the revolting mechanics of electrical power and water; a UN hygiene official had explained it to me, equally coldly, 24 hours earlier: when electricity is cut – which it is every three hours, for example, in Basra – the pumps stop and the pressure in the leaking water pipes falls. Into the vacuum is sucked sewage which runs out of the taps. Even the original source of the water is now contaminated in Iraq.[14]

Dr Hoskins notes that, 'Contaminated water supplies and poor sanitation have created health conditions enabling diarrhea to emerge as the leading child killer during the postwar period. During both 1991 and 1992, mortality due to diarrhea was estimated at more than three times the 1990 levels.'[15]

Reuters reported that after the biggest power plant in southern Iraq was bombed, Basra 'came close to drowning in its own filth'. The power plant was then bombed twelve more times. It was 'completely incapacitated' after the first attack, according to the chief engineer, '[so] we thought that would be it, there would be no further attacks. But they came back and struck again, and again, and again.' The final attack came on 28 February, half an hour before the cease-fire. By then, most of the facility was apparently a 'scrap heap'.[16] Perhaps this was the Al Hartha plant, used as a dumping ground for US Air Force bombers returning home.

Dr Leon Eisenberg of Harvard Medical School noted that the destruction of the country's power plants in 1991 'brought its entire system of water purification and distribution to a halt, leading to epidemics of cholera, typhoid fever, and gastroenteritis, particularly among children'. Death rates doubled or tripled among children admitted to hospitals in Baghdad and Basra. Cases of marasmus, a disease of acute malnutrition, appeared for the first time in decades. An International Study Group supported by the United Nations Children's Fund (UNICEF) carried out a comprehensive study in mid-1991, interviewing members of households selected to represent the Iraqi population: 'There were approximately 47,000 excess deaths among children under five years of age during the first eight months of 1991. The deaths resulted from infectious diseases, the decreased quality and availability of food and water, and an enfeebled medical care system hampered by the lack of drugs and supplies.'[17]

Much was made of the (fabricated) story of incubators being stolen from Kuwait by Iraqi forces. Little was said of the incubators in Iraq that were effectively stolen by the cutting off of electricity supplies.

In brief, the deliberate destruction of the civilian infrastructure by US-led forces, coupled with the effects of economic sanctions (which were re-imposed after the war largely at the behest of the United States and Britain) caused the deaths of 47,000 children under the age of five in less than a year. Deliberately destroying the means of containing water-borne disease is equivalent to the use of a biological weapon. It seems fair to say, then, that 47,000 children were killed in Iraq in the first eight months of 1991 by biological warfare instigated by Britain and the United States.

LEVERAGE

And for what purpose were these children killed? In June 1991, US Air Force officers reportedly said that the targeting of Iraq's infrastructure had been related to an effort 'to accelerate the effects of sanctions.'[18]

According to a detailed history of the war, 'the air commanders hoped to send a signal to the Iraqi people: "Hey, your lights will come back on as soon as you get rid of Saddam." '[19] US General Buster Glosson, responsible for compiling the target lists for the US-led bombardment, 'commented that after the war the US and its allies expected to rebuild the damaged infrastructure', according to an interview with the *Chicago Tribune*.[20] General Glosson's colleague Colonel John Warden explained after the fighting was over that, 'Saddam Hussein cannot restore his own electricity. He needs help. If there are political objectives that the UN Coalition [in other words, the US] has, it can say, "Saddam, when you agree to do these things, we will allow people to come in and fix your electricity."[21] Children were killed for political leverage, in this view.

INDISPENSABLE OBJECTS

An Additional Protocol to the Geneva Conventions says,

> It is prohibited to attack, destroy, remove or render useless objects indispensable to the survival of the civilian population, such as foodstuffs, agricultural areas for the production of foodstuffs, crops, livestock, drinking water installations and supplies and irrigation works, for the specific purpose of denying them for their sustenance value to the civilian population or to the adverse Party, whatever the motive, whether in order to starve out civilians, to cause them to move away, or for any other motive.

The US human rights group, Middle East Watch, notes that, 'insofar as the civilian population is concerned, it makes little or no difference whether [a civilian facility] is attacked or destroyed, or is made inoperable by the destruction of the electrical plant supplying it power. In either case, civilians suffer the same effects – they are denied the use of a public utility indispensable for their survival.'[22]

According to the official version of events, then, the long-term damage to Iraq's electricity system was unintentional. The intention was to knock out Iraq's electricity system only in the short term. It was expected that the damage would be reversed within months by a US-led reconstruction effort, on condition that Iraq experienced political changes dictated by Washington (in other words, 'leadership change').

Whether short- or long-term, however, damage to the electricity system, which rendered useless irrigation systems, drinking water installations, and sections of the Iraqi agricultural and livestock industries, was illegal according to the laws of war as they are codified in Additional Protocol I to the Geneva Conventions.

CATASTROPHE, 2002?

If US and British missiles and bombs are directed at the deteriorating civilian infrastructure of Iraq once more, the consequences are like to be enormous. Perhaps the intention once again will be to do only 'short-term' damage. But the risk exists that history will repeat itself, and massive long-term damage will be done to Iraq's public health infrastructure, deepening the immediate humanitarian disaster.

In February 1998, UN Secretary-General Kofi Annan referred to the continuing 'threat of a complete breakdown' in power generation, stating that the humanitarian consequences of such a breakdown 'could potentially dwarf all other difficulties endured by the Iraqi people'.[23] Such a breakdown could be triggered by a single power station being shut down unexpectedly by a fire, the Secretary-General warned. A missile strike on a power station, whether deliberate or accidental, could have the same effect.

Save the Children UK has noted that in northern Iraq, food stocks in the autonomous Kurdish zone 'would not last more than a few weeks if communications broke down' between the autonomous region and the food warehouses in Kirkuk and Mosul. Furthermore, there are 'unprecedented levels of dependency' in Iraq, as families rely on government food rations for survival. Save the Children UK warns that, 'dependency levels are so high that any shock to the system would lead directly and inevitably to a humanitarian disaster'.[24] The British aid agency believes that,

> military action [against Iraq] that disrupts the food pipeline and results in damage to essential civilian infrastructure will have a catastrophic effect on the health and well-being of an extremely vulnerable population. Any military action that further compromises the human security of the population, would, we believe, constitute a breach of International Humanitarian Law. Of particular relevance in this regard is the First Additional Protocol to the Geneva Convention (1977) concerning the destruction or 'rendering useless' of objects indispensable for the survival of the civilian population.[25]

Iraq is generally agreed to be experiencing a humanitarian emergency or crisis. The shock of war on the fragile support systems that exist in Iraq would turn a humanitarian crisis into a humanitarian disaster for 23 million people. If vital elements of the public health infrastructure were damaged, including the electricity sector, the disaster would be deepened.

Washington says it will not take 'yes' for an answer. The people of Iraq could pay a very heavy price for the US determination to effectively block the return of UN weapons inspectors, to undermine negotiations and diplomacy, to pursue the 'decapitation' of the Iraqi leadership at all costs, and to impose a more obedient Saddam-clone on the long-suffering people of Iraq.

REASON 5
Unsafe Haven

Endangering The Kurds

Since mid-1991, three of Iraq's eighteen 'governorates' or states have been a country-within-a-country, housing an autonomous Kurdish zone run by an independent Kurdish administration in conjunction with the United Nations. The northern zone was set up by the United States and Britain after hundreds of thousands of Kurds fled from the Iraqi Government's retaliation in the wake of the failed postwar uprisings. Now, three and a half million Kurds enjoy a version of self-rule in an enclave which is itself partitioned – one domain is run by the Patriotic Union of Kurdistan (PUK), the other by the Kurdish Democratic Party (KDP). During a February 2002 visit, US journalist Jeff Goldberg found that President Bush's State of the Union address had had an electric effect on every Kurd he met who heard the speech. President Bush referred in his speech to the Iraqi Government murdering thousands of its citizens, 'leaving the bodies of mothers huddled over their dead children'. This was a clear reference to the experience of the Kurds, and to Halabja in particular.

General Simko Dizaqee, chief of staff of the Kurdish guerrillas (or *peshmerga*), told Mr Goldberg, 'Bush's speech fill our hearts with hope'. Mr Goldberg found that Kurds throughout the autonomous zone 'were enthusiastic about the idea of joining an American-led alliance against Saddam Hussein, and serving as the northern Iraqi equivalent of Afghanistan's Northern Alliance.'[1]

Despite grassroots enthusiasm, Kurdish leaders have been publicly rebuffing US war plans. Massoud Barzani, leader of the KDP, signalled his non-cooperation in June 2002, saying, 'The Iraqi issue won't be solved by military action or covert action. We cannot stop the US [from taking covert action], but we would like there to be transparency and clarity, and for there to be no covers or curtains to hide behind.'[2] Both Mr Barzani and Jalal Talabani, leader of the PUK, 'are cautious of committing the Kurds to helping to remove President Saddam without clear guarantees from Washington.' A *Guardian* reporter comments, 'The Kurds still harbour bitter memories from 1975, when the withdrawal of US and Iranian support caused an abrupt end to their armed struggle against Baghdad.'[3] There are memories also from 1963, and 1991, and 1995.

A close aide of Mr Barzani's, Sami Abdurrahman, says, 'We are not interested in overthrowing Saddam if he is only to be replaced by another dictator. We want to be full and equal partners in a democratic Iraq, where the Kurds are granted federal status.'[4] The KDP has drawn up a draft constitution which formalises the current situation, dividing Iraq into a large Arab region, and an Iraqi Kurdistan to the north. Each region would have its own parliament and president elected by secret ballot, in addition to a federal assembly. Baghdad would maintain control of internal security and a federal army, but the Kurdish region would have wide-ranging powers, including taxation and the freedom to initiate international relations.[5]

At a CIA conference in April 2002 in Virginia, the KDP and the PUK met CIA officials and General Wayne Downing, the president's military adviser on counter-terrorism (who has since resigned). Mr Talabani and Mr Barzani were asked whether they would agree to the establishment of CIA stations at the headquarters in Irbil and Sulaimaniyah. They refused. According to one account, Mr Barzani and Mr Talabani asked for more money than the CIA was prepared to offer. According to a Kurdish account, the meeting failed for a more fundamental reason: a lack of trust after being betrayed so many times.[6] Another version of events has the Kurds demanding a major role in any future Iraqi government, rather than just regional rights, in return for co-operation.[7]

The principal concern of the Kurdish leaders is the protection of the gains they have won over the past eleven years. Surrounded and outgunned by Iraqi forces, the Kurds are in a precarious position. Nasreen Barwari, the Harvard-educated Minister of Reconstruction and Development in Iraqi Kurdistan, 'We have really created something here, against all the odds. We have a lot to lose' from a US war on Iraq. Her concerns are another current in the Kurdish response to the gathering war clouds. Goldberg comments, 'The Kurdish leadership worries, in short, that an American mistake could cost the Kurds what they have created, however inadvertently: a nearly independent state for themselves in northern Iraq.'[8]

In the event of a US assault, 'Saddam would have every incentive to crush the Kurds.' Iraqi Kurdistan has been protected in part by the threat of the US and British aircraft patrolling the no-fly zone above the 36th parallel. According to Kenneth Pollack, a former US National Security Council official, once there is a major air war going on, 'that threat will no longer work, and Saddam would likely move to reoccupy the north – with all of the attendant slaughter and repression that would entail.'[9]

> With Iraqi troops and tanks massed around strategic points near the enclave it is easy to understand the Kurds' concern. Aid workers in the region agree that American warmongering could, as one put it, prompt Saddam to hit first.

'That is a real risk', said the aid worker. 'Iraqi Kurdistan is unprepared for the humanitarian disaster that would almost certainly ensue.'[10]

REASON 6
Crime Time[1]

War Would Be Illegal

As the *Economist* has observed, 'The US does not, to date, have a legal mandate for serious military intervention' in Iraq.[2]

PROHIBITING THE USE OF FORCE

The United Nations Charter forbids the use of force. Article 2, paragraphs 3 and 4, state in full:

> 2(3) All Members shall settle their international disputes by peaceful means in such a manner that international peace and security, and justice, are not endangered.
>
> 2(4) All Members shall refrain in their international relations from the threat or use of force against the territorial integrity or political independence of any state, or in any other manner inconsistent with the Purposes of the United Nations.[3]

There are only two exceptions to this prohibition recognised in international law, and in the UN Charter in particular: for individual or collective self-defence, and for the restoration of international peace and security – when authorised by the UN Security Council.

THE REQUIREMENT TO NEGOTIATE

Before any recourse to force, the UN Charter explicitly requires that in the resolution of any dispute, 'the continuance of which is likely to endanger the maintenance of international peace and security', the parties to the dispute 'shall, *first of all,* seek a solution by negotiation, enquiry, mediation, conciliation, arbitration, judicial settlement, resort to regional agencies or arrangements, or other peaceful means of their own choice' (Article 33, emphasis added). In contrast, the Bush Administration is doing its best to undermine efforts to achieve a peaceful solution through negotiation (see pages 60–62).

'Should the parties to a dispute of the nature referred to in Article 33 fail to settle it by the means indicated in that Article, they shall refer it to the Security Council,' says Article 37. Once again, a violation by London and Washington.

SELF-DEFENCE

There is a right under international law for nations to defend themselves by force. Article 51 of the UN Charter states in full:

> Nothing in the present Charter shall impair the inherent right of individual or collective self-defence if an armed attack occurs against a Member of the United Nations, until the Security Council has taken measures necessary to maintain international peace and security. Measures taken by Members in the exercise of this right of self-defence shall be immediately reported to the Security Council and shall not in any way affect the authority and responsibility of the Security Council under the present Charter to take at any time such action as it deems necessary in order to maintain or restore international peace and security.

Note that the responsibility for peace and security lies with the Security Council as a whole. The definition of 'armed attack' in the Charter refers to a military (or paramilitary) attack across a national border, on a member state of the United Nations. A State under attack may call on others for assistance, in which case it becomes a matter of 'collective self-defence'. The right of self-defence does not apply to military expeditionary forces sent out of the home country.

British Defence Secretary Geoff Hoon has said that a war against Iraq would be legally justified, 'Not least because those weapons of mass destruction might well be capable of posing a threat to the United Kingdom, in which case we would be entitled to act in self-defence.'[4] If any action in Hoon's scenario constitutes 'armed attack' as defined in international law, it is the invasion of Iraqi territory by the US and Britain – against which attack Iraq presumably has a right of self-defence under Article 51.

The use of armed force in self-defence is justified only when the need for action is 'instant, overwhelming, leaving no choice of means, and no moment for deliberation'. This wording comes from US Secretary of State Daniel Webster in the mid-nineteenth century, condemning a British act of claimed 'self-defence' which sent a US ship over the Niagara Falls. This definition has stood the test of time, and was relied upon at the Nuremburg Tribunal.[5]

The threat to the United States and Britain from Iraq is not of this kind.

There is disagreement among legal scholars over the legality of pre-emptive attacks, or 'anticipatory self-defence'.[6] The wording of Article 51 of the UN Charter, however, allows only self-defence against armed attacks that have already occurred. Louis Henkin, the US legal scholar, remarks in his classic *How Nations Behave* that the framers of the UN Charter 'recognised the exception of self-defence in emergency, but limited to actual armed attack, which is clear, unambiguous, subject to proof, and not easily open to misinterpretation or fabrication... nations should not be encouraged to strike first under pretext of prevention or pre-emption.'[7]

What is clear is that an act of self-defence must be capable of warding off the attack; must be directed to warding it off (rather than being a punitive raid); and must be proportional to the attack being defended against. Examining the intended assault on Iraq against these tests, the war does not appear to meet either the second or the third requirements. The proposed invasion does not satisfy the conditions for self-defence, whether 'anticipatory' self-defence is legally permitted or not.

SECURITY COUNCIL AUTHORISATION

The Security Council can authorise the use of force to 'maintain or restore international peace and security'. Authorisation has rarely been granted, however. Lord Healey, once Defence Secretary in a Labour Government, and a leading right-winger within the Labour Party, said in December 1998 that there was 'no question' that Operation Desert Fox was unlawful: 'It is illegal to attack with bombs targets in a sovereign country without direct authorisation from the Security Council.'[8]

David Hannay, British Ambassador to the UN in 1991 and now a Lord, argues that direct authorisation is available for a new war: 'Iraq is in breach of the mandatory 1991 Security Council Resolution that was the basis for the Gulf War ceasefire.'[9] Then Foreign Office Minister Ben Bradshaw spoke for the Government in March 2002, 'The legal view, with which I have some sympathy, is that Iraq is in flagrant breach, not just of UN resolutions, but of the ceasefire agreement that it entered into at the end of the Gulf War.'[10] If Iraq is judged not to be compliant with Resolution 687, on this analysis, the ceasefire is off and the war can legally resume, despite the fact that the Iraqi invasion was reversed over ten years ago. One version of the argument was offered in a British newspaper in July 2002:

> The basis of this claim is [UN Security Council Resolution] 678 of November 1990 authorising the US and others 'to use all necessary means to uphold and implement resolution 660 (1990) *and all subsequent relevant resolutions and to restore international peace and security in the area.*' That last provision covers the post-Gulf War Resolution 687 of April 1991, setting up the current system for inspecting and destroying Iraq's weapons of mass destruction. By refusing to have the UN inspectors back, it is said, President Saddam is in breach of this resolution and thus liable to attack under 678. International policy lawyers are divided on precisely this point.[11]

So, the argument runs:

1) Resolution 678 authorised the use of force to expel Iraq from Kuwait in 1990;

2) Resolution 678 also authorised the use of force in support of the objectives and demands contained in Resolution 687, in April 1991;

3) Iraq has breached Resolution 687;

4) by breaching Resolution 687, Iraq has re-activated the authorisation to use force originating in Resolution 678; and

5) the authorisation to use force remains delegated to the United States and Britain, without reference to the Security Council.

1) Taking the first proposition, it is not at all clear that Resolution 678 authorised the use of force. Resolution 678 authorised Member States of the UN cooperating with the (exiled) Government of Kuwait to use 'all necessary means' to reverse the Iraqi occupation – 'Acting under Chapter VII of the Charter'.[12] However, Chapter VII does not deal only with military enforcement.

According to Article 39, action should be taken after the Security Council has detected a 'threat to the peace, breach of the peace, or act of aggression'. No such declaration has been made.

Article 40 enables the Security Council to call upon the parties concerned to comply with 'provisional measures' to restore peace. Article 41 empowers the Security Council to impose 'measures not involving the use of armed force', including economic sanctions. Acting under Chapter VII could mean merely these provisions. There is no specific authorisation of the use of force.

Article 42 states that, 'Should the Security Council consider that measures provided for in Article 41 [economic and other non-military sanctions] would be inadequate or have proved to be inadequate, it may take such action by air, sea, or land forces as may be necessary to maintain or restore international peace and security.' But Resolution 678 does not state that the economic sanctions imposed on Iraq were inadequate, had failed, or would inevitably fail to secure the expulsion of Iraq.

Article 46 says, 'Plans for the application of armed force shall be made by the Security Council with the assistance of the Military Staff Committee.' The Military Staff Committee, according to the next Article, is there to 'to advise and assist the Security Council on all questions relating to the Security Council's military requirements for the maintenance of international peace and security, the employment and command of forces placed at its disposal, the regulation of armaments, and possible disarmament', and consists of 'the Chiefs of Staff of the permanent members of the Security Council or their representatives.' The Military Staff Committee was not formed in 1990 or 1991, gave no advice or assistance, and certainly did not draw up the plans for the application of armed force used in the US-led war.

In July 1950, after the onset of the Korean War, Security Council Resolution 84 noted that a number of countries had offered military assistance to the Government of South Korea as it defended itself, and recommended that those countries providing military forces 'make such forces and other assistance available to a unified command under the United States of America.' Resolution 84 also requested that Washington 'designate the commander of such forces' which were permitted to fly the UN flag. This does not sound like an 'authorisation' of the use of force, rather it appears to be a 'recognition' of an ongoing act of collective self-defence. The Security Council failed to follow this precedent – which may be connected to Article 51 rather than Article 42 in 1990.

While Western legal opinion appears generally to regard Resolution 678 as having authorised the use of force, a plain reading of the UN Charter suggests otherwise. The procedures laid down in the UN Charter for the use of force were not followed, and no explicit authorisation of military action was granted. The Korean precedent of explicitly recognising an international military coalition headed by the United States was also ignored. Noam Chomsky has rendered what appears to be the appropriate judgement: 'under US pressure, the Security Council was compelled to wash its hands of the matter, radically violating the UN Charter by leaving individual states free to act as they chose.'[13]

2) As for the second proposition, it is not possible to twist Resolution 678, whatever it authorised in November 1990, to cover military action in support of a disarmament process begun in April 1991. True, Paragraph 2 of the Resolution does call on Member States to use all necessary means to uphold and implement Resolution 660 'and all subsequent relevant resolutions and to restore international peace and security in the area,' but this refers to the ten Resolutions passed between the passing of Resolution 660 and the adoption of Resolution 678. These Resolutions are spelled out in the preamble to Resolution 678, which refers to them as the 'relevant resolutions'.[14]

Paragraph 4 of Resolution 686 states that the Security Council 'Recognizes that during the period required for Iraq to comply with paragraphs 2 and 3 above, the provisions of paragraph 2 of resolution 678 (1990) remain in force.' These paragraphs dealt with the aftermath of the Kuwait war, and the designation of Iraqi military commanders to meet with Kuwaiti and US commanders 'to arrange for the military aspects of a cessation of hostilities at the earliest possible time'. There is no hint that Resolution 678 has any other objective other than the expulsion of Iraq from Kuwait.[15]

3) On the issue of 'breach', let us, for the sake of argument, accept that Iraq's behaviour has violated legally-binding obligations properly imposed by Resolution 687.

4) However, as international lawyer Glen Rangwala points out, if the 1991 war was carried out under the authority of the UN Security Council, as the US and Britain are arguing, it follows that the ceasefire 'treaty' embodied in Resolution 687 is between the Government of Iraq and the Security Council. It is for the Security Council to decide whether Iraq's behaviour constitutes a 'material breach' which effectively ends the ceasefire or whether it is a less serious form of violation. According to Mr Rangwala,

simply finding that there has been a 'material breach' is also not enough; the Security Council would also have to explicitly suspend the ceasefire resolution.

Furthermore, the suspension of the ceasefire would not by itself constitute authorisation to use force. Because of the general prohibition on the use of force contained in Article 2(4) of the UN Charter, a ceasefire between two parties returns them to a state of peace, and any prior right to use force is terminated. Mr Rangwala points out that the ceasefire agreements between Israel and its neighbours in 1949 were not thought to be nullified by the Israeli invasion of Egypt in 1956, allowing Cairo to legally resume its military campaign seven years after the armistice.[16]

5) Turning to the final element of the Government argument, all of the Resolutions available make it clear that the decision on whether or not to use force against Baghdad in pursuit of the disarmament objectives of Resolution 687 rests with the Security Council. The final paragraph of Resolution 687 itself states that the Security Council 'Decides to remain seized of the matter and to take such further steps as may be required for the implementation of the present resolution and to secure peace and security in the area.' Professor Colin Warbrick of Durham University points out that there is no provision for enforcement in Resolution 687: 'It's for the Security Council to decide what action to take.'[17]

Resolution 1154, passed in March 1998, states that any failure to allow 'immediate, unconditional and unrestricted access' to UN inspectors 'would have the severest consequences for Iraq'. Paragraph 5 of this Resolution holds that the Security Council 'Decides, in accordance with its responsibility under the Charter, to remain actively seized of the matter, in order to ensure implementation of this resolution, and to secure peace and security in the region.' In other words, any further violations of the inspection regime would be dealt with by the Security Council itself. There was no phrase that could be interpreted as delegating the use of force to any individual state.

Donald Anderson, the highly respected chair of the House of Commons Defence Select Committee regards the legal basis for an attack on Iraq as 'pretty shakey'.[18] Donald Macintyre, writing in the *Independent* in April 2002, suggests that the question of a new Resolution is an 'unresolved question within the Government', with a significant body of opinion within Whitehall taking the view that a fresh Security Council resolution might indeed be required in international law.[19] *The Sunday Times* has reported that British Government lawyers have recommended seeking a new Resolution, to settle the issue of legality once and for all.[20] The *Independent* put the matter more strongly, stating that 'highly confidential' legal advice warned the Government that participation in an invasion of Iraq would be illegal without a new UN mandate.[21]

The political pressure is set to grow. Denzil Davies MP, a former Labour Shadow Defence Secretary, has said, 'many of us in the Parliamentary Labour Party would look for an underpinning in terms of a fresh UN resolution.'[22] An extraordinary coalition of voices is calling for a new UN Resolution, including Douglas Hurd, former Conservative Foreign Secretary, who has 'insisted that there should be no military strike unless authorised by the UN Security Council'; British Cabinet minister Clare

Short; King Abdullah of Jordan; Malcolm Harper, Director of the British United Nations Association; President Chirac of France; Chancellor Schroeder of Germany; and even the leader of the Supreme Council for Islamic Resistance in Iraq (SCIRI), the most effective opposition guerrilla group in Iraq, who has warned the United States 'not to take military action against Saddam Hussein without United Nations approval.'[23] The Kuwaiti Defence Minister, Sheikh Jaber al-Hamad al-Sabah, has signalled his Government's opposition to a US war on Iraq by calling for a new Resolution: 'Kuwait does not support threats to hit Iraq or to launch an attack against it. Our acceptance for this matter is conditional on an international blanket decision within the global organisation.'[24]

Despite such calls, a 'Washington source' said in July 2002 that Britain and the US were both opposed to seeking a new UN Resolution to justify an attack on Iraq.[25] In fact, there are complex divisions on the British side. The Prime Minister is 'believed to have urged caution, seeking action under UN resolutions' – perhaps a new Resolution – during his meeting with President Bush in Crawford in April 2002.[26] On the other hand, 'Sources close to Jack Straw, the Foreign Secretary, favour going back to the UN, but Mr Blair's advisers take a more hawkish view.'[27]

Whatever his position may have been before and during the Crawford conference in April 2002, Mr Blair has since made it clear that he would refuse to commit Britain to seeking a fresh UN mandate before any escalation of military action against Iraq.[28] 'British sources believe a return to the UN for a specific mandate for military action would end in failure, largely due to Russian opposition.'[29] Perhaps it was a similar fear that led the Soviet Union not to seek UN authorisation for its invasion of Afghanistan in 1979.

THE OBJECTIVE SOUGHT

The war is directed primarily at the overthrow of Saddam Hussein. As Mr Bush said at the Crawford war conference with Mr Blair in April 2002, 'I explained to the prime minister that the policy of my government is the removal of Saddam and that all options are open.'[30] This objective is not mentioned in either Resolution 678 or Resolution 687. An invasion directed to the overthrow of a political leader cannot be justified by Resolutions which are concerned with reversing an illegal occupation or maintaining an internationally-validated disarmament process.

It has not been stated by the Security Council, let alone proved, that the continued rule of Saddam Hussein constitutes a threat to international peace. It is therefore difficult to see how the proposed war can be consistent with the UN Charter.

IMMEDIACY AND REMOTENESS

British Defence Secretary Geoff Hoon has said that a war against Iraq would be legally justified, 'Not least because those weapons of mass destruction might well be capable of posing a threat to the United Kingdom, in which case we would be entitled to act in self-defence.'[31] Ann Widdecombe, the former Conservative Minister, has said, 'If Saddam is stockpiling weapons of mass destruction, it is not vengeance, but self-defence to stop him.'[32] Richard Haas, Director of Policy Planning in the State Department, has said of the intended assault on Iraq, 'We'd be able to make the case that this isn't a discretionary action, but one done in self-defence.'[33]

Three points suggest themselves immediately. Is there legally watertight evidence that Iraq possesses weapons of mass destruction? The available evidence at the time of writing is that there is not only an absence of evidence; there is little conviction even among those pressing for war. Notice the conditional nature of the comments by Mr Hoon and Ms Widdecombe. Secondly, is there legally watertight evidence of an Iraqi intent to use whatever weapons it possesses on the United States or Britain (or on one of their allies)? Few adults would accept a child's explanation that it was necessary to attack another child simply because they might be 'stockpiling' a knife or a stick. It is not a legal justification, as you conspire to attack someone in cold blood, to allege that your intended victim may possess weapons which they may or may not use against you at some unknown point in the future.

In the present circumstances, there is no hard evidence that the weapons exist, and there is no evidence of an intention to use such weapons against the United States or Britain at some time in the future. Congressperson Henry Hyde, chair of the House International Relations Committee, and a senior Republican, said in mid-2002, 'You hit the other guy first, but only if you know he's going to hit you.'[34]

According to Professor Warbrick, the self-defence argument is 'too remote' because Washington could not convincingly portray Iraq's alleged weapons of mass destruction as an immediate threat.[35] The Security Council is not above international law. A World Court judge once observed, 'one only has to state the proposition thus – that a Security Council resolution may even require participation in genocide – for its unacceptability to be apparent'.[36] The Geneva Conventions define the legal principle of 'proportionality' as prohibiting any attack which may be expected to cause incidental loss of civilian life, injury to civilians, or damage to civilian objects 'which would be excessive in relation to the concrete and direct military advantage anticipated.' The authoritative legal commentary on the laws of war states:

> A remote [military] advantage to be gained at some unknown time in the future would not be a proper consideration to weigh against civilian loss... The advantage concerned should be substantial and relatively close... There can be no question of creating conditions conducive to surrender by means of attacks which incidentally harm the civilian population.[37]

No military action in modern times better fits the description 'a remote advantage to be gained at some unknown time in the future' than President Bush's much-proclaimed war against Iraq.

REASON 7
Ring Of Anger

Iraq's Neighbours Fear Bush, Not Saddam

In the spring of 2002, the British Foreign Secretary Jack Straw said, 'The whole world has made a decision that Iraq poses a very serious threat to the security of the region and to the security of the world.'[1] In reality, the world has made a decision that it is the United States that poses a threat to regional security.

IRAQ'S NEIGHBOURS

Iraq has borders with Saudi Arabia, Jordan, Syria, Turkey, Iran, and Kuwait. Are these countries in fear of Iraqi weapons of mass destruction, and ready to support a war on Iraq? Crown Prince Abdullah, the effective ruler of Saudi Arabia, referred to the proposed US war on Iraq a few days after Mr Straw's bold claim. The Crown Prince said, 'I do not believe it is in the United States' interests, or the interests of the region, or the world's interest'. Earlier, Prince Abdullah had told Thomas Friedman, Diplomatic Correspondent of the *New York Times*, 'Any attack on Iraq or Iran should not be contemplated at all because it would not serve the interests of America, the region or the world, as there is no clear evidence of a present danger. Iraq is contemplating the return of the inspectors, and the U.S. should pursue this because inspectors can determine if Iraq is complying with the UN resolutions.' The message was reinforced at the Arab Summit in March 2002, when 'Live television pictures beamed back to Iraq from the Beirut summit showed a public display of harmony and reconciliation, with Crown Prince Abdullah of Saudi Arabia embracing and kissing Iraqi delegation head Ezzat Ibrahim.' This is not a recent phenomenon. The Saudi Arabian defence minister, Prince Sultan bin Abdulaziz, expressed Saudi Arabia's opposition to an attack on the Iraqi people during the crisis of February 1998. Saudi dissent is motivated in part by domestic pressure from a population hostile to the Western troops stationed in the kingdom. In November 2001, senior Foreign Office advisers were reported to be concerned that 'the real cancer in the Middle East' was not Afghanistan but Saudi

Arabia, where there is now a 'real prospect of a coup.' Apart from domestic anxieties, the Saudis remain anxious about the regional situation: 'Despite their dislike of Saddam Hussein, they are unlikely to feel comfortable with any scenario in which Iraq is destabilised enough to allow powerful neighbours like Iran or Turkey to extend their influence.'[2]

To the north, King Abdullah of Jordan said that, 'striking Iraq represents a catastrophe to Iraq and the region in general, and threatens the security and stability of the region.' British newspapers reported in July 2002 that Jordan had agreed to host US forces during a war on Iraq, a claim bitterly denied by the Jordanian Government. Hashem Gharaybeh, head of the Jordanian Council of Professional Associations, expressed the astonishment of middle class Jordanians: 'It is inconceivable even to speak of such a thing.' Adnan Abu-Odeh, a political adviser to the late King Hussein during the crisis of 1990–1991, notes, 'The whole atmosphere is different now from in 1990. In 1990 blood was on the ground. The Iraqi army was in Kuwait and the whole world wanted to do something. Now only one country wants to try to do something about Iraq. Iraq has been under siege for 12 years, and Arabs are also much more disaffected with America than they were in 1990, because of the Palestinian issue.' The powerful Islamist movement has declared a boycott of US businesses in Jordan, forcing branches of McDonalds and Burger King to lay off staff, and even highly westernised families have given up Coca-Cola. The Secretary-General of the Islamic Action Front said that if the Jordanian Government were to host US forces, 'it will be very dangerous, and no one can predict what the outcome will be. Such an immoral decision will definitely stir strong reactions.' The authorities have insisted that Jordan is opposed to the overthrow of the Iraqi Government, 'and is determined to remain strictly neutral in the event of a future US-led action against its neighbour.'[3]

Even in Kuwait, in July 2002, Muhammed al-Sabah, the foreign minister, told a local newspaper 'that US troops stationed in the emirate were there solely to defend Kuwait's sovereignty and not as a offensive force against Iraq.' This is very unlikely to be true, but it may be a reflection of the deep hostility felt in the tiny state. An opinion poll in March 2002 found 'more than 40 per cent of its citizens are hostile to Washington's policies.' That same month, an agreement between Iraq and Kuwait was negotiated on the sidelines of the Arab League summit, and endorsed in a 'Beirut Declaration' issued by the summit that welcomed 'Iraq's confirmation to respect the independence, sovereignty and security of the state of Kuwait and guarantee its safety and unity to avoid anything that might cause a repetition of what happened in 1990'. Speaking on his return to Kuwait City, Kuwaiti Foreign Minister Sheikh Sabah al-Ahmed al-Sabah said he was completely satisfied with the agreement with Iraq . Kuwait seems to be facing two ways. On the one hand, Kuwait has apparently provided bases for the US to launch a war against Iraq; on the other the emirate has also been making friendly gestures to the Iraqis, one outcome of which was Baghdad's agreement to return Kuwait's entire official archives, seized in 1990. In July 2002, as we have seen, the Kuwaiti Defence Minister explained that, 'Kuwait does not support threats to hit Iraq or to launch an attack against it. Our acceptance for this matter is conditional on an international blanket decision within the global organisation.'[4]

Returning to the north, Syria was reportedly 'infuriated' by a CIA survey of airfields in northern Iraq. Damascus and Tehran are both apparently 'concerned that an American attack on Iraq will endanger their own security.' The Iranian President, Mohammad Khatami, has said, 'We wish to caution the great powers against further interfernce in the region and against the exacerbation of the flames of war. No one has the right to decide for the people of Iraq. The people of Iraq should decide for themselves'. The President said Iran condemned any 'foreign interference' in Iraq.[5]

Turkey's Prime Minister Bulent Ecevit called the threat of a US attack on Iraq a 'nightmare'. He said, 'We feel that Iraq should not be the subject of military attacks because it would upset the whole Middle East.' Mr Ecevit 'argued that Saddam Hussein did not constitute a threat to his neighbours.' Mr Ecevit's ill health, and the prospect of early elections, precipitated a political crisis which might yet lead to difficulties for Washington. The US had judged that despite deep reluctance Turkey would finally acquiesce in the use of its bases for an assault on Iraq. Then Mr Ecevit's illness brought on the collapse of the ruling coalition. The political crisis opens the way for an Islamic party to gain entry into government in the November 2002 elections – which would leave the US 'highly concerned', according to the *Financial Times*. The Islamic 'Justice and Development Party' has the support of nearly a fifth of voters in polls, nearly double that of any other party, and could theoretically win all the seats in parliament. The crisis could also lead to the US having to lend Ankara $18 billion to replace an IMF loan (Turkey is the IMF's largest borrower) in order to cement Turkish support for the war. The mid-July 2002 visit by US Deputy Defence Secretary Paul Wolfowitz, in which he met Mr Ecevit, now a lame duck Prime Minister, in order to gain 'perspectives' on Turkish attitudes to the war on Iraq, seems rather forlorn in the circumstances.[6]

The United States' main friends in the region – Turkey and Saudi Arabia – have been the most outspoken of Iraq's neighbours in opposing a US-led assault on Iraq. Any large-scale US military operation against Iraq would depend on access to bases in Saudi Arabia, Turkey or Kuwait 'and all three countries remain anxious over the impact of an Iraqi campaign on their security and internal security.'[7]

WIDER OPINION

Editorials in Gulf newspapers have 'uniformly condemned any assault on Iraq.' US Vice-President Dick Cheney's tour of the Middle East in March 2002, designed to mobilise support for a war on Iraq, was an abject failure. The *Independent* observed, 'Rarely can an American vice-president have met such a rebuff from America's Arab allies. Not a single Arab king, prince or president has been prepared to endorse a US attack on Iraq. Even the small United Arab Emirates had no time for the Cheney argument.' 'One Arab leader after another urged the US not to mount a direct attack against Iraq.' They emphasised that the Israeli-Palestinian crisis was more serious and should take priority. Egyptian President Hosni Mubarak stressed 'the sovereignty of Iraq is a must for regional stability', 'which appeared to throw cold water on any fast-track US plan to overthrow the Iraqi leader.'[8]

The *Economist* described the position of Arab leaders: 'In 1990, they feared what Mr Hussein might do next if he were allowed to swallow Kuwait. This time they seem more frightened about the possible anti-American reaction on their own streets.' For all these countries, the Israel-Palestine conflict has much greater urgency than the murky possibility that Iraq might possess weapons of mass destruction. The *Financial Times* observed in March 2002 that the US believes the question of Iraq can be divorced from the other crisis in the region; the Arab-Israeli conflict can be contained; and the region's authoritarian regimes can suppress popular opposition to a campaign against Baghdad. The *FT* suggested, 'That is doubtful.' According to one analysis, the debate within the Bush Administration over Palestine has resulted in a new synthesis: 'The President has concluded that, far from being the key to peace, Palestine is a lock without a key. It must be forced open by other changes. Mr Bush believes that the key to opening a door to peace is to be found well to the east of Palestine.' The overthrow of Saddam will encourage 'moderates' in the Middle East (those willing to accommodate to US power, in other words), and create for the first time the opportunity for an Arab-Israeli peace.[9] The President seeks to effect total Arab despair and surrender in the face of overwhelming force, and a collapse of all resistance.

According to the *Daily Telegraph*, 'Even Israel, which was the victim of 40 Iraqi Scud missiles during the Gulf War, does not seem keen on America taking on Saddam. It maintains that Iran poses a far greater and more immediate danger.' In April 1992, General Amnon Shahak-Lipkin, soon to become Chief of Staff of the Israeli Army, expressed his preference for 'a boycotted Iraq with Saddam' over 'an Iraq without Saddam again supported by the entire world'.[10] Israel has no particular interest in a US war on Iraq. The central goal of Israeli policy for many years has been to try to trigger a US assault on Iran, which remains a powerful and unruined counter-force.

Kofi Annan, Secretary-General of the United Nations, said in February 2002, 'I am on record as saying any attack on Iraq at this stage would be unwise,' a statement he repeated in August 2002. Romano Prodi, President of the European Commission echoed this concern: 'My position is one of deep worry about a possible attack on Iraq because of the potential expansion of the conflict.'[11] Germany, France and even Italy have all signalled their hostility to the war, as have Russia and China, the remaining permanent members of the UN Security Council.

Jack Straw may choose to believe that the world has made a decision that 'Iraq poses a very serious threat to the security of the region and to the security of the world.' The facts are otherwise. There is deep scepticism about the alleged Iraqi 'threat', and there is great fear of the consequences of US violence. There is a ring of anger around Iraq, but it is burning against Washington, not Baghdad.

REASON 8
GI Joe Says No

US And British Generals Oppose The War

'PACIFIST' GENERALS, 1991

In 1990, during the build-up of US forces in the Gulf preparatory to the war on Iraq, General Norman Schwarzkopf was interviewed by *Life* magazine. The head of the US-led forces in the Gulf said, 'In a lot of ways I am a pacifist – though that might be too strong a word. But I know what war is. I am certainly anti-war. But I also believe that there are things worth fighting for.' According to veteran US journalist Bob Woodward, in 1990 General Schwarzkopf told General Colin Powell, the head of the US Joint Chiefs of Staff that, 'he was not sold on an offensive operation as the solution' to the occupation of Kuwait. Pushing Saddam out of Kuwait at this point would be dirty and bloody. 'Do they know that back in Washington?' Back in Washington were the civilian politicians, who did not know 'what war is'. General Schwarzkopf gave an interview in October 1990 in which he said, 'Now we are starting to see evidence that the sanctions are pinching. So why should we say, "Okay, gave'em two months, didn't work. Let's get on with it and kill a whole bunch of people?" That's crazy. That's crazy.' The general continued by describing how, in Vietnam, the United States would pound villages from the air and nevertheless find determined Vietnamese fighters rising out of their holes when US troops entered the area. 'War is a profanity because, let's face it, you've got two opposing sides trying to settle their differences by killing as many of each other as they can,' said the commander-in-chief.[1]

General Schwarzkopf was not the only military officer with doubts about going to war with Iraq. At the end of September 1990, the top military officer in the US Armed Forces, General Colin Powell lobbied his civilian superiors to consider allowing sanctions to work for a longer period. In early October, he personally presented the case for sanctions rather than war to President George Bush Sr: 'There is a case here for the containment or strangulation policy ... This is an option that has merit. It will work some day. It may take a year, it may take two years, but it will work some day.'[2]

The civilian leadership rebuffed the advice of the military professionals and the war was fought.

'PACIFIST' GENERALS, 2002

The idea of a major assault on Iraq was proposed at the highest levels of the US Government on the day after 11 September. US Defence Secretary Donald Rumsfeld asked President Bush 'Why shouldn't we go against Iraq, not just al Qaeda?' General Colin Powell, now US Secretary of State, 'countered that they were focused on al Qaeda because the American people were focused on al Qaeda, and the president agreed,' according to the *Washington Post*. 'Bush made it clear it was not the time to resolve the issue.'[3] From that moment on, a contest began between the war clique and the military professionals, a contest similar to that played out in 1990, but at a much higher level of intensity.

On one side were the civilian politicians such as Mr Rumsfeld, his deputy Paul Wolfowitz, and Vice-President Dick Cheney. On the other were the Joint Chiefs of Staff and the State Department led by Colin Powell. Edward Luttwak, senior adviser at the Centre for Strategic and International Studies in Washington, points out that 'Ever since the trauma of Vietnam, and as late as the Kosovo war in 1999, the persistent opposition of military chiefs to almost any combat that risked casualties compelled the State Department to become the leading advocate of military action ... Paradoxically, it is the former soldier Powell who has now re-established the proper role of the secretary of state as the advocate of diplomatic solutions.'[4] From another point of view, General Powell is simply demonstrating the resistance of military professionals to the reckless use of force. The conflict within the Administration could be seen as one between adventurist civilians, who sit thousands of miles from the conflict, and the Vietnam veterans who know 'what war is'. Curiously, as early as November 2001 there was speculation that another war veteran was advising the President to take the cautious path – President George Bush Sr.[5]

THE HAWKS

The early debate spilled out into public view, with Paul Wolfowitz stating within a week of 11 September that the 'war on terrorism' would include 'ending states who sponsor terrorism'.[6] Mr Wolfowitz was then reined in as the Administration prepared for the onslaught against Afghanistan. Mr Wolfowitz continued to be influential, however, through his sponsors Donald Rumsfeld and Dick Cheney. Pentagon insiders said in late September 2001 that 'it would be hard to underestimate Mr Wolfowitz's influence. Apart from Mr Rumsfeld, he is the only defence official trusted to speak to the press about the current operation.'[7] Curiously, in the autumn of 1990, Mr Wolfowitz had been somewhat agnostic on the subject of military action. Pressed by General Powell, the then Under Secretary for Policy stated that containment by sanctions was a defensible position – if sanctions were indefinite. 'Wolfowitz said he thought it was a hard call; probably 55 per cent of the merit was for one side, 45 per cent for the other.'[8]

Another critical player in the debate for many months was the Iraqi National Congress (INC), an umbrella group for a bewildering variety of Iraqi oppositionists. The INC had strong links with the US Congress, which resulted in the Iraq Liberation Act of October 1998, authorising the expenditure of $97 million to overthrow the Iraqi Government. The INC had built a relationship with the Wolfowitz clique based on their shared desire for a military defeat of the Baghdad regime. Drawing on advice from US Special Forces General Wayne Downing, the INC drew up an imaginative war plan. Revised after 11 September, the plan called for:

(1) military training and arms for 5,000 Iraqi dissidents,
(2) an invasion of southern Iraq by this force (supported by thousands of US Special Forces troops and some mercenaries),
(3) the declaration by the US of a 'no-drive' zone in southern Iraq, banning the movement of Iraqi tanks and armoured vehicles, to protect the invasion force,
(4) support and participation from Iran,
(5) an uprising by Shi'ites in the south, and
(6) preparations for attack by Kurdish groups in the north of Iraq.

According to investigative journalist Seymour Hersh, 'If all went as planned, dissent would quickly break out inside the Iraqi military, and Saddam Hussein would be confronted with a dilemma: whether to send his elite forces south to engage the Americans or, for his own protection, keep all his forces nearby to guard against an invasion from the north.'[9] The whole purpose of this strategy was to provoke a retaliation from Baghdad's heavy armour. A US adviser to the INC (General Downing, one presumes) told Mr Hersh that success depended on tempting an Iraqi military response: 'if he doesn't come, you go home and say we failed.' On the other hand, if the Iraqi tanks did come, they would be destroyed by US airpower. The fall-back position would be, if the tanks didn't come, but the INC managed to capture Basra, then 'that's the end. You don't have to go to Baghdad. You tie up his oil and he'll collapse.'[10] (The consequences for the humanitarian oil-for-food programme of ending the sale of oil for an extended period do not seem to receive a great deal of consideration.)

The Downing plan was then augmented and modified by a Pentagon planning group on the orders of Deputy Defence Secretary Paul Wolfowitz, and sent to the US Joint Chiefs of Staff (JCS) for evaluation. The JCS ordered their staff to come up with a counter-proposal – one that did *not* involve the INC – but that might involve Kurdish opposition groups in northern Iraq. A US Air Force consultant said, 'Everything is going to happen inside Iraq, and Chalabi is going to be on the outside.'[11]

THE BAY OF GOATS

The JCS's professional assessment is that a major war would be required to ensure the overthrow of the current regime. One JCS study suggests putting 50,000 US troops on Iraq's southern border; another 50,000 US troops on its northern border; then sending the two forces toward Baghdad in the middle. 'But planners doubt that even that force would be enough to take Baghdad.'[12] Just days before 11 September, Lieutenant General Paul Mikolashek, commander of US ground forces in the region, estimated that to take Baghdad and overthrow the regime would require forces 'at least at the level' of Desert Storm in 1991 – when around 169,000 US combat troops were deployed (along with twice that number of support troops). *Time* magazine reported that a classified study (perhaps the report containing the Mikolashek estimate just mentioned) 'has just concluded that absent a long war – of the sort the World War II Allies fought against Germany and Japan – it is almost impossible for a military intervention from outside to impose changes that stick' in Iraq.[13] The civilians have not taken kindly to this advice. A former government official told Seymour Hersh, 'These guys are being squeezed so hard.' *Newsweek* reports that the JCS have been 'under heavy political pressure'.[14] The hawks want a less costly war plan. The least costly option is simply to offer air support to an indigenous rebel force, as in Afghanistan. However, as noted earlier, a 'senior Administration official' told Seymour Hersh that the Administration had no intention of allowing 'a bunch of half-assed people to send foreigners into combat'. Of Chalabi and his supporters in and out of government, the senior official, almost certainly Colin Powell, said, 'Who among them has ever smelled cordite? These are pissants who can't get the President's ear and have to blame someone else. We're not going to let them lead others down the garden path.'[15]

US Marine Corps General Anthony Zinni, then the outgoing chief of US Central Command, later President Bush's special envoy to the Middle East, wrote in the *United States Naval Institute Proceedings* in 2001 that it would take a great deal to 'drive a stake' through the heart of someone like Saddam Hussein:

> You must have the political will – and that means the will of the administration, the Congress, and the American people. All must be united in a desire for action. Instead, however, we try to get results on the cheap. There are congressmen today who want to fund the Iraqi Liberation Act, and let some silk-suited, Rolex-wearing guys in London gin up an expedition.
>
> We'll equip a thousand fighters and arm them with ninety-seven million dollars' worth of AK-47s and insert them into Iraq.
>
> And what will we have? A Bay of Goats, most likely.[16]

The Bay of Pigs invasion of Cuba remains one of the most embarassing failures of the United States military in the postwar era.

THE GENERALS SABOTAGE THE PLAN

According to Mr Chalabi, 'The people who are opposed – the way they are trying to screw it up is by taking control of how to do it.'[17] Much of the tension, as in 1990, has revolved around force levels. In October 1990, General Schwarzkopf was instructed to draw up plans for driving Iraq out of Kuwait with the 200,000 troops he then had under his command. He responded that this was not possible. He was instructed once again to draw up a strategy. When he presented the resulting plan, he later revealed, it was immediately followed by a statement which said: 'That is not what the commander in chief of Central Command is recommending. It is a weak plan and it is not a plan we choose to execute. And here are the things that are wrong with it: A, B, C, D, E, F, G, H, I, J, and a lot more ... and if, in fact, we are serious about ejecting them from Kuwait what we need is more forces to be able to execute a proper campaign.'[18] All the signs are that a very similar dynamic has been at work since December 2001, with civilian superiors instructing the generals to draw up plans which they do not believe in. At the time of writing, it appears that the generals may have succumbed.

THE AFGHAN MODEL

The ideal is a plan that can meet what has been described as 'the Afghan test': 'a low-cost, speedy assault that has a high probability of toppling President Saddam Hussein.'[19] President Bush is caught between two imperatives. His State of the Union speech in January 2001, and his subsequent remarks, have committed him to taking action to overthrow Saddam Hussein before the end of his term of office – before the end of 2003 in reality, as that is when the President's re-election campaign will begin. On the other hand, as Geoffrey Kemp, formerly a member of President Reagan's National Security Council, puts it, 'Bush cannot embark on a mission that fails. Given what happened to his father, and the hype in this Administration, it would be the end.'[20]

One possibility was to follow the Afghan route, relying on local opposition forces supported by US airpower, essentially the INC strategy. The generals' position has been to favour instead a long-standing invasion plan that calls for a force of 200,000 troops to be assembled over a period of up to three months. The intermediate option (and therefore the most likely plan) would be 'a comparatively compact assault on Baghdad by three divisions comprising 50,000 troops who could be deployed in weeks'.[21]

The 'Afghan model' of supporting an indigenous uprising is 'superficially seductive' for the President, as an *FT* columnist points out. From a US point of view, it would deal with Saddam Hussein 'at minimum risk to American forces.'[22] But US generals believe that any comparison between Iraq and Afghanistan is naive. The Iraqi opposition is 'fragmented, largely untested, and faced with an Iraqi army much larger and more sophisticated than the one the Northern Alliance helped vanquish in Afghanistan.' In Afghanistan, the military balance between the opposition and the Taliban was 'quite close', according to Kenneth Pollack, former Deputy Director of the US National Security Council (1999–2001), 'which is why US actions were able to tip the scales decisively'. In Iraq, however, 'the gap in capabilities between the regime and the opposition is much wider.'[23]

According to Pollack, 'If the United States were to provide the Kurds with weapons, training, funds, and massive air support, at some point they would probably be able to hold their territory against an Iraqi assault – but even then they would have great difficulty translating such a defensive capability into the offensive power needed to overthrow Saddam.'[24] According to Judith Yaphe, who was for twenty years the senior analyst for Middle Eastern and Persian Gulf issues within the CIA Directorate of Intelligence, the idea of defeating Baghdad through the Iraqi opposition movements is 'a dream': 'It's going to be 99% American effort.'[25]

This was accepted by the INC in March 2002. The umbrella group acknowledged then that, 'Whatever we do we will be marginalised in the actual regime change.' The coalition foresaw a political rather than a military role for itself.[26] General Downing, author of the INC war plan, held on in his post as anti-terrorism adviser to President Bush until the end of June 2002 when he finally resigned – 'a blow to those arguing for Saddam to be tackled sooner rather than later.'[27]

However, the exclusion of the INC is not exactly the same as the abandonment of the Afghan model. The CIA has apparently been trying to form a separate axis involving four opposition groups who are considered to have significant military capacties, the so-called 'Gang of Four': the Patriotic Union of Kurdistan (PUK), the Kurdish Democratic Party (KDP), the Supreme Council for Islamic Revolution in Iraq (SCIRI), and the Iraqi National Accord (INA). There have been difficulties in recruiting all these groups, quite apart from the feasibility of the plan.

QUICK STRIKE

Another problem for the Afghan model is that according to one US military source, the only way to convince wavering allies of American resolve is to put a column of US Army tanks on the road to Baghdad: 'Once Bush's prestige is on the line, and there is no going back, then a call to rebellion stands a reasonable chance of success. It doesn't matter very much how many tanks we send – it's the symbolism that counts.' According to this source, a force of 40,000 to 50,000 troops could be on the ground in Iraq within a month.[28] Later versions of this option have ranged up to 80,000 troops.

This medium-sized force could be assembled on US aircraft carriers and in Kuwait, without having to force unwilling allies in the region to provide bases. It could also be built up faster, lessening the opportunities for international opposition to develop. 'A force of three American divisions – one airborne, one mechanised and one marine – could strike swiftly at Baghdad, possibly provoking an immediate coup'.[29] By July 2002, such planning had evolved into the concept of marshalling 50,000 troops at the Kuwaiti border in roughly a week, airlifting them in, and bringing in their tanks and heavy equipment on ships through the Strait of Hormuz. 'We could have a situation where on Monday, it first looks like there will be a war, on Friday troops are in Kuwait, and by [the next] Thursday they're in Baghdad,' according to John Pike, a defense analyst in Washington.[30]

This has several advantages for the US. It would give Baghdad just a few days' notice, rather than the six months it took for US forces to slowly build up before the 1991 war. A quick strike could also eliminate any need to rely on bases in neighbouring countries like Saudi Arabia or Jordan, whose governments are hostile to the invasion, and extremely reluctant to be involved. A lightning attack could also minimise the risk of plunging the Middle East into chaos. US planners also apparently believe they would have 48 hours 'to find and kill or capture Saddam' before he tried to deploy any nuclear, biological or chemical weapons he may have.[31]

The main flaw, however, is that, as Associated Press reports, 'Such a surprise attack also might fall short of the main goal of toppling Saddam, requiring a backup plan involving thousands more American troops.'[32] Kenneth Pollack points out that in 1991 the US hit some Republican Guard divisions with more than 1,000 bombing raids each, using up twice as many precision-guided missiles as were used in Afghanistan in 2001. 'But the key Iraqi divisions never broke and fought hard, although not particularly well, during the coalition's subsequent ground campaign.' If the elite forces retain these qualities, they could survive and quell any rebellion, Pollack suggests.[33]

THE GENERALS SABOTAGE THE WAR

So we return to the upper end of the intervention spectrum. Another reason for looking at large numbers of US troops is the political signal they give. While it was suggested earlier that the number of US tanks heading to Baghdad was immaterial, Kenneth Pollack says that a high-ranking official from a Gulf state told him, 'when you are ready to use all of your forces, we will be there for you, but we're not interested in letting you try out theories about air power.'[34] The head of the Middle East Institute in Washington DC, Edward Walker says, 'Allies have to know that the US Administration really means it this time, or no one will stick his neck out.' The United States must show it is willing to accept serious US casualties if necessary.[35] The President and his inner circle are clearly nervous of such a possibility. They may not take much comfort from a press report that a 1999 study by the 'Triangle Institute for Security Studies' 'showed that the [US] public would tolerate thirty thousand deaths in a military operation to prevent Iraq from acquiring weapons of mass destruction.' 58,000 US soldiers were killed in the Vietnam War.[36]

The 200,000 troop scenario also has problems, some of which were hinted at earlier. 'The Iraqis aren't just going to sit on their butts while we put in 250,000 people,' one military analyst told the *New York Times*.[37] Furthermore, 'By the time that the US invasion force was ready, the region could already be embroiled in conflict.'[38] The political costs of a slow deployment of troops could be huge: the process maximises the opportunities for political unrest in the Middle East, in Europe and back home in the US. 'Those suggesting it, their opponents argue, are doing so for tactical reasons, and really want nothing to happen.'[39] Hence Mr Chalabi's complaint that the people opposed to the war are trying to 'screw it up' by taking control of how to do it.

Having rumbled away in the background for months, the debate sprang onto the front pages on 24 May 2002, when the *Washington Post* published a report under the headline 'Military Bids to Postpone Iraq Invasion': 'The uniformed leaders of the US military believe they have persuaded the Pentagon's civilian leadership to put off an invasion of Iraq until next year at the earliest and perhaps not to do it at all, according to senior Pentagon officials.' A top general said he thought that the 'Iraq hysteria' he had detected last winter in some senior Bush officials had been diffused.

NIGHTMARE SCENARIOS

The generals identified three particular concerns, one political, the other two broadly military. The political concern discussed in the *Post* centred on some of the Chiefs' 'misgivings about the wisdom of dislodging an aging, weakened Hussein who, by some accounts, has behaved better than usual in recent months': 'Their worry is that there is no evidence that there is a clear successor who is any better, and that there are significant risks that Iraq may wind up with a more hostile, activist regime.' The wrong kind of regime change, in other words.[40]

As for the other issues, one of them revolves around Iraq's suspected weapons of mass destruction, already alluded to. In the event of a US invasion designed to kill him, there would be absolutely no incentive for Saddam Hussein to refrain from the use of whatever weapons of mass destruction he may possess. According to John Pike of GlobalSecurity.org, speaking in March 2002, 'Pentagon planners are having a very hard time coming up with a workable plan which does not include chemical or biological weapons versus Israel',[41] with all the upheaval that would follow – including almost certain Israeli nuclear retaliation.

Another military nightmare scenario involves having to fight block-by-block through Baghdad. 'That's when it could get messy', a senior Ministry of Defence official has said.[42] If there were a guerrilla resistance by Iraqi forces, US casualties could be in the hundreds, perhaps the thousands, according to former US Marine Scott Ritter. Iraqi deaths could be in the tens of thousands.[43]

These are the some of the motivations for the military resistance to civilian war plans. According to *Time* magazine, 'Senior Administration officials at the highest levels of planning say there are few good options.'[44] In March 2002, the Republican chair of the Senate Foreign Relations Committee, Joseph Biden, spoke of 'incredible division' in the heart of the Administration as to Iraq, 'And that is before anyone has come up with a convincing blueprint for a post-Saddam Iraq.'[45] Leaks and counter-leaks continue to plague the Administration. *Time* magazine comments, 'For all the tough talk along the Potomac, the only war now being waged is the one involving the White House, State Department and Pentagon over how and when to move against Saddam Hussein.'[46] The Foreign Editor for the *Times* newspaper, Bronwen Maddox, observed acidly in March 2002, 'Both Bush and Cheney showed that, for the moment, sound and fury is the preferred weapon against potential enemies.'[47]

BRITISH GENERALS

In the middle of March 2002, the *Observer* reported, 'Britain's military leaders issued a stark warning to Tony Blair last night that any war against Iraq is doomed to fail and would lead to the loss of life for little political gain.' The senior officers 'urged "extreme caution" over any moves to war, saying servicemen faced being bogged down in a perilous open-ended commitment.' Claiming that the Government had yet to give any clear political direction over committing troops, the *Observer*'s sources warned that Arab countries were likely to rebel over any Western assault on Iraq in the absence of a Middle East peace deal. Furthermore, 'Senior armed forces figures will warn the Prime Minister this week that without a leader-in-waiting to take over from Saddam, there is little chance of any successful move to overthrow the Iraqi dictator.'[48]

A few days earlier, another high-ranking official had warned that in the absence of any set objective, without territorial targets or an identified range of targets, and with only Kuwait offering bases, 'Given these uncertainties, conditions are nowhere near right to plan a military campaign.' The official added, 'You have to build a case publicly and legally. That has not yet been done.'[49] The *Financial Times* added, 'Defence chiefs in London – and some in the Pentagon – are concerned about an open-ended commitment without a clear exit strategy, about logistical problems if Arab states do not cooperate, and about the danger of relying on a divided opposition.'[50] As in the US, British military leaders have more than simply narrow military concerns.

After their earlier warnings failed to make a dent in the Prime Minister's determination, top British military officials used another standard device, voicing their concerns through retired officers such as former Chief of Defence Staff Field Marshal Lord Bramall, who warned that invading Iraq would pour 'petrol rather than water' on the flames, providing more recruits for al Qaeda. Lord Bramall extended his critique beyond the practical, saying, 'You're supposed to get UN backing. Some lawyers will say you have that, as Saddam has defied UN resolutions. But I think the moral question is not open and shut.' The Field Marshal drew parallels with the disastrous British invasion of Egypt in 1956.[51] Former head of the SAS, and former chief of UN forces in Bosnia General Sir Michael Rose warned 'The evidence seems to be that we are heading for an assault on Iraq without, on either side of the Atlantic, anything like enough open debate about the moral justification or military practicality of doing so.' Sir Michael advised that British soldiers should not participate in the war without approval from the UN Security Council, and added, 'It is almost designed to create instability and a lack of security. Is that what Bush wants?'[52]

DON'T LEAVE PEACE TO THE GENERALS

It is worth noting, perhaps, that despite his reservations the 'pacifist' General Schwarzkopf did carry out the mission he was ordered to carry out. There is no reason to believe that today's military leadership on either side of the Atlantic will show any greater moral courage. If this invasion is to be halted, it will be by public pressure from civilians as well as military professionals. This is yet another case of war – and peace – being too important to be left to the generals.

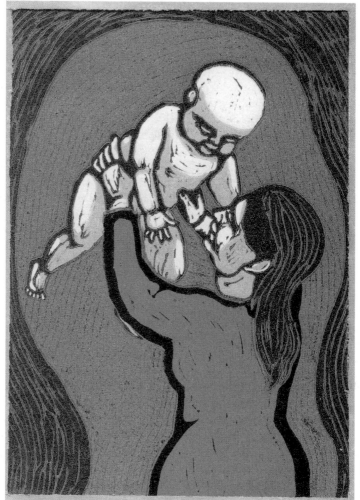

Emily Johns

REASON 9
No Mandate

58% Of UK Opposes War

The Prime Minister 'has been too slow' in preparing British public opinion for the coming conflict with Iraq, *The Times* warned in February 2002: 'He had better start closing the gap now.'[1] The major propaganda initiative coming out of Downing Street, the famously missing 'dossier', stalled before it was launched, and the passing months have not been kind to the war party. In March 2002, Donald Macintyre observed in the *Independent* that there was some unease about the looming war among ministers – not only Robin Cook and Clare Short – 'compounded by fears that public opinion may not be as solid as it was over war in Afghanistan'. Downing Street apparently found these fears 'much exaggerated'.[2] A *Guardian*/ICM poll a week later discovered that these concerns were far from exaggerated. Hugo Young, the *Guardian* columnist, remarked on the 'surprising majority' of respondents opposing war on Iraq: 'All kinds of voices can be heard, as the issue looms into view, which deny the existence of a national consensus for another war.'[3] Quite the reverse, there appears to be an emerging national consensus against another war on Iraq.

Mr Blair was asked a pointed question relating to the *Guardian* poll by NBC television in April 2002: 71 per cent of the British people had supported Mr Blair's response to 11 September earlier; now only 34 per cent of people in Britain supported the idea of going to war on Iraq. The Prime Minister was evasive: 'It is hardly surprising frankly if people are concerned about military action at this present time because we are not suggesting it at this present time.'[4]

In February 1991 and February 1998, *Guardian*/ICM polls found that 80 and 56 per cent of respondents, respectively, were in favour of bombing Iraq.[5] Now the majority of ICM respondents – 51 per cent of those asked – are opposed to military action, an extraordinary turn-around considering the years of demonisation of Saddam Hussein, and the shocking events of 11 September. A *Guardian* editorial in July 2002 suggested that the level of opposition might be higher still.[6] An increase in British opposition to the war had actually been registered in April, in a MORI poll carried out

British public attitudes to war on Iraq

Chart 9.1 51 per cent say no to war

Q. Do you approve or disapprove of British backing for US military action against Iraq?

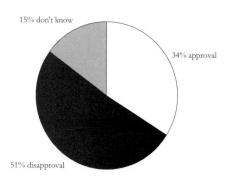

15% don't know

34% approval

51% disapproval

Source: ICM poll,
Guardian, 19 March 2002

Chart 9.2 Should the US go to war?

Q. On balance, do you think the American government would be right or wrong to step up military action in Iraq, the country run by Saddam Hussein?

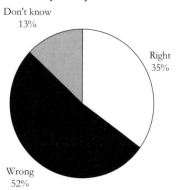

Don't know
13%

Right
35%

Wrong
52%

Source: MORI poll,
Time, 1 April 2002

Chart 9.3 56 per cent say no war on Iraq

Q. On balance, do you think the British government would be right or wrong to join the Americans in stepping up military action in Iraq, the country run by Saddam Hussein?

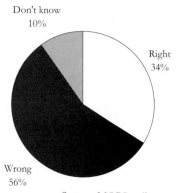

Don't know
10%

Right
34%

Wrong
56%

Source: MORI poll,
Time, 1 April 2002

Chart 9.3 58 per cent say no war on Iraq

Q. Do you think the US under present circumstances would be justified in taking military action against Iraq?

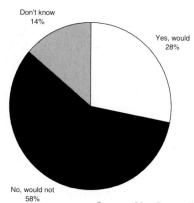

Don't know
14%

Yes, would
28%

No, would not
58%

Source: YouGov poll
Daily Telegraph, 12 August 2002

for *Time* magazine – which found that 56 per cent of British respondents were now opposed to the idea of going to war with Iraq. A YouGov poll in August 2002 for the *Daily Telegraph* found that 58 per cent of respondents did not believe war on Iraq was justified.[7]

There are three other polls to note. Online YouGov polls found that opposition to the war in Britain increased from 43 per cent in March 2002 to 51 per cent in July 2002. Support for war fell by five per cent to 40 per cent, while the proportion of people believing that Mr Blair was the 'puppet' of President Bush grew to 49 per cent of respondents. The later poll found that 51 per cent of those questioned supported action to overthrow Saddam Hussein, so a significant body of opinion – perhaps 10 per cent of the population – may support military or covert action short of war.

The final poll, an NOP poll for Channel 4, came in August 2002, showing that 52 per cent of people questioned in Britain opposed British forces being involved in a war on Iraq, and, once again, that only 34 per cent supported such action.[8]

It is interesting that the July YouGov result is similar to other polls, as YouGov has consistently positioned the Labour Party lower in terms of popularity than other polling organisations. For example, in June 2002, YouGov said that Labour had the support of only 38 per cent of voters, only three points ahead of the Tories. Other polls put Labour ten points ahead. Gallup, MORI, NOP and ICM conduct their polling by telephone – YouGov is online. It has been suggested that the difference in methodology may allow 'quiet Conservatives' to express their views more freely.[9]

Chart 9.5 British public attitudes to war on Iraq - by party affiliation

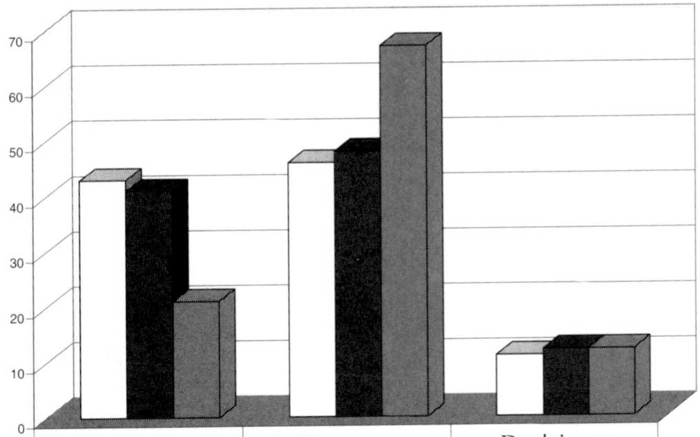

	Approve	Disapprove	Don't know
☐ Labour voters	43	46	11
■ Conservative voters	41	48	12
▦ Liberal Democrat voters	21	67	12

Source: ICM poll, published in the *Guardian,* 19 March 2002

Chart 9.6 British public attitudes towards the Prime Minister's wars
Q. Do you approve or disapprove of the way British Prime Minister Tony Blair is handling the British response to the terrorist attacks on 11 September?

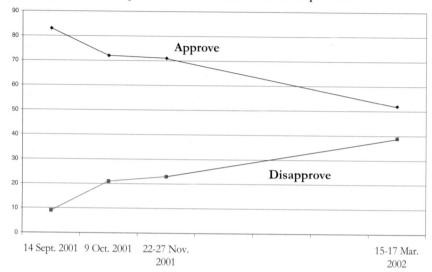

(Source: MORI polls for *The News of the World, The Times, The Mail on Sunday, Time*)

Chart 9.7 British public attitudes towards President Bush's wars
Q. Do you approve or disapprove of the way US President George W. Bush is handling the US response to the terrorist attacks on 11 September?

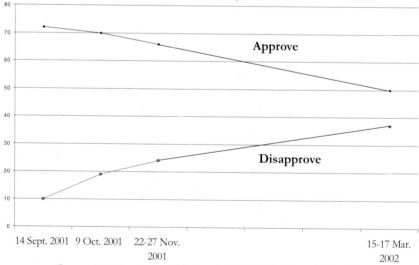

(Source: MORI polls for *The News of the World, The Times, The Mail on Sunday, Time*)

Increasing opposition to war on Iraq was also detected across the Atlantic, with a Gallup poll in November 2001 finding 74 per cent of US respondents in support of sending troops against Iraq, falling to 59 per cent in July 2002. On the other hand, 75 per cent of US respondents supported the idea of a presidential directive to the CIA to use deadly force to overthrow the leadership of Iraq. Strangely, the same poll found that only 54 per cent of US respondents supported official attempts to assassinate Saddam Hussein – a lower figure than for going to war with Iraq.[10]

GREATER TORY OPPOSITION

One of the peculiarities of the groundswell of opposition to the war is that a greater proportion of Conservative voters than Labour voters is opposed to war on Iraq. 48 per cent of Conservative voters are against going to war with Iraq, while 46 per cent of Labour voters feel the same way. A striking 67 per cent of Liberal Democrat voters are hostile to the US-led war drive (see chart 9.4).

Whether it is due to party loyalty to the Blair leadership, a greater degree of hostility to the Baghdad regime in Labour ranks, or an unwillingness to publicly disagree with Downing Street, only a narrow majority of Labour voters is opposed to war on Iraq – 46 per cent opposed, 43 per cent in favour. The margin of opposition is 7 per cent for the Conservatives and 46 per cent for the Liberal Democrats, compared to Labour's 3 per cent.

From another viewpoint, taking the population as a whole, and ignoring the 'don't knows', 60 per cent of people in Britain with an opinion are opposed to war on Iraq.

Chart 9.8 Support for President Bush: The British Gender Gap
Levels of approval among British people of President Bush's response to 11 September – by gender

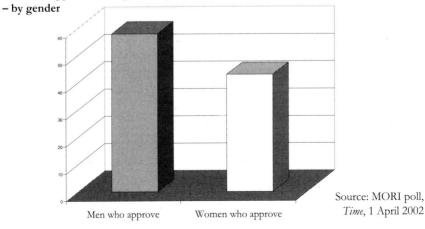

Source: MORI poll, *Time*, 1 April 2002

NOT ANTI-AMERICANISM

Approval rates for President Bush's handling of 11 September was high to begin with (see Chart 9.7). In the MORI poll of April 2002, 52 per cent of British respondents opposed the US Government going to war with Iraq, and only 4 per cent more of them opposed British participation in the war. In other words, it was not that British people were content to let Washington fight the battles and take the risks, while conserving British lives and resources.[11] The August 2002 YouGov poll for the Daily Telegraph complicates the picture, however (see Table 9.2, below).

US QUALMS

The US public are very concerned at the idea of being politically isolated – polls in the US in June and August 2002 found that while more than half of Americans would approve of military action against Iraq if the US wins some allied support, that number shrinks to a minority if the United States had to go it alone.[12] Hence the importance of detaching Britain from the US war effort. In March 2002, one US poll found seven out of ten North Americans preferring only airstrikes, rather than a full-scale invasion.[13] No one should assume that the US public is baying for a major war on Iraq.

Table 9.1 The Poodle Index:
British public attitudes to the Blair Government's support for the US Government
Q. Some people say that in the present crisis, Mr Blair looks increasingly like President Bush's poodle. Do you think that is... ?

Yes, a fair description	54%
No, not a fair description	39%
Don't know	7%

Source: YouGov poll, *Daily Telegraph*, 12 August 2002

Table 9.2 British opposition to military participation in a US war on Iraq
Q. If the US does decide to take military action against Iraq, should the UK... ?

Join the US in taking military action	19%
Support the US diplomatically but not militarily	32%
Distance itself from the US but not condemn it	29%
Condemn the US publicly for taking such action	17%
Don't know	3%

Source: YouGov poll, *Daily Telegraph*, 12 August 2002

REASON 10
It's The Economy, Stupid

War Could Trigger
A World Recession

A POLITICAL INHERITANCE

In February 1991, President George Bush Sr. won the Gulf War against Iraq. In November 1992, President George Bush Sr. lost the election against Bill Clinton. The glow of military victory had faded, and a tide of economic difficulties had eroded the President's public support. As the Clinton team summarised their campaign theme, 'It's the economy, stupid.' This stark reversal is the political inheritance of the present President.

CRISIS AND OIL PRICES

On 5 April 2002, Iranian supreme leader Ayatollah Ali Khamenei called for a symbolic one-month oil embargo against countries which support Israel, in order to protest against Israel's brutal reoccupation of Palestinian areas. On Monday 8 April, Iraq announced it was stopping its UN-permitted oil sales for 30 days, 'or until the Zionist entity's armed forces have unconditionally withdrawn from the Palestinian territories.' Ali Rodriguez, secretary-general of the Organisation of Petroleum Exporting Countries (OPEC), 'warned that Iraq's action, coupled with labour trouble that cut Venezuelan oil exports, could provoke an oil crisis.'[1]

Joe Stanislaw, president of Cambridge Energy Research, commented, 'The psychological impact of this cannot be underestimated. It adds to the fear and uncertainty in the market and unless someone makes up the shortfall prices could be heading to $30 a barrel.' Iraq exports 2 million barrels of oil a day, about 4 per cent of internationally-traded supplies. It is the sixth largest oil supplier to the United States.

'The two key questions are: who will join Iraq, and who will compensate for the fall in supplies', noted Leo Drollas, chief economist at the Centre for Global Energy Studies.[2] No one joined Iraq in the embargo, not even Iran (which doesn't actually supply any oil to the US) – one London analyst suggested, 'They're too commercially astute to join Iraq with prices as high as they are.'[3]

Saudi Arabia is the traditional 'swing' producer of oil, ready to make up any deficit in the market. In early 2002, Saudi oil production was running at around 7.4 million barrels a day (mbd), with close to 3 mbd of spare capacity. Two US oil analysts comment that this spare capacity is usually enough to 'entirely displace the production of another large oil-exporting country if supply is disrupted or a producer tries to reduce output to increase prices.' Edward Morse and James Richard observe that, 'Saudi spare capacity is the energy equivalent of nuclear weapons, a powerful deterrent against those who try to challenge Saudi leadership and Saudi goals.'[4] If Iraqi oil production for international markets ceases for any reason, spare Saudi capacity should be able to make up the shortfall.

Another buffer is the range of national and international oil stocks held by consumer nations. During the 1991 Gulf War, the International Energy Agency made 2.5 mbd available, 'slightly more than the 2 million barrels that Iraq currently exports.'[5]

At the time of the Iraqi oil embargo, oil prices had reached roughly the same level as before 11 September 2001. There are different categories of oil traded on the international market. The price of Brent crude oil is used as a standard for gauging the level of the market, and the price of Brent crude had returned to around $26 per barrel. Oil prices had risen 35 per cent during March 2002. According to Chakib Khelil, Algeria's energy minister, the price then – $24.48 per barrel of Brent crude – included a premium of $3 a barrel because of the geopolitical tensions, mainly around Iraq.[6] After the Iraqi cut-off, oil jumped $1.01 per barrel, to $27 per barrel.

There are two plausible scenarios for the future: oil prices 'high', but below $30 per barrel, on the one hand, and oil prices jumping to over $40 per barrel.

PESSIMISM AND OPTIMISM

Opinion is divided over the effects on the world economy of staying at the current, sub-$30 level. Larry Elliott of the *Guardian* is gloomy: 'periods of high oil prices mean an initial surge of inflation followed by recession': 'It happened in 1973. It happened in 1979. It happened in 1990. And it could well be happening again.'[7]

At the optimistic end of the spectrum, Roger Bootle, the well-known City economist, suggests that current prices are not a serious threat: the dire effects of higher oil prices were largely caused, 'not by the direct impact of higher oil, but rather by the passing on of this impact through a spiral of higher wages and prices that ultimately brought both havoc and high interest rates.' This is unlikely with oil prices as they are, because there is now more use of substitute energy sources, more emphasis on service industries (which use less energy), and inflation is more under control.[8]

PESSIMISM

Alan Blinder, a former vice chair of the US Federal Reserve, says, 'I can't imagine that somebody isn't telling George Bush that one possible consequence of a real shooting war in Iraq could be a spike in the price of oil and a return to recession in the US': 'a real spike to $40 or $50 a barrel would have the potential, indeed the likelihood, of derailing the whole world recovery.'

Despite the existence of Saudi spare capacity, the *Financial Times* warns that in the event of war and the loss of Iraqi oil, 'increased supply from other countries would take time to come on stream, and speculation is bound to send oil higher in the short term at least ... Even a fairly short-lived price leap could have a serious economic impact.'[9]

In the early 1990s, the Federal Reserve might have been able to prevent recession in the US if it had not been for the high oil prices (over $40 per barrel) caused by the oncoming war against Iraq. The *Financial Times* comments, 'Mr Bush's determination to overthrow Mr Saddam looks like determination to complete his father's unfinished business. His fear must be that he might reproduce the recession that led to his father's ejection from office.' There is a 'potentially irreconcilable conflict between foreign and economic policy'.[10]

THE £4 BILLION WAR

Apart from the wider issues, there is the cost. The 1991 Gulf War is estimated to have cost $80 billion at today's prices – with roughly $63 billion paid to the US by Saudi Arabia, Kuwait and Japan.[11] None of these countries is expected to pay anything towards the cost of a new war. (Incidentally, it was estimated by the Congressional Budget Office that US war costs were actually two-thirds of the official claim, meaning that the US may have made a profit on the 1991 war.[12]) For Britain alone, the initial campaign is expected to cost £1 billion, according to Major Charles Heyman, the editor of *Janes World Armies*.[13] The Chancellor estimates that the war could cost Britain up to £4 billion all told, according to the *Sunday Mirror*. Mr Brown is said to have had 'blistering' discussions with the Prime Minister, pointing out that paying for the war could be a body blow to the spending plans for health, education, and transport.[14] This could have damaging effects on Labour's re-election chances, quite apart from their impact on public health and society at large.

THE WIDER EFFECTS

The re-election fortunes of the Republicans and New Labour are hardly the most significant issue here. The effects of an unnecessary world recession on the employment, real incomes, and simple survival of people all around the world could be enormous. War may be the health of the State, as Randolph Bourne argued, but this war may lead to a sickness of the world economy, and poverty and disease for millions.

Emily Johns

CHAPTER XI
Sanctions Kill

SWEENEY'S ERROR

On 23 June 2002, journalist John Sweeney published an article in the London *Observer* and broadcast a documentary on BBC2 television, attempting to cast doubt on the claim that sanctions have caused death and suffering in Iraq. Mr Sweeney had two topics: he interviewed a child and several adults with horrifying stories of torture; and he collected evidence that mass funerals of babies' bodies were 'faked'. On the first subject, Baghdad's human rights record is not a matter of controversy in Britain or in the United States. There is unanimity across the political spectrum on the nature of what one Iraqi exile calls 'The Republic of Fear'. What is a matter of controversy, and a matter of serious political dispute, is whether the economic sanctions imposed on Iraq are causing massive suffering and death, particularly among children.

This has been denied by the British and US Governments. However, a Humanitarian Panel of experts appointed by the UN Security Council concluded in March 1999 that, 'Even if not all suffering in Iraq can be imputed to external factors, especially sanctions, the Iraqi people would not be undergoing such deprivations in the absence of the prolonged measures imposed by the Security Council and the effects of war.' In June 2001, one of the world's leading human rights non-governmental organisations, Human Rights Watch – who certainly have no love for the regime in Iraq – admonished the US Government to 'stop pretending that the sanctions have nothing to do with the dire public health crisis confronting millions of Iraqis.'[1]

Mr Sweeney's 'evidence' that economic sanctions are not causing death and suffering on a large scale consisted of two parts. Firstly, he collected evidence that 'the regime's propaganda has faked mass baby funerals'. He disparaged this ' "evidence" of the 7,000 children under five the regime claims are being killed each month by sanctions.'[2] However, contrary to Mr Sweeney's insinuation, no critic of the economic sanctions has relied on the mass baby funerals as 'evidence' of the level of suffering among children in Iraq. 'Revelations' concerning the mass funerals do nothing to invalidate the judgement of Julian Filochowski, director of the British Catholic aid agency CAFOD, who helped to launch a report on the sanctions by leading European Catholic aid agencies in February 2001 with these angry words: 'The sanctions are humanly catastrophic, morally indefensible and politically ineffective. They are a failed policy and must be changed.'[3]

MASS KILLING

In August 1999, UNICEF revealed that in the south/centre of Iraq – home to 85 per cent of the country's population – the death rate among children under five had more than doubled during the period of sanctions. The death rate had gone from 56 deaths per 1000 live births (1984–1989) to 131 deaths per 1000 live births (1994–1999). Infant mortality – defined as the death of children in their first year – had increased from 47 to 108 deaths per 1000 live births within the same time frame.

UNICEF Executive Director Carol Bellamy noted that there had been a substantial reduction in child mortality throughout Iraq during the 1980s. If this had continued through the 1990s, there would have been half a million fewer deaths of children under five in the country as a whole during the eight year period 1991 to 1998.[4] 500,000 children died who would otherwise have lived. This estimate is Mr Sweeney's second target.

SOLID EVIDENCE

Mr Sweeney writes of the 500,000 figure, 'The projection is open to question.' He points out that, 'All but one of the researchers used by UNICEF were employees of the Ministry of Health.'[5] Mr Sweeney appears to be have made no attempt to assess the rigorous procedures used by UNICEF. It so happens that UNICEF was involved in all aspects of the surveys – from survey design through to data analysis. Specifically, UNICEF had direct input to the design of the surveys, which were based on the internationally respected household survey format, the DHS (Demographic and Health Survey) format; UNICEF was involved in the training of all survey supervisors; UNICEF conducted field visits to every governorate (major administrative unit in Iraq) while the survey was being conducted; UNICEF oversaw the process of data entry; UNICEF had full access to the hard copies of the interview records and the complete data sets for both surveys at all times.

UNICEF also convened a panel of experts to examine the surveys and the findings in July 1999. This panel included senior personnel from DHS, Macro International, the World Health Organisation, and senior UNICEF officials from the Regional Office in Amman and New York Headquarters. UNICEF said that if the Iraqi Government had attempted to manipulate the data by influencing the survey interviewers to over-record the number of deaths or by directly manipulating the survey data on the computer, 'this would have been detected by analyzing the spread of births and deaths. The panel of experts who reviewed the survey methodology and results looked for this, but it was not found.' Internal cross checking of data failed to detect any manipulation of the results of the survey, by the surveyors themselves or by anyone else.[6]

Given these facts, it is irrelevant to point out that the surveyors were members of the Iraqi Ministry of Health. They were conducting a survey designed by UNICEF, supervised by UNICEF, cross-checked by UNICEF, and assessed for signs of manipulation by international experts in a review commissioned by UNICEF.

UNICEF acted professionally and carefully, and built a solid case based on the evidence. Unfortunately, Mr Sweeney has not followed this excellent example.

It is important to note that UNICEF were careful not to attribute all these deaths to economic sanctions. However, the UN agency did emphasise the judgement of the Security Council's own Humanitarian Panel, quoted above. Given that economic sanctions have been the major persistent damaging factor during the period 1991–1998 (the Gulf War only lasted six weeks), it seems reasonable to conclude that most of the 500,000 excess child deaths were caused by the economic sanctions.

JUDGING SANCTIONS

The primary focus of this book is the planned invasion of Iraq. However, it is impossible not to include some mention of the economic sanctions regime, which Save the Children has called a 'silent war on Iraq's children'.[7] Whether or not the United States and Britain launch their military campaign, this war continues.

The economic sanctions on Iraq were re-imposed by the Security Council on 3 April 1991, a month after Iraq was expelled from Kuwait. The punitive nature of the sanctions was revealed by the vagueness of a critical element of Resolution 687. Paragraph 21 of the Resolution said restrictions on exporting to Iraq would be lifted by the Security Council after considering 'the policies and practices' of the Government of Iraq. Paragraph 22 was rather clearer, saying that the restrictions on Iraq's exports and 'the financial transactions related thereto', would be lifted once Iraq had complied with internationally-supervised disarmament of its weapons of mass destruction. However, by 1994, the US and UK had moved the goalposts, arguing that sanctions should remain in place until other, unspecified, resolutions were also complied with – resolutions not mentioned in Resolution 687.[8] Together, the two paragraphs add up to a set of goalposts that can be moved indefinitely, a matter not improved by the demand for undefined 'cooperation in all respects' in the later Resolution 1284.

If it was focused on changing future behaviour rather than punishing past behaviour, the sanctions regime would offer the gradual lifting of restrictions in return for moves towards desired behaviour. In the case of Iraq, there has been considerable relaxation of the sanctions over the years, but only as a result of international pressure, never in order to reward Iraqi compliance.

Sanctions can also be judged in terms of how 'targeted' they are. The UN Security Council's Humanitarian Panel observed in March 1999, 'the humanitarian situation in Iraq will continue to be a dire one in the absence of a sustained revival of the Iraqi economy.'[9] Hanny Megally, director of the Middle East and North Africa division of Human Rights Watch, remarked in August 2000, 'An emergency commodity assistance program like oil-for-food, no matter how well funded or well run, cannot reverse the devastating consequences of war and ten years of virtual shut-down of Iraq's economy.'[10] Shutting down an economy harms the entire population. Sanctions can hardly be more indiscriminate.

Sanctions can also be judged in terms of their effects on human rights. Two US analysts with links to the US Government write that, 'Iraq's population has been devastated socially, economically, and psychologically': there has been a 'dramatic rise in corruption and bribery in a government which prided itself on being one of the least corrupt in the region.' 'Social ills such as theft, begging, prostitution and rural thievery that were rare or "efficiently" controlled in this once well-policed authoritarian state have become widespread'.[11] US epidemiologist Richard Garfield notes in particular the decline in adult literacy from 80% to 58%, suggesting that this is 'perhaps at least as condemning a statement about humanitarian conditions in Iraq as data on mortality', a dramatic deterioration in the 'long-term assets' of Iraqi society.[12]

The sanctions regime has been extremely punitive, highly indiscriminate, and has had a devastating effect on the human rights of Iraq's civilian population, and on children in particular. The New York-based Center for Economic and Social Rights has observed that, 'As a matter of fundamental principle, human rights are based on the inherent dignity and worth of every human person, and are owed directly to individuals. These rights are not forfeited because of a government's misconduct'.[13]

PUBLIC HEALTH INFRASTRUCTURE

In September 2000, the UN Food and Agriculture Organisation estimated that 800,000 Iraqi children under the age of five were chronically malnourished.[14] Chronic malnutrition can lead to life-long physical and mental stunting. Anupama Rao Singh, then UNICEF's director in Baghdad, pointed out that chronic malnutrition is 'extremely difficult to reverse, if not irreversible.'[15] One key factor is the lack of clean drinking water. In March 2000, the International Committee of the Red Cross identified the 'collapse of the public health system' and 'the water problem' as the two 'major threats' to the health of the Iraqi population.[16]

The 'water problem' is only the most acute aspect of a general breakdown of the public health infrastructure. The Arab Monetary Fund estimated the value of destroyed infrastructure and economic assets during the 1991 war at $232 billion.[17] (By comparison, the decade-long Iran-Iraq war caused only $67bn worth of economic damage.[18]) For over five years Iraq was completely prevented from exporting oil, and was thus denied tens of billions of dollars of revenues, sharply deflating the economy, and preventing reconstruction.

The effect of sanctions on the supply of clean drinking water has not been simply in terms of impeding imports of water purification and pumping equipment and supplies of chlorine. There is also the underlying problem of electricity. As we have seen, Robert Fisk learned in 1998 that, 'when electricity is cut – which it is every three hours, for example, in Basra – the pumps stop and the pressure in the leaking water pipes falls. Into the vacuum is sucked sewage which runs out of the taps. Even the original source of the water is now contaminated in Iraq.'[19] Recall that the electrical power system is in disrepair because it was deliberately targeted by the United States in 1991.

UNICEF adviser Dr Eric Hoskins remarks that, 'Contaminated water supplies and poor sanitation have created health conditions enabling diarrhea to merge as the leading child killer during the postwar period. During both 1991 and 1992, mortality due to diarrhea was estimated at more than three times the 1990 levels.'[20] UNICEF observed in 2000 that the 'case fatality rate' due to diarrhoeal diseases in children under five years 'has remained high at 2.4%': 'Diarrhoea leading to death from dehydration, and acute respiratory infections together account for 70 percent of child mortality.'[21] This is due in large measure to the deliberate destruction of Iraq's electricity system in the 1991 war, and the deliberate prevention of reconstruction by comprehensive economic sanctions in the years thereafter.

Estimates of the sums required for reconstruction of the civilian infrastructure in Iraq range from $50bn to $100bn, 'of which $30bn must be spent on imported equipment, machinery and spare parts'.[22] Over the five and a half years from December 1996 to July 2002, oil-for-food generated a total of $55.4 billion, of which a large proportion was diverted to compensation – as of April 2002, $14.8 billion had been paid out in compensation.[23] On the humanitarian side, supplies and equipment worth $23.5 billion have been delivered to Iraq for humanitarian relief as of July 2002.[24] The need to purchase consumables – food, medical supplies, and so forth – every year has meant that only a tiny proportion of Iraq's oil earnings since 1996 have been available for purchasing capital goods for reconstruction of the infrastructure.

The Economist, the leading international journal of business, spoke out strongly against the economic sanctions in a passionate editorial:

> Slowly, inexorably, a generation is being crushed in Iraq. Thousands are dying, thousands more are leading stunted lives, and storing up bitter hatreds for the future. If, year in, year out, the UN were systematically killing Iraqi children by air strikes, western governments would declare it intolerable, no matter how noble the intention. They should find their existing policy just as unacceptable.[25]

The Economist commented on the so-called "smart sanctions" introduced by Britain and the United States: 'although the country would be able to import more, it would still be denied the free movement of labour and capital that it desperately needs if it is at last to start picking itself up ... Iraq needs massive investment to rebuild its industry, its power grids and its schools, and needs cash in hand to pay its engineers, doctors and teachers. None of this looks likely to happen under smart sanctions.'[26] 'To recover from its 11 years under the sanctions battering-ram – which has crushed the country's industrial and agricultural infrastructure – Iraq needs the freedom, and overseas investment, of a huge reconstruction effort ... the British proposal of "smart sanctions" offers an aspirin where surgery is called for.'[27]

Without foreign investment and foreign loans there cannot be a serious reconstruction effort. Without a serious reconstruction effort, children will continue to sicken and die from contaminated drinking water and unhealthy living conditions. Reconstruction and the restoration of decent standards of public health depend on the lifting of economic sanctions.

FAMILY PURCHASING POWER

The UN Food and Agriculture Organisation (FAO) reported in 1995 that the solution to the nutritional crisis in Iraq lay in part in restoring the viability of the Iraqi Dinar, the local currency, and in 'creating conditions for the people to acquire adequate purchasing power'. In other words, generating jobs. 'But these conditions can be fulfilled only if the economy can be put back in proper shape enabling it to draw on its own resources, and that clearly cannot occur as long as the embargo remains in force,' said the FAO.[28] Four years later, the Humanitarian Panel observed that, 'the humanitarian situation in Iraq will continue to be a dire one in the absence of a sustained revival of the Iraqi economy.'[29] The *Financial Times*, the world's leading business newspaper, observed of later US/UK "smart sanctions" proposals, 'the US plan will not revive Iraq's devastated economy while control over Iraq's oil revenues remains in the hands of the UN, and foreign investment and credits are still prohibited.'[30]

The economic sanctions have shut down the economy. The shut down of the economy crushes the earning capacity of millions of ordinary families. The economy cannot be revived till the economic sanctions are lifted. The humanitarian crisis caused by mass poverty cannot be solved until the economic sanctions are lifted.

A DISTRACTION

The argument about economic sanctions on Iraq is not about food and medicines, it is not centred on the (scandalous) behaviour of the Sanctions Committee. The first concern must be to recreate a healthy environment for children to grow up in – by permitting the reconstruction of Iraq's public health infrastructure, including the electricity sector. The second priority must be to restore breadwinners' capacities to provide for their families by generating jobs and real incomes which Iraqi families can live on – by permitting the re-inflation of the Iraqi economy. The expert consensus is that neither of these crucial steps to solving the humanitarian crisis can take place while the economic sanctions continue. The Iraqi peoples also have other needs apart from the need for survival – education, cultural expression, dignity. Bertrand Russell wrote many years ago, in relation to Germany after Versailles, 'No man [or woman] thinks sanely when his [or her] self-esteem has suffered a mortal wound, and those who deliberately humiliate a nation have only themselves to thank if it becomes a nation of lunatics.'[31] This has not happened to the people of Iraq. Yet.

Mr Sweeney and his baby funerals merely distract attention from the serious issues. Flailing accusations do not advance the public debate. Rather, they help to delay the full awakening of public outrage at the atrocities that have been committed in the name of the peoples of Britain and the US, and the appropriate changes in policy.

THE 'OIL-FOR-FOOD' DEAL

SCOPE The term 'oil-for-food' is misleading. In the beginning, in 1997, much of the revenues were spent on food and medicines, but since 1999 the scope of the programme has broadened to include agriculture, housing, education, sewage and sanitation, the electricity sector, telecommunications, and the oil industry itself. All are sectors of vital humanitarian need. Without a functioning oil industry, for example, Iraq could not afford to purchase either medicines or food.

FINANCES Iraq is allowed to sell oil on the open market. The purchaser deposits money in a special UN-controlled 'escrow' account in a bank in New York. Iraq has no direct access to these oil revenues, but can order civilian goods to be paid for out of the escrow account. 59 per cent of revenues are available for humanitarian purchases for the Baghdad-controlled south/centre; 13 per cent goes to the Kurdish north; 25 per cent is diverted for war compensation; 2.2 per cent covers UN administration costs; and 0.8 per cent funds UNMOVIC.

THE AMBER LIST As a result of Resolution 1409, passed in May 2002, Iraq is allowed to import all civilian goods without having to seek the permission of the UN Sanctions Committee. Iraq need only notify the UN of the import of these goods, and they will be paid for out of the escrow account. However, the Sanctions Committee does intervene in the case of 'dual-use' goods which have been identified (by the United States, in reality) as having a possible military use as well as a civilian one. There is an extensive 'Goods Review List' naming and describing these suspect items. Items on this 'Amber List' are not necessarily banned as they would be on a 'Red List', but their purchase by Baghdad has to be approved by the Sanctions Committee.

THE COMMITTEE The Sanctions Committee was set up by UN Security Council Resolution 661 in August 1990 (hence the name '661 Committee'). The fifteen members of the Committee are the members of the Security Council. Because membership of the Security Council is temporary and rotating (except for the permanent five members – Britain, China, France, Russia and the United States), the composition of the Sanctions Committee is also always changing.

HOLDS Members of the 661 Committee can seek further information (which delays delivery); and/or put an item on 'hold'. Holds can last indefinitely, do not have to be justified, and can be imposed by a single country. Goods on hold increased in value from $3.71bn on 14 May 2001 to $5.17bn on 17 May 2002 – 17.9 per cent of the value of all applications. The US has placed almost all these holds. At the time of writing, there are insufficient funds in the escrow account to pay for all goods on hold if they were approved, and this has been true for some months. More information can be found at www.un.org/Depts/oip/

THE FIRST OIL-FOR-FOOD DEAL: DESIGNED TO BE REFUSED

The moral level of the countries imposing economic sanctions cannot really be understood without recalling the genesis of the 'oil-for-food' deal. For many years London and Washington blamed Baghdad for the suffering in Iraq, pointing out that the Iraqi Government rejected an oil-for-food deal for four years in the first half of the 1990s. However, the US and UK are careful to conceal their own share of responsibility for this rejection. The offer they were instrumental in creating was designed to be refused.

The value of oil sales offered was a fraction of the resources Iraq urgently needed; the humanitarian 'oil-for-food' deal was bundled in with paying for hated UN weapons inspectors and resented war compensation; the language of the Resolution was unnecessarily humiliating; the Resolution was restrictive in specifying the pipeline that should be used to transport Iraqi oil; and the creation of a new UN-controlled bank account for oil-for-food transactions was humiliating and unnecessary. This was not a humanitarian offer, it was a propaganda weapon, and a very successful one.

OFFERING A FRACTION OF THE NEED

Following the passage of Resolution 687 re-imposing economic sanctions on Iraq, the UN Secretary-General sent an 'Executive Delegate', Prince Sadruddin Aga Khan, to visit Iraq and to report on humanitarian conditions. Prince Sadruddin reported in July 1991, estimating that it would cost $22bn to restore the power, oil, water, sanitation, food, agriculture and health sectors to pre-war levels. (Twelve years of deterioration have since increased the cost.) He recommended that Iraq should be allowed to sell $6.9bn over one year to restore the health services to full capacity; the electrical sector to 50 percent of its prewar capacity; the water and sanitation services to 40 per cent operation; northern oil facilities to a limited extent (to be able to supply more oil in the future, to fund humanitarian purchases). This money would be needed also to rehabilitate agriculture, and to provide subsistence food rations to the entire population.

As a short-term measure, Prince Sadruddin proposed an initial sale of $2.65bn worth of oil over the first four months (a third of the total amount, plus a small sum for start-up costs), to be renewed if arrangements were satisfactory.

During discussions in the Security Council, the period for the one-off oil sale was lengthened to six months, which under the Executive Delegate's formula would have required $3.8bn worth of oil sales (half the annual amount, plus start-up costs of $350m).

The UN Secretary-General, seeing the way the argument was drifting, argued for Iraq to be allowed $2.4bn worth of oil sales. This is a drop of over 36 per cent in terms of the value of oil sales – and only a proportion of this was to be available for humanitarian goods. The Security Council had decided by then that 30 per cent of all Iraqi oil revenues should be reserved for war compensation payments – a small proportion was also set aside for UN costs, including those for the weapons inspectors.

Under the Secretary-General's proposal, instead of Iraq receiving $3.8bn for humanitarian spending over the six months, as suggested by the Secretary-General's own Executive Delegate, Iraq would receive only $1.6bn for humanitarian aid – just over 40 per cent of its assessed needs.

This proposal was rejected by the UN Security Council – by the United States, in effect – as too generous. Resolutions 706 and 712, the latter passed in September 1991 actually offered Iraq only $1.6bn in total oil sales over the six months. The sum available for humanitarian aid had been reduced to roughly $930 million over six months – less than 25 per cent of the UN's expert assessment of humanitarian needs.[32]

According to an aid agency staff member involved in the discussions in Baghdad, UN officials had already become convinced by late July 1991 that 'the US intention was to present Saddam Hussein with so unattractive a package that Iraq would reject it and thus take on the blame, at least in western eyes, for continued civilian suffering'.[33] This objective was achieved: Iraq did reject the offer contained in Resolutions 706 and 712, and did take on the blame for the humanitarian crisis.

James Fine, who was in Iraq in 1991 as a consultant to the American Friends Service Committee on relief and reconstruction later revealed that, in July 1991 'Iraqi officials told UN humanitarian administrators in Baghdad that Iraq would accept the Executive Delegate's recommendations.'[34] But they refused the 25 per cent offer.

AN OFFENSIVE BUNDLE

Apart from the monetary value of the offer, there was also the curious way in which the Resolution bundled together into one account funding for the humanitarian programme, war reparations, and funding for UNSCOM weapons inspectors. Humanitarian observers, according to Sarah Graham-Brown, 'argued that humanitarian needs should have been entirely separated from questions of compensation and payment for the work of UN weapons inspectors'. The latter issues were for the Iraqi state alone, and government resistance to paying for these items should not have been allowed to affect the condition of the civilian population. Ms Graham-Brown says there were 'many humanitarian observers who felt that the "package" deal offered under Resolutions 706 and 712 was one which it could have been anticipated Iraq would refuse.'[35] Iraq did refuse, and negotiations were stalemated for over four years of suffering.

INFRINGING SOVEREIGNTY

Much of the Iraqi hostility to Resolution 706 lay in the infringement of Baghdad's sovereignty. When the Security Council did finally agree an oil-for-food deal with Iraq under Resolution 986, some of the most offensive language was amended. For example, UN staff were asked to 'monitor' the distribution of oil-for-food goods in Resolutions 706 and 712; under Resolution 986, UN officials were to 'observe' the distribution of humanitarian goods.[36] Similarly, as the then UN Secretary-General pointed out, Resolution 986 took into account some of Iraq's concerns over Resolution 706 by reaffirming 'the commitment of all Member States to the sovereignty and territorial integrity of Iraq' and by describing the new exercise as 'temporary'. This was an implicit admission that some Iraqi objections to Resolution 706 could have been accommodated back in 1991. This contradicts the hardline position taken by the Security Council – for over three years – that Iraq bore 'full responsibility' for the suffering of its civilian population.[37]

THE TURKISH PIPELINE

Resolution 712 specified that oil must be transported by the Kirkuk-Yumurtalik pipeline passing through Turkey. 'This was meant not only to benefit Ankara, but also to give a lever to the anti-Saddam leaders in Iraqi Kurdistan which had been placed under the Western air umbrella since June 1991.'[38] Iraq protested against this inflexibility. This diktat was also dropped three and a half years later in Resolution 986.

THE ESCROW ACCOUNT

Another device used to make the first oil-for-food offer unpalatable to the Iraqis involved the financial arrangements for the scheme. Sadruddin Aga Khan had proposed that Iraq's existing oil revenue accounts in the United States be used for the channelling of funds for the new humanitarian programme. According to Fine, privy to the discussions among international humanitarian staff in Baghdad, 'Under these proposed control and monitoring safeguards, Iraq would have had no more opportunity to divert or misuse relief supplies than under the very similar arrangements eventually mandated by the Security Council in August [Resolution 706] and September [Resolution 712]' of 1991.[39]

However, instead of using Iraq's existing State Oil Marketing Organisation (SOMO) account, the Resolutions established a new UN 'escrow' account, through which Iraq's oil wealth would flow. 'The escrow account afforded the UN no greater measure of security of control, but provocatively raised the issue of national sovereignty by taking direct possession of Iraqi national resources.'[40]

NEARLY ACCEPTED

Despite this, and all the other unnecessarily insulting arrangements, according to Sarah Helms, diplomatic editor for the London *Independent*, 'President Saddam might have accepted the resolution if the higher sum [proposed by Sadruddin Aga Khan] had been agreed'.[41] Perhaps one day an epidemiologist will calculate how many hundreds of thousands of children died in Iraq because of these US and British manoeuvres.

THE GOAL

In July 1991, a US official was quoted as saying that the first oil-for-food proposal was 'a good way to maintain the bulk of sanctions and not be on the wrong side of a potentially emotive issue.'[42] That public relations effort continues today with the latest reforms of oil-for-food. The goal is 'leadership change', whatever the human cost.

CHAPTER XII
Nuking Iraq

HOON'S THREATS

Just before he left on a 'peace mission' to India and Pakistan, Jack Straw was asked on Radio 4's *Today* programme why the two countries should pay any attention to a country which had never itself renounced the first use of nuclear weapons. The Foreign Secretary said that everyone knew the prospect of Britain (and the US and France) using nuclear weapons was 'so distant as not to be worth discussing'. *Guardian* columnist Hugo Young commented that Straw's response was 'about as misleading an answer as can be found in the entire record of Britain's conduct as a nuclear power.'[1] British Defence Secretary Geoff Hoon has given several indications that the use of British nuclear weapons against Iraq is far from distant:

On 20 March 2002, the Defence Secretary told the House of Commons Select Committee on Defence that states like Iraq 'can be absolutely confident that in the right conditions we would be willing to use our nuclear weapons.'[2] On 24 March, Geoff Hoon appeared on ITV's Jonathan Dimbleby show and 'insisted that the government "reserved the right" to use nuclear weapons if Britain or British troops were threatened by chemical or biological weapons.'[3]

Finally, during a debate on 29 April 2002 in the House of Commons, Mr Hoon said in response to a question about his nuclear threats: 'ultimately and in conditions of extreme self-defence, nuclear weapons would have to be used.' Diane Abbott MP pressed the Defence Secretary for an explanation of what these 'conditions of extreme self-defence' might be. Hoon refused to be specific. The Defence Secretary confined himself to saying that it was 'important to point out that the Government have nuclear weapons available to them, and that – in certain specified conditions to which I have referred – we would be prepared to use them.'[4]

NON-PROLIFERATION PROMISES

MPs have expressed concern as to whether Hoon's threats might be in contravention of international commitments given by the UK. In 1978, the five declared nuclear powers promised that they would refrain from using their nuclear weapons against non-nuclear-weapon states. The US and British promises – or 'negative security assurances' (NSAs) – were full of exceptions and loopholes.

Restated in 1995, the British NSA said, 'The United Kingdom will not use nuclear weapons against non-nuclear-weapon States Parties to the Treaty on the Non-Proliferation of Nuclear Weapons except in the case of an invasion or any other attack on the United Kingdom, its dependent territories, its armed forces or other troops, its allies or on a State towards which it has a security commitment, carried out or sustained by such a non-nuclear weapon State in association or alliance with a nuclear-weapon State.' (This was looser wording than given in 1978.)

In contrast, the 1995 NSA from China said, 'China undertakes not to be the first to use nuclear weapons at any time or under any circumstances. China undertakes not to use or threaten to use nuclear weapons against non-nuclear-weapon States or nuclear-weapon-free zones at any time or under any circumstances.'

In 1989, Nigeria proposed an international treaty banning the use of nuclear weapons against any non-nuclear-weapon State which had signed the Non-Proliferation Treaty, unless that State had nuclear weapons stationed on their territory. Britain and the other nuclear powers have resisted such proposals.

BROKEN PROMISES

Iraq is a member of the Non-Proliferation Treaty, does not possesses nuclear weapons so far as is known, and is not allied with any nuclear weapon state. Therefore, unless the British Government claims that Iraqi military action against British and US troops in any coming war is 'in association' with China, France, Russia, India, Pakistan and/or Israel, the 1995 Negative Security Assurance ought to rule out the possibility that Iraq could be attacked by British nuclear weapons.

Hence the question from Malcolm Savidge MP to Mr Hoon on 29 April: did the Defence Secretary's comments signal 'a change of Government policy, whereby Britain is reneging on assurances given to non-nuclear weapons states under the nuclear non-proliferation treaty?' Hoon avoided answering the question, despite the fact that the promise not to use nuclear weapons against non-nuclear-weapon States is fundamental to the Non-Proliferation Treaty. A French diplomat was asked about Hoon's comments, 'Don't you think that all this might encourage small countries that are still developing nuclear arms to acquire atomic bombs themselves and therefore ruin all the efforts so far to eliminate nuclear weapons of mass destruction?' The representative of the French Mission to the UN replied, 'The danger you point out is real. We've drawn the attention of our partners and allies to this difficulty many times.'[5]

The fear in the Pentagon and the Ministry of Defence is that if, somehow, Iraq does have chemical or biological weapons, there would be no reason for Saddam Hussein to hold back from using them against British and US troops (and perhaps Israel) if Washington and London launched a war aimed at deposing and killing him. The only option available is the nonsensical strategy of trying to deter the Iraqi President from using his weapons of mass destruction by threatening to use British or US weapons of mass destruction in retaliation. A leaked US policy document – the 'Nuclear Posture

Review' – 'is understood to identify three circumstances in which nuclear weapons could be used: against targets able to withstand non-nuclear attack; in retaliation for the use of nuclear, biological or chemical weapons; and "in the event of surprising military developments".[6] Iraq is mentioned as a possible target.

VITAL INTERESTS

Tory Defence Secretary Malcolm Rifkind said in November 1993 that because the threat of an all-out nuclear assault might not be 'credible' against certain enemies, it was important for Britain to be able to 'undertake a more limited nuclear strike' to deliver 'an unmistakable message of our willingness to defend our vital interests to the utmost.'[7] This limited strike would be carried out by a single 'Tactical Trident' missile fired from a Trident submarine, probably carrying a single 5–20 kiloton nuclear war-head. (Hiroshima was destroyed by a bomb of about 15 kilotons.) The policy of using nuclear weapons to defend 'vital interests' was confirmed by New Labour's 'Strategic Defence Review', which concluded in July 1998 that Britain's nuclear arsenal should be the minimum needed to 'deter any threat to our vital interests' (Chapter 4, paragraph 61). The Review explained that 'our vital interests are not confined to Europe. Our economy is founded on international trade ... We invest more of our income abroad than any other major economy ... We depend on foreign countries for supplies of raw materials, above all oil' (Chapter 2, paragraph 19). So, 'vital interests' include economic and financial interests abroad as well as national survival.

FOUR SCENARIOS

According to the respected military journal *International Defense Review* Tactical Trident has four possible roles:

> At what might be termed the "upper end" of the usage spectrum, they could be used in a conflict involving large-scale forces (including British ground and air forces, such as the 1990–91 Gulf War) to reply to enemy nuclear strikes.
>
> Secondly, they could be used in a similar setting, but to reply to enemy use of weapons of mass destruction, such as bacteriological or chemical weapons, for which the British possess no like-for-like retaliatory capability.
>
> Thirdly, they could be used in a demonstrative role, ie aimed at a non-critical, possibly [!] uninhabited area, with the message that if the country concerned pursued its present course of action, nuclear weapons will be aimed at a high-priority target.
>
> Finally, there is the punitive role, where a country has committed an act, despite specific warning that to do so would incur a nuclear strike.[8]

Only one of these scenarios involves striking an enemy possessing nuclear weapons.

NUCLEAR THREATS, 1991

After the invasion of Kuwait, President Bush Sr. warned Iraq on 8 August 1990 that the use of chemical weapons would be intolerable 'and would be dealt with very, very severely'.[9] On 10 August, 'Whitehall sources made it clear that the multinational forces would be ready to hit back with every means at their disposal ... [including] tactical nuclear weapons.'[10] On 21 August, US Defence Undersecretary Paul Wolfowitz says, 'If we have to fight a war, we're going to fight it with all we have.'[11] On 30 September, a senior officer with the British 7th Armoured Brigade says that if attacked with chemical weapons, British forces would retaliate 'with battlefield nuclear forces'.[12] On 26 October, a senior British minister was quoted: 'If we were prepared to use tactical nuclear weapons against the Russians, I can't see why we shouldn't be prepared to use them against Iraq.'[13] *Guardian* journalist Hugo Young reports hearing a minister say the war might have to be ended with 'tactical nukes'.[14] On 6 December, Prime Minister John Major says the use of nuclear weapons is 'not likely, remotely'.[15] On 5 January 1991, President Bush Sr. writes to Saddam Hussein warning that in response to 'unconscionable acts' 'you and your people will pay a terrible price'.[16] On 14 January, *Newsweek* reveals that General Schwarzkopf requested permission to detonate a nuclear bomb over Iraq in order to generate an electromagnetic pulse that would shut down every electrical device in the country. On 15 January, Mr Major says he does not 'envisage needing to use' nuclear weapons.[17] On 3 February, 'Mr Hurd said that if Iraq responded to an allied land assault by using chemical weapons, President Saddam would be certain to provoke a massive response – language the US and Britain employ to leave open the option of using chemical or nuclear weapons.'[18] Also on 3 February, US Defence Secretary Dick Cheney says, 'I would not at this point advocate use of nuclear weapons.'[19] On 5 February, President Bush Sr. refuses to rule out the use of nuclear weapons: 'I think it's better never to say what you may be considering.'[20]

History repeats itself.

NUCLEAR THREATS, 1961

Britain formally granted 'independence' to Kuwait in 1961, but manufactured an 'Iraq-poised-to-invade' crisis to give British forces an opportunity to emphasise Britain's continuing military role in the Gulf. The Air Officer Commanding (Middle East) at the time later acknowledged that no serious threat from Iraq was detected.[21] According to an RAF historian, British strategic nuclear bombers in Malta were placed at readiness; two knowledgeable commentators claim that a British aircraft carrier with nuclear-capable Scimitar aircraft was also deployed to the Gulf.[22] Intelligence insider Anthony Verrier states that the nuclear mobilisation was 'directed against Nasser and, by extension, Russian ambitions in Arabia',[23] in other words, Arab nationalism.

History repeats itself.

'Men with no respect for life should never be allowed to control the ultimate instruments of death.' President George W. Bush, 11 March 2002.

CHAPTER XIII
Resisting Thought Control

MENTAL RESISTANCE

For much of 2002, the US-led war against Iraq has been a propaganda war. Politicians and generals alike now realise that securing the home front is a critical element in fighting wars. Control of the media has been a hotly disputed issue during many of the wars since Vietnam. It is misleading, however, to focus on the bureaucratic devices used to try to limit media access to battlefield realities. The real problems are far more profound.

Why, for example, was there only a single report, in a single newspaper, of the conclusion of the Czech police that Mohammed Atta, the 11 September ringleader, did not meet any Iraqi diplomats in Prague in 2001? The information was effectively buried – cast down the 'memory hole' Orwell invented in 1984. Why was Bronwen Maddox of *The Times* one of the few British journalists, if not the only journalist, to remark on the limits of the 'evidence' being offered by Mr al-Haideri, the Iraqi defector? Going back to the war on Afghanistan, why was there only a single report, in a single newspaper (the *Daily Telegraph*, once again) that the Taliban actually agreed the extradition of Osama bin Laden to Pakistan? Why did no other newspaper pick up the story, and why did the *Telegraph* let that story wither, just as it did the Prague report?

These examples can be multiplied a dozen times, simply from the material in this book. Other studies have provided thousands of pages of documentation of similar systematic distortions in media coverage of significant issues.

Crucial pieces of information, with great bearing on the major decisions being made by Government, appeared in the British broadsheets – fleetingly. The information was effectively suppressed, almost as if a Government censor had indicated the boundaries of the acceptable and journalists had halted at this border. There is no such Government censor. There is, however, a real problem of freedom of expression and of freedom of thought in Britain and in the United States, two of the freest societies ever to have existed.

Noam Chomsky and Edward Herman have set out a 'Propaganda Model' of the media, in which they explain how the private mass media in Western countries provide a 'guided-free-market' in ideas and reporting. Mass media corporations are large, privately-owned, profit-seeking enterprises, which are interlocked with, and have considerable common interests with, other major corporations, banks, and the Government. The private mass media is also constrained by its need for advertising, which also comes from corporations. Professor Chomsky remarks, 'Like other businesses, the mass media sell a product to buyers. Their market is advertisers, and the "product" is audiences, with a bias towards more wealthy audiences with improved advertising rates.'[1] From all this, one would expect an institutional imperative within the mass media for reporting to favour the interests of corporations, the State, and the rich. This is, indeed, a detectable pattern in media coverage.

Crucially, this institutional imperative informs recruitment and promotion practices, as one would expect, so that only those with the right attitudes are selected. Those selected require no instruction and few, if any, attempts at censorship, because they have already internalised the correct attitudes long before being hired or promoted. Noam Chomsky notes that questioning basic assumptions can be costly in terms of personal advancement; can provoke vilification from others; and is generally unpleasant, as the answers to honest inquiry are often ugly. Thus there is a pressure to censor oneself.

The interaction of institutional imperatives and individual self-censorship (based on lifelong indoctrination) drastically limits the range of expressible opinion in the mass media – and indeed in academia.

THE LIMITS OF THE EXPRESSIBLE

Professor Chomsky has remarked that the most important role in the propaganda system is played by 'liberal' critics, who define the outer limits of respectable opinion. Once properly framed, 'debate' has a system-reinforcing character. So long as all the participants obey the ground rules, vigorous debate can help to buttress the fundamental principles of state propaganda. These principles are, in essence, that the State is Good, it is pursuing noble aims, and that it only acts violently in self-defence. These general principles are applied in particular circumstances in different ways.

In the present crisis, it is assumed that: (1) the US and Britain are trying to force Iraq to accept UN weapons inspectors and Iraq bears the entire burden of responsibility for the failure to re-establish the inspection system; (2) the US and Britain are sickened by the 'vile' Government in Iraq, and are seeking 'regime change'; and the basic propaganda move: (3) the only choice is between inaction and military action.

The fundamental principle is that the US and British Governments are entitled to use force in pursuit of the perceived interests of those who hold power in these States, regardless of morality and law. The only judgements that count are cost and benefit. By this measure, some of those speaking out as 'anti-war' figures are actually pro-war. They accept the right of the United States and Britain (alone among the nations of the world) to carry out violence outside of international law. In this case, however, these 'critics', such as those quoted at the start of this book, perceive the costs of war to outweigh its benefits, and to be greater than the costs of nonviolent alternatives.

During the Vietnam War, Professor Chomsky remarked on the role played by establishment liberal Arthur Schlesinger, who opposed the war, but said that he prayed that those who supported the war were right in predicting victory. Schlesinger's opposition was based on his judgement that the United States was unlikely to be able to defeat the Vietnamese resistance at an acceptable cost, not on a question of principle. Mr Schlesinger and his fellow 'doves' played an important role in reinforcing the unspoken assumption that the United States (alone of all nations) should enjoy the right to impose political arrangements on other societies by force.

HONESTY AND ACCURACY

If the mass media performs as if it were an enormous state propaganda machine, how is that books such as this one can be written? How does it come about that the mass media provides such ammunition against dominant propaganda? Edward Herman and Noam Chomsky remark,

> That the media provide some information about an issue ... proves absolutely nothing about the adequacy or accuracy of media coverage. The media do, in fact, suppress a great deal of information, but even more important is the way they present a particular fact – its placement, tone, and frequency of repetition – and the framework of analysis in which it is placed.

There is so much information in the media system, some error and leakage is inevitable. Professor Chomsky says, 'the enormous mass of material that is produced in the media and books makes it possible for a really assiduous and committed researcher to gain a fair picture of the real world by cutting through the mass of misrepresentation and fraud to the nuggets hidden within.'

> That a careful reader, looking for a fact can sometimes find it, with diligence and a skeptical eye, tells us nothing about whether that fact received the attention and context it deserved, whether it was intelligible to most readers, or whether it was effectively distorted or suppressed.[2]

To escape from the mental traps set by the propaganda system requires an awareness of the propaganda devices being used, a willingness to look at the facts with an open mind, to put simple assumptions to the test, and to pursue an argument to its conclusion, and a determination to be a careful reader. With these tools, you have all the equipment you need to engage in what Professor Chomsky calls 'intellectual self-defence'. Collective intellectual self-defence can protect us from war propaganda, can help mobilise public outrage at the impending war, and may have a role, therefore, in saving lives in Iraq. The propaganda war is a real war.

Emily Johns

CHAPTER XIV
Turning Back The War

There is substantial evidence that the fear of domestic disruption has inhibited murderous plans. One documented case concerns Vietnam. The [US] Joint Chiefs of Staff recognized the need that 'sufficient forces would still be available for civil disorder control' if they sent more troops to Vietnam after the Tet Offensive, as Pentagon officials feared that escalation might lead to massive civil disobedience, in view of the large-scale popular opposition to the war, running the risk of 'provoking a domestic crisis of unprecedented proportions'.

A review of the internal documents released in the Pentagon Papers shows that considerations of cost were the sole factor inhibiting planners, a fact that should be noted by citizens concerned to restrain the violence of the state. In such cases as these, and many others, popular demonstrations and civil disobedience may, under appropriate circumstances, encourage others to undertake a broader range of conventional action by extending the range of the thinkable, and, where there is real popular understanding of the legitimacy of direct action to confront institutional violence, may serve as a catalyst to constructive organization and action that will pave the way to more fundamental change.

Noam Chomsky[1]

STOPPING NUCLEAR WAR

In 1985, former President Richard Nixon revealed that he had considered using nuclear weapons to end the war in Vietnam.[2] Matters actually went beyond merely 'considering' the option. In August 1969, the United States began a sequence of threats against North Vietnam, beginning with an ultimatum personally delivered by Henry Kissinger stating that if by 1 November 1969 there had been no ceasefire by the Vietnamese resistance, 'we will be compelled -with great reluctance - to take measures of the greatest consequences.'[3] Two nuclear bombs would be dropped on North Vietnam. To demonstrate his intentions, President Nixon ordered a full-scale nuclear alert, raising US nuclear forces to their highest level of alertness, DEF CON 1, for 29 days.

On 13 October 1969, one of Nixon's aides sent a Top Secret memorandum to Henry Kissinger warning that 'The nation could be thrown into internal physical turmoil', requiring the 'brutal' suppression of 'dissension'.[4] The US anti-war movement was organising a massive wave of demonstrations and mobilisations culminating in the Vietnam Moratorium demonstration in Washington. President Nixon later wrote in his memoirs, 'A quarter of a million people came to Washington for the October 15 Moratorium... On the night of October 15, I thought about the irony of this protest for peace. It had, I believe, destroyed whatever small possibility there may have existed for ending the war in 1969'. The key factor in his decision not to drop an atomic bomb on North Vietnam was that 'after all the protests and the Moratorium, American public opinion would be seriously divided by any military escalation of the war'.[5] Mobilised public opinion averted the world's second nuclear war.

ONE DETERMINED PERSON

In his State of the Union address, George Bush once again referred to the final recorded words of Todd Beamer, uttered just before he and other passengers thwarted the plans of the hijackers of United Airlines Flight 93, which came down in Pennsylvania on 11 September: 'Let's roll.' There are now bumper stickers and baseball caps with these words on them all over North America. Erwin Staub, a University of Massachusetts psychologist who specialises in heroism and violence, has suggested that the growing deification of those on board the United Airlines plane was a response to people's feelings of hopelessness when faced with such a threat to their security. Against an enemy who threatens to strike anywhere and at anybody, the actions of Mr Beamer and his fellow passengers makes people feel they are not helpless: 'It shows that one determined person has enormous power,' says Mr Staub.[6]

THE PLEDGE OF RESISTANCE

'I pledge to take part in, or to support, nonviolent civil disobedience in the event of a major US/UK attack on Iraq or any other country in the course of the "war on terrorism".' This Pledge of Resistance initiated by ARROW has, at the time of writing over 1000 signatories (please see www.justicenotvengeance.org).

Actions must be chosen carefully. Noam Chomsky has observed, 'In undertaking some form of action, we must ask ourselves what the consequences will be for the people who are at the wrong end of the guns, for the people who can't escape. Even a very well intentioned act, if it strengthens the forces of repression, is no gift whatsoever to those whose fate we, in some sense bear in our hands.'

Mass civil disobedience and mass demonstrations helped to bring the war in Vietnam to an end. Mass civil disobedience and mass demonstrations helped to prevent direct US military intervention in Central America in the 1980s (in part through an enormously successful Pledge of Resistance). Nonviolent resistance has the power to constrain British participation in the US "war on terrorism", and to make it more difficult for the United States to carry out further illegal military assaults.

What future do Zahra's sisters and brothers face in Iraq if each of us does not take the action that we can?

CHAPTER XV
War Plan Iraq

At the time of Tony Blair's conference with President Bush in Crawford in April 2002, few would have believed that four months later the United States Government would only just be agreeing the basis for a war plan against Iraq. In a briefing to the US President on 5 August 2002, however, the head of US Central Command, General Tommy Franks, seems to have finally conceded defeat, and proposed a compromise plan. It may be useful to review the divisions between the two main factions within the Administration with their radically different proposals for overthrowing the Iraqi leader.

The group led by US Defence Secretary Donald Rumsfeld and his deputy Paul Wolfowitz – referred to as the 'jihadist' wing of the Administration by *Time* magazine[1] – has favoured the 'Afghan model' of supporting an internal insurgency with a few thousand US Special Forces troops, along with massive US airstrikes. The mainstream of the foreign policy establishment, led by Secretary of State Colin Powell and his fellow generals in the Joint Chiefs of Staff, has counselled the use of overwhelming force for minimum US casualties – which would have required the use of over 200,000 US troops. Democratic Senator Jack Reed has described the factional strife in these terms: 'All along there has been this division within the Administration between those who see Iraq as something that has to be done regardless of the cost, and those who ask, "What are the costs?" '[2] Questions of principle and legality have been irrelevant in these debates.

The two camps have divided over whether the Iraqi opposition was militarily significant or politically reliable (from the point of view of US interests), a matter discussed earlier. They have also disagreed over the ease with which the United States could impose its will.

At the optimistic end of the spectrum is Kenneth Adelman, former Pentagon official, who believes that the war will be a 'cakewalk'.[3] On the other hand, the generals were shocked by Operation Prominent Hammer, a secret war game played in the Pentagon, which revealed that shortages of equipment could seriously hamper the lives of US troops and Iraqi civilians. One-third of US Air Force refuelling aircraft were undergoing repair in May 2002. There were also believed to be shortages of trained pilots, base security staff, electronic warfare equipment, and precision-guided munitions or "smart bombs" – and as US Air Force General John Jumper pointed out, 'We never sized ourselves to have to do high force protection levels at home and overseas at the same time.'[4] These problems might not be too significant, depending on the needs of the plan. As arch-hawk Richard Perle of the US Defence Advisory

Board said in June 2002, 'It's hard to separate the readiness issue from the strategy. And I don't think a strategy has been settled on yet.'[5]

The generals are also concerned by 'nightmare scenarios' including a retreat into the cities by elite Iraqi forces, requiring bloody urban warfare which could cost thousands of US lives, according to Michael O'Hanlon of the liberal Brookings Institution.[6] Then there is the possibility that Baghdad will order the use of any weapons of mass destruction that it may possess. In 1991, the Iraqi leadership refrained from their use, hoping to survive the war. In this proposed war, however, the objective is to kill the Iraqi leadership. As influential US Congressperson Joseph Biden, chair of the Senate Foreign Relations Committee, said at the end of July 2002, 'Some fear that attacking Saddam would precipitate the very thing we are trying to prevent.'[7] Former commander-in-chief of Central Command, General Joseph Hoar testified before the Senate Foreign Relations Committee that 'the possibility of him using WMD [weapons of mass destruction] goes up considerably if the regime is about to fall' – 'a grave risk'. US military estimates for US casualties in the event of a chemical warhead artillery assault range from 10,000 to 35,000 dead or wounded soldiers.[8]

Field Marshal Lord Bramall, formerly Chief of Britain's Defence Staff, warned in August 2002 that Iraq was 'much more likely' to use biological weapons against Israel in the event of an Anglo-American assault: 'By attacking him, you're encouraging him to use them.'[9] Israel is likely to respond to a biological strike on one of its cities by launching nuclear missiles against all Iraqi cities not occupied by US troops, according to influential US military analyst Anthony Cordesman.[10]

Interestingly, despite the repeated allegations by US and British officials that Iraq is attempting to acquire a nuclear weapons capability, 'Pentagon planners do not yet appear concerned that any such weapon is likely to be deployed against them', according a report in July 2002. British troops training in Kuwait in July 2002 were said to be wearing the chemical and biological warfare suits that they would use once an invasion is launched.[11] It seems highly unlikely that Iraq has any useable weapons of mass destruction, but if they exist, the most likely situation in which they would be used is precisely in the event of a US-led invasion of Iraq.

Returning to the evaluation of Iraqi military strength and the ease of US/UK victory, military analyst Anthony Cordesman completed a 92-page estimate of Iraqi military readiness in late July 2002. Mr Cordesman said, 'to be perfectly blunt, I think only fools would bet the lives of other men's sons and daughters on their own arrogance and call this force a cakewalk or a speed bump or something you can dismiss.'[12]

The dispute between the 'jihadists' and the 'pragmatists' within the Bush Administration has resulted, as one would expect, in a compromise, with force levels expected to be below 80,000 US troops, according to a report of General Franks' briefing of the President on 5 August 2002. The head of Central Command is said to have proposed an outline plan conforming closely to the so-called 'inside-out' strategy championed by the Wolfowitz faction: a lightning airborne strike at Baghdad, with further attacks radiating outwards from the Iraqi capital.[13]

There are difficulties with such an intermediate-weight invasion force, as John Keegan, the well-informed Defence Editor for the *Daily Telegraph* pointed out: 'Weak and ineffective though Saddam's army is, it could quite possibly find the strength and competence to fight decisively against an intervention force that it outnumbered.'[14] While General Franks is said to have conceded defeat in his struggle against the 'jihadists', commentators have reported that the 'palpable' tension between the two factions had been growing, not fading in the run-up to this crucial meeting with the President.[15]

The modified 'Afghan test' for a US assault requires, above all else, certain victory, but also demands that the victory be won at low cost and with minimum build-up (to lessen time for opposition to develop). The method chosen must also ensure that Iraq continues to be a unitary state after the war – a state managed by someone willing obey the United States, and acceptable to US allies in the region. These are difficult contradictions to manage. Thus the comment on the US President's choices from a diplomat in Washington in July 2002: 'I know he wants to do it, but when you look at everything involved, I still don't see how he does it.'[16]

REAL ISSUES

Noam Chomsky once remarked that those aspects of international relations that receive the most attention tend to be the least significant. In the case of the proposed invasion of Iraq, it is irrelevant to the legality or morality of the military action whether it is carried out by 250,000 or 80,000 or 80 troops (backed up by devastating air strikes and, over the horizon, US and British nuclear weapons). It is irrelevant whether the invasion force pushes simultaneously up from the Basra region and down from Iraqi Kurdistan, or parachutes immediately into the suburbs of Baghdad.

Given the immense devastation caused by US airstrikes on the Iraqi civilian infrastructure in 1991, and quite likely to be repeated under all of these scenarios, it is not at all clear that the human cost of the invasion will differ greatly if the number of invading soldiers is 250,000 or 25,000. The degree of disruption of the 'oil-for-food' civilian support system and the impact of infrastructural damage may be relatively insensitive to the kinds of strategic and tactical choices being debated so seriously in Washington. It would be a significant achievement if the opponents of the war can force the US Air Force to exempt critical elements of the public health infrastructure, such as the electricity sector, but these are gains that can be won whichever of the strategies is chosen.

For Iraq's Kurds, however, if there is a war, the choice of strategy could be highly significant. An 'inside-out' strategy might well leave them undefended against Iraqi retaliation. Whatever the strategy, there is a real risk that Kurdish territory would be absorbed by Turkey in a 'buffer zone' of the kind operated by Israel in southern Lebanon for many years – as a quid pro quo for Turkish support for the war. The experience of Kurds under Turkish rule has hardly been a pleasant one.

THE MAN ON THE WHITE HORSE

One issue being quite widely debated is of considerable significance for the Iraqi people: the question of what – or who – will come after Saddam Hussein, in the event of US victory. The concern in the mainstream debate is over the cost and dangers of the post-Saddam aftermath. In testimony to the Senate Foreign Relations Committee, Scott Feil, a retired US colonel, and co-director of a project studying post-conflict resolution at the Association of the US Army, estimated that Iraq would need a security force of 75,000 troops, costing an estimated $16.2bn (£10bn) a year. The force would be needed for at least a year, but the US would have to maintain a significant military presence, more than 5,000 strong, for up to ten years, 'if the reconstruction effort is to succeed.'[17] According to a senior aide to President Bush, speaking in August 2002, the British Government keeps asking how the United States proposes to keep law and order the day after victory; 'And when there's no concrete answer, the question comes back: "OK, how long are we going to be occupying Iraq?" ' 'No one has any answer to that question,' according to the aide.[18]

At its core, the question is whether the United States is really prepared to allow the people of Iraq to build a democratic society, or whether the US intends to impose some form of military rule on the country. All of the evidence suggests that Washington is intent on an authoritarian solution, preferably stabilising and maintaining the current regime.

John Simpson recalled in July 2002, 'I shall not quickly forget the tears of the Iraqi Shia general who told me in July 1991 how he went to his own base, now occupied by the Americans, to beg them for the Iraqi weapons stored there. They refused; and he and his men had to face Saddam's avenging forces unarmed. The general was one of the very few survivors.'[19] In 1991, the US spared key elements of the Republican Guard at the war's end; permitted Iraq to use its helicopter forces to put down rebels; withheld arms from Iraqi opposition forces; rebuffed an unwelcome coup attempt linked to opposition forces; and held the rebels at arm's length, refusing to meet with opposition leaders. After calling on the Iraqi people to take matters into their own hands and to overthrow their leader, President George Bush Sr. did everything to support the repression of the uprising short of ordering US tanks and aircraft to fire into the crowds.

In the years that followed, the United States concentrated on trying to install a friendly replacement-Saddam, selected from the 'Iraqi centre', and channelled through the Iraqi National Accord, a group of exiled generals who have carried out indiscriminate terrorist attacks both on Iraqi civilians and almost certainly on their fellow oppositionists in the Iraqi National Congress.

In the current war drive, the Wolfowitz faction has publicly trumpeted its support for the Iraqi National Congress, and the need for a 'democratic' Iraq. One must distinguish between a serious attempt to foster genuine democracy, and the institution of shallow democratic forms – as in the Afghan *loya jirga*, the Pakistani 'referendum', or in the Central and Latin American 'democracies'. Whatever the meaning of the right-wing support for the Iraqi National Congress, the focus of Administration energies appears to have been on the search for 'A Man on a White Horse', a new totalitarian leader to replace the present incumbent.

Time magazine reported in August 2002 that because of the practical problems associated with all-out war, 'the war party is looking for a silver bullet strategy – a lucky first strike on Saddam, say, or a manufactured coup by Iraqi dissidents – that would forestall an old-fashioned deployment of hundreds of thousands of troops and tanks.' The generals discount such 'dream schemes', apparently.[20] If this report is accurate, the 'war party' led by Mr Wolfowitz and Mr Rumsfeld has no serious commitment to a democratic Iraq, despite the public rhetoric. Given their roles in the 1991 Bush Administration which helped crush the uprisings, this would be completely unsurprising.

One plausible scenario would be the creation of an Afghan-style double-act, with a Hashemite king and a Sunni general (possibly an exile, possibly one of the current stars of the regime) being installed to effectively continue the rule of the Ba'ath party – though under a new signboard, no doubt. The reinstallation of a Hashemite king would reassure both the Gulf principalities and Jordan. The reinstallation of a military strongman would reassure Turkey and all of Iraq's neighbours that the three Ottoman provinces of Iraq are to be kept tightly bound together in 'the best of all possible worlds'. The British pioneered this paired system of colonial domination in Iraq in the 1920s; it would be entirely appropriate for the new imperial power to adopt the same device for controlling Iraq in the new century.

DECISIONS, DECISIONS

World opinion in mid-2002 was generally of the view that the pressing issue of the moment in the Middle East was the resolution of the escalating Israel/Palestine crisis, rather than the lingering Iraqi inspection crisis. A French official summed up the divergence neatly: 'The important thing is to build a coalition for peace in the Middle East, not to build a coalition for war in Iraq.'[21] This may well be Mr Blair's private preference also. The British Prime Minister is said to have urged President Bush to accept the primacy of the Middle East peace process, and to have been rebuffed.[22] Outwardly Mr Blair is the staunch ally of the United States. Behind the scenes he appears to be pleading for a flexibility that simply does not exist in the Bush Administration. Hence his constant refrain that 'no decisions have been made' throughout 2002, despite the fact that the Government had quite clearly made a number of important decisions regarding British military deployments and readiness.

British troops were suddenly pulled out of two major exercises for the NATO ACE Mobile Force Rapid Reaction Corps in Germany and the Ukraine scheduled for the autumn of 2002. The 1 (UK) Armoured Division, with its 3000 troops, 'Britain's main fighting force', was withdrawn from a tank exercise in Poland. The bulk of British forces were also rapidly withdrawn from Afghanistan and Bosnia. Most of the UK's 2,400 troops were withdrawn from Kosovo – a move that surprised a British diplomat in its suddenness and scale. The withdrawal also surprised France and the Netherlands, who share responsibility for Kosovo. A senior NATO official in Brussels told the *Financial Times* in July 2002 that the British Ministry of Defence was 'mentally preparing for new challenges'. Asked if that meant Iraq, the official retorted, 'Well, what do you think?' Members of the SAS and the SBS were said to be deployed in northern Iraq at the time, liaising with Kurdish forces and carrying out reconnaissance of potential Iraqi targets, along with CIA 'special activities' teams. HMS Ocean, the pride of the Royal Navy, was to have been the main attraction at the Plymouth Navy Days at the end of August 2002, but was instead withdrawn for a 'highly unusual' and unscheduled overhaul to be ready for active service. Security was tightened up at the British Central Ammunition Depot at Kineton, near Warwick at the end of July 2002, with public access to the arms dump suddenly cut off. A mass mobilisation of key British reservists, including pilots, medical staff, special forces, intelligence and signals personnel, was expected for September 2002.[23]

It was not simply a slip of the tongue when the Prime Minister answered a question on the war from Tam Dalyell MP: 'When the decision is made, we will consider the best way of consulting the House, in the normal way and in the normal circumstances.'[24] When, not if. A Whitehall source confirmed in July 2002 what had been apparent all year, 'President Bush has already made up his mind. This is going to happen. It is a given. What we are waiting for is to be told the details of how and when and where.'[25] And Prime Minister Blair has also made up his mind, and had set the wheels in motion for military preparedness in July 2002.

INSPECTION IS AN OPTION

In public, Washington and London insist that the conflict with Iraq is over disarmament. In reality, however, 'disarmament' is a cover for the overthrow of Saddam Hussein. Thus when Iraq invited the head of UNMOVIC to Baghdad for talks, and then invited US Congresspeople to bring weapons experts and inspect all suspect sites, the US position was that 'There's no need for discussion. What there is a need for is for the regime in Baghdad to live up to its commitment to disarm.'[26] This commitment can only be fulfilled and verified by inspections, but it is clear that the United States is wholeheartedly opposed to the return of weapons inspectors and is doing everything in its power to undermine any initiative which could lead to this 'nightmare scenario'. For the United States, the two central objectives are restoring 'credibility' by finally defeating a rebel against US power, and re-establishing US control over Iraqi oil reserves. Power is the objective. War is the means. UN weapons inspectors are an obstacle from this perspective: part of the problem, not part of the solution.

For those who have a genuine concern for the suffering of the Iraqi people, and for the security of the Middle East, the two central objectives must be the solution of the humanitarian crisis in Iraq, and a regional disarmament process which could begin with the re-establishment of a UN monitoring and inspection regime in Iraq. The means to achieve these objectives are: the lifting of economic sanctions against Iraq, and the return of UN weapons inspectors – the only way to ensure that Iraq does not develop weapons of mass destruction.

Whether or not inaction is an option – it is the option that has been pursued by President Bush since his State of the Union speech in January 2002 – one thing is certain. Inspection *is* an option.

UN weapons inspectors carried out the disarmament of Iraq's weapons of mass destruction, something that was not achieved by US bombing in the 1991 Gulf War. There are three reasons why the inspection and monitoring regime no longer exists in Iraq. Firstly, the US penetrated and used UNSCOM for its own spying/assassination/coup purposes, including the coordination of an UNSCOM inspection with a CIA-backed coup attempt in June 1996. This damaged UNSCOM beyond repair when the truth became known in late 1998 and early 1999. Secondly, the US manipulated UNSCOM inspections and the final UNSCOM report in November and December 1998 to create an atmosphere of confrontation. Thirdly, the US ordered the withdrawal of all UNSCOM staff in December 1998 in order to make it politically possible to carry out Operation Desert Fox. The cumulative impact of these three US interventions was to destroy UNSCOM, and remove the one sure means of preventing Iraq from developing weapons of mass destruction.

VICTORY FOR BIN LADEN

Former UN weapons inspector Scott Ritter has suggested that a US-led war on Iraq 'will effectively mean that Osama bin Laden will have won. Whatever the faults of Saddam Hussein, and he is a brutal dictator, his regime is also secular. If Saddam does indeed fall, which Bush and Blair want, it is highly likely that an Islamist regime will take over after US troops leave, as they will sooner or later.' This could have knock-on effects on Kuwait, Saudi Arabia, Jordan and even Egypt: 'The invasion of Iraq is the quickest path to losing the war on terror and giving legitimacy to the criminal who attacked the US and the entire freedom of the world on 11 September.'[27] While few other commentators are predicting a fundamentalist regime in Iraq, many informed observers share Mr Ritter's belief that al Qaeda's political base woiuld be enlarged considerably by US/UK military action.

Former Chief of the British Defence Staff, Field Marshal Lord Bramall has warned that in the event of a US/UK invasion of Iraq, 'Petrol rather than water would have been poured on the flames, and al-Qaeda would have gained more recruits.'[28] Republican Senator Richard Lugar, five terms in the Senate and the most influential Republican congressperson on foreign affairs, has expressed his fear that establishing 'liberal democracy' in Iraq 'might even lead to more terrorists being spawned out of the process'.[29]

President Bush said in August 2002, 'There's no telling how many wars it will take to secure freedom in the homeland'[30] – yet another indication that the President is entirely sincere about the 'axis of evil'. If he is able to go to war with Iraq, and to prevail at what he considers an acceptable cost, he has every intention of pursuing further unilateral and illegal wars against other enemy states.

THE ATTACK ON SUDAN

At the same time, it is clear that these wars do not increase the security of the US homeland. It was revealed in early August 2002 that relations between Osama bin Laden and the Taliban regime in Aghanistan deteriorated sharply in the two years after bin Laden took refuge in Afghanistan. By the summer of 1998, the leader of the Taliban, Mullah Omar, was so fed up with his unwanted guest that he had struck a secret deal with the Saudis to expel him. But just before Mullah Omar's order to oust the 'arrogant, publicity-seeking' bin Laden was carried out, President Clinton launched an illegal missile strike on Afghanistan and Sudan in retaliation for the bombing of US Embassies in Africa. Prince Turki al-Faisal, the head of Saudi intelligence who had brokered the deal, said, 'The Taliban attitude changed 180 degrees.' When he returned to Afghanistan a month after the missile attacks, Mullah Omar was 'absolutely rude' to the Prince, and the deal to expel bin Laden – which could have had significant benefits for US homeland security – was in tatters.[31]

The US airstrike on Sudan also had other consequences. It destroyed half of Sudan's pharmaceutical supplies. The targeted factory specialised in producing drugs to kill the parasites which pass from herds to herders, 'one of Sudan's principal causes of infant mortality'.[32] A year after the attack a US journalist reported that, 'without the lifesaving medicine [the destroyed facilities] produced, Sudan's death toll from the bombing has continued, quietly, to rise ... Thus, tens of thousands of people – many of them children – have suffered and died from malaria, tuberculosis, and other treatable diseases.' Sanctions against Sudan made it impossible to import adequate amounts of medicines required to cover the serious gap left by the plant's destruction.[33] Noam Chomsky remarks that, proportional to the US population, it is as if the bin Laden network, in a single attack on the US, caused 'hundreds of thousands of people – many of them children – to suffer and die from easily treatable diseases'.

Professor Chomsky also notes that, according to the *Financial Times*, the US bombing 'appears to have shattered the slowly evolving move towards compromise between Sudan's warring sides' and terminated promising steps towards a peace agreement to end the civil war that had left one and a half million people dead since 1981, which might have also led to 'peace in Uganda and the entire Nile Basin.' The attack apparently 'shattered ... the expected benefits of a political shift at the heart of Sudan's Islamist government' towards a 'pragmatic engagement with the outside world,' along with efforts to address Sudan's domestic crises, to end support for terrorism, and to reduce the influence of radical Islamists.[34]

The human cost of the 1998 missile attack on Sudan – which did not advance, but which set back US homeland security, so far as the bin Laden network is concerned – was greater in both relative and absolute terms than the enormous atrocity that was inflicted on New York on 11 September 2001.

It is often assumed by the proponents of war that negotiation and diplomacy are the equivalent of inaction. The case of bin Laden, both in terms of the Saudi-negotiated expulsion order of 1998 and Pakistani-negotiated extradition order of October

2001, shows that diplomacy – in this case with a supposedly mindless fundamentalist regime – was able to achieve what military action could not and did not achieve. These two cases also demonstrate that the determination of the US to pursue military confrontation and achieve military victory has set back US homeland security. This is no service to the relatives of the victims of 11 September, or to the relatives of future victims of terrorist attack, whether in the US homeland, elsewhere in the West, in the Sudanese homeland or in Iraq's ancient homeland.

PREVENTING MASS DESTRUCTION

The way forward must involve solving both the humanitarian crisis and the inspection crisis – without making the former dependent on the latter. The United States and Britain must stop making the health of millions of families dependent on the disarmament of weapons they had no part in developing. The human rights of the ordinary people of Iraq must come first. With the lifting of economic sanctions, whoever controls Iraq is certain to try to use some of the country's newly-restored wealth to re-arm, but there are nonviolent means of restraining proliferation: there could be an ongoing UN inspection and monitoring system, and greater cooperation and restraint by supplier nations. This disarmament effort can only be successful if it is extended to Israel and Iran and others, as suggested in UN Security Council Resolution 687. A rigorous, universal inspection regime for all weapons of mass destruction, throughout the world, would be necessary to persuade the states of the Middle East to accept such restraints. An absolute, unconditional, and legally-binding 'Negative Security Assurance' treaty signed by all the nuclear weapon states, including the United States, stating that none of them will use or threaten to use nuclear weapons against any non-nuclear weapon state under any circumstances, would help to remove another motive for proliferation.

Economic sanctions against Iraq have been a weapon of mass destruction. Britain and the United States share a special responsibility for the human toll. The most appropriate response to that crime for the people of Britain is not merely to dissent from sanctions and war against Iraq – as they already do in large numbers in the case of war – but to actively and nonviolently resist the drive to war, and to demand the complete lifting of economic sanctions. With public opinion turning decisively against war, dissent must build into resistance. Nonviolent resistance has been effective in restraining US violence in the past; it can and it must be effective again. Iraq does not need more Western bombs, or more Western-imposed leaders. Iraq needs a war – a war on poverty. It needs to be able to reconstruct those 'objects indispensable to the survival of the civilian population' still reeling from 1991. Mr Blair must obey his party and his people. The overwhelming majority of people in Britain believe that this country should not participate militarily in a war against Iraq. Britain must withdraw all political and military support for an illegal, immoral, unjustified, unpopular and anti-democratic war for US domination, and call instead for the lifting of economic sanctions. This withdrawal of support stop the US war drive in its tracks.

Emily Johns

LAST WORDS

There is no doubt that the Iraqi people have suffered at the hands of their leader and that the vast majority of Americans believe they deserve to live in a free, prosperous and open society. I believe that history will judge America harshly if we stand by and allow a war criminal to starve and terrorize his people. We have often called ourselves the indispensable nation on the global stage. We cannot and should not stand by while the Iraqi people are left to suffer their fate. But is a US invasion the right response? The answer I believe is no. **The US cannot legitimately claim to be advancing the peace and security of the world by unilaterally invading Iraq, and if we do we should be condemned as Iraq was when it invaded Kuwait.**

All societies rely on the use of force to maintain order and permit individuals to pursue the widest possible goals. When the activities of one violate societal norms the police are empowered to legitimately intervene, with force if necessary, to restore order. Vigilantism, the illegitimate use of force, must be controlled for the common good. Even the use of police powers must be monitored to ensure that excesses are kept to a minimum. Certainly I think that force might legitimately be used in this situation, but it matters profoundly how we go about it.

It's true that international society is less mature than many domestic societies. There is no global police force empowered to knock on Mr. Hussein's door and arrest him. But there are processes in place to deal with violators of international law. The Security Council is empowered to decide when the global peace and security are threatened and force can be used. Granted, it's not a perfect system, but to by-pass it entirely is to bolster those who would agree that the US behaves as a rogue nation, that its actions are illegitimate.

Further, having rejected the International Criminal Court it is more difficult to argue that the US is on the side of law and order. That the ICC does not enjoy the support of the US is especially unfortunate since the Balkan model, the use of force as a way to get criminals before the Tribunal at the Hague, is working remarkably well. The idea that leaders who would develop weapons of mass destruction in violation of international law could be brought before the ICC should not be lightly dismissed.

Which brings up a final point. We in the US like international law. Specifically, we like other states to obey. However, it is the height of hypocrisy to demand that others live up to their obligations while we aggressively reject the notion that we should submit to a legitimate international system of laws as part of a community of nations.

Robin S. Theurkauf, Visiting Fellow,
Department of Political Science, Yale University, and
widow of Tom Theurkauf

Will the invasion of Iraq really bring us closer to a more peaceful global community?

I know from personal experience what the violent death of a family member does to the human spirit.

To be honest, I am tired of the violence here and abroad. There has to be a better way.

> Amber Amundson,
> widow of Craig Scott Amundson

APPENDIX

The Nineteen Questions

On 7 March 2002, the Iraqi Foreign Minister Naji Sabri presented 19 questions to the Secretary-General of the United Nations. The Iraqi News Agency released what it claimed were the text of these questions on 10 July 2002. This document is taken from the CASI website – www.casi.org

1. What is your assessment and what is your evaluation of the stage we have reached following seven years and seven months of Iraq's cooperation with the Special Commission and the International Atomic Energy Agency? How will this cooperation be built on?

2. Since one or two permanent members of the Security Council are saying that they are not convinced that the disarmament phase has ended, we would like to know what is it that they want to verify? What are they looking for and how long will it take? Not only the Security Council but we too should be convinced in order to continue to cooperate with the Security Council. If they have any suspicions about a certain site or a specific activity, we too should know about it.

3. How can you explain the stand of a permanent member of the Security Council officially proclaiming that it wants to invade Iraq and impose an agent regime on its people by force? Is this not a blatant violation of the resolutions of the Security Council? The resolutions of the Security Council clearly stipulate respect for Iraq's sovereignty, independence, and territorial integrity. They also provide for respect to the rules of international law and the charter of the United Nations. How can this permanent member state demand from Iraq to implement the resolutions of the Security Council?

4. Does the Security Council adhere seriously to its mandate and to the resolutions it had passed, especially Resolution 687 of April 1991? Does it seriously adhere to a fair and legal reading and interpretation of this resolution? The Security Council is submitting to the interpretation of the United States and to unilateral US decisions regarding Iraq.

5. How can the relationship between Iraq and the Security Council be normalized in light of the present public policy of the United States that is seeking to invade Iraq and change the national political regime in Iraq by force?

6. The United States keeps proclaiming that the economic sanctions imposed on Iraq will remain so long as the national political regime in Iraq remains. What is the position of the Security Council on this policy that violates the pertinent Security Council resolutions?

7. What guarantees can the United Nations give to prevent a linkage between Iraq's relationship with the United Nations and the hostile political US objectives?

8. The principle of 'concurrence' in implementing the reciprocal commitments stipulated in the Security Council resolutions pertaining to Iraq is necessary and essential to restore confidence between Iraq and the Security Council. What is your opinion on the commitments pertaining to Iraq's rights, especially regarding lifting the sanctions, respecting Iraq's sovereignty, independence, and territorial integrity, and removing weapons of mass destruction from the Middle East region? The Security Council should abide by these commitments in order to start a new page of cooperation between Iraq and the United Nations. And, how can a mechanism be formed to guarantee concurrence in the implementation of the commitments by the two sides?

9. Do you think it is fair to ask the government of Iraq to implement the resolutions of the Security Council and not to make the same request from a permanent member of the Security Council? This permanent member continues to violate these resolutions, especially those pertaining to respect for Iraq's sovereignty, independence, and territorial integrity. It is officially proclaiming that its policy is to invade the Republic of Iraq and impose an agent government on its people.

10. The espionage activities of the inspectors of the former Special Commission and the IAEA – as came in the confessions of some of its members, statements by US sources and permanent members of the Security Council, and as also admitted by the General Secretariat – have been revealed. Following these revelations, would it be fair for such inspectors to return to Iraq? These inspectors would spy on Iraq and its leadership in order to update their information on Iraq's vital economic installations so they could be targeted in a forthcoming aggression.

11. Can the United Nations guarantee that those who may come to Iraq are not spies and will not carry out any espionage activities?

12. Can the United Nations guarantee an end to the two no-fly zones? Can it guarantee that the inspection process would not be a prelude to an aggression on Iraq, as happened in 1998? Can the United Nations guarantee that the United States would not launch an aggression on Iraq while the inspection process is proceeding, as happened in the past seven years and seven months between May 1991 and December 1998?

13. What is the opinion of the Secretary General regarding the required period of inspection so that the inspection teams would be convinced that Iraq does not keep weapons of mass destruction and would inform the Security Council of this fact? What are the methods of inspection that the United Nations is thinking of adopting? To what extent are these methods compatible with international agreements concluded in this regard?

14. How can inspectors from countries that are openly and officially threatening Iraq's national security and threatening to invade Iraq apply 'a neutral international mandate in Iraq'? How can such inspectors respect the provisions of the Security Council resolutions and abide by the limitations of their duties in accordance with the UN charter? The American and British inspectors in the Special Commission and the IAEA helped the United States and Britain to gather intelligence information and to select the targets of their aggression. All the sites that were inspected by the inspection teams were attacked near the end of 1998, including the presidential sites. These attacks took place although the inspectors confirmed these sites did not contain weapons of mass destruction. Moreover, the United States and Britain bombed all the industrial sites that were under constant supervision based on information provided to them by the spy inspectors.

15. What is the Secretary General's opinion on the formation of UNMOVIC? Can it include members who have previously violated the neutral mandate of their organization, breached their duties, and undermined the reputation of the United Nations with their espionage activities against Iraq?

16. What will be UNMOVIC's point of reference? The documents and statements by the United Nations regarding this point of reference are still vague. What are the powers of the UNMOVIC chairman and where do they stop? What are the powers of the general body of commissioners? What is the form of the Secretary General's supervision of its activities and to what extent is this supervision? What are the guarantees that this commission would not transgress on Iraq's sovereign rights?

17. The use of 120,000 tons of bombs – including 800 tons of depleted uranium – against Iraq during the aggression in 1991, the aggressions that followed, and the total blockade over the past 12 years have almost totally destroyed the economic, health, education, and services infrastructures. When the sanctions are lifted, Iraq will need to devote all its resources to rebuild its basic infrastructures. The issue of reparations and the high rate of reparations stand as a major obstacle to accomplishing this goal. What does the Secretary General think can correct this situation? Does he intend to send a team of experts to Iraq to discuss the reconstruction process and how much it will cost? Will the Secretary General prepare what is required to urge the Security Council to reconsider the issue of compensations?

18. The blockade and the military attacks that the United States and Britain have been launching against Iraq since 1991 have led to huge material and human losses in Iraq. To what extent is it possible to look into a framework for a comprehensive solution based on justice to compensate Iraq for the material, human, and psychological losses sustained by its people on the same basis as the one adopted by the Security Council regarding the issue of reparations?

19. Iraq has the full right to defend itself in accordance with Article 51 of the UN Charter. However, the Security Council has not abided by its pledges to respect Iraq's sovereignty, independence, and territorial integrity. This situation encouraged parties in the region and outside the region to violate Iraq's national security. What is your opinion on Iraq's right to self-defense and its right to have defensive weapons as guaranteed by international law and the UN Charter?

NOTES

Please note that newspapers are London newspapers unless otherwise identified. Editions of *Newsweek* and *Time* magazines are European editions.

1 Cited in in Andrew Cockburn and Patrick Cockburn, *Out of the Ashes: The Resurrection of Saddam Hussein* (New York, HarperCollins, 1999), p. 37.
2 *Time* magazine, 13 May 2002, p. 38.
3 *Daily Mirror*, 16 July 2002.

THE BREADTH OF OPPOSITION

1 *Daily Telegraph*, 19 March 2002, p. 25.
2 *Guardian*, 16 March 2002, p. 5.
3 *Sunday Telegraph,* 24 March 2002, p. 1
4 *Sunday Times*, 21 March 2002, p. 15.
5 The full text is available from Pax Christi, St Joseph's, Watford Way, Hendon, London NW4 4TY.
6 *Independent*, 8 April 2002, p. 4.
7 *Hansard,* 12 March 2002, col. 745.
8 *Guardian*, 8 April 2002, p. 2.
9 Michael Quinlan, 'War on Iraq: a blunder and a crime', *Financial Times,* 7 August 2002, p. 15.
10 *Independent*, 20 November 2001, p. 4.
11 Letter, *The Times*, 1 November 2001, p. 21.
12 Letter, *The Times*, 5 September 2002, p. 25.
13 *Daily Mirror*, 5 August 2002, p. 5; *Times*, 5 August 2002, p. 1.
14 Wesley Clark, 'Why war should be America's last resort', *Times*, 29 August 2002, p. 17.
15 *New York Times*, 25 August 2002, cited in *Independent*, 27 August 2002, p. 10.
16 *Wall Street Journal*, 16 August 2002, cited in *Sunday Telegraph*, 18 August 2002, p. 23.
17 *Sunday Telegraph*, 18 August, 2002, p. 23; David E. Sanger, 'For the president, summer of discontent', *International Herald Tribune*, 4 September 2002, p. 4.
18 Bronwen Maddox, 'Read my lips: it's time for war on Iraq – maybe,' *Times*, 28 August 2002, p. 12.
19 James Drummond, 'Moussa warns attack would open "gates of hell" ', *Financial Times*, 6 September 2002, p. 8
20 'Schroeder leads EU chorus of dissent', *Times*, 5 September 2002, p. 16.
21 James Blitz et al., 'Mandela sharply criticises Bush's policy on Iraq', *Financial Times*, 3 September 2002, p. 11; Alice Lagnado and Philip Webster, 'No alternative to Iraq attack, Blair will tell critics', *Times,* 3 September 2002, p. 11.
22 *Daily Mirror*, 6 September 2002, p. 5.
23 Letter, 'Iraq: war is not the way', *Guardian*, 5 September 2002, p. 25.

ACHILLES' HEEL

1 Tim Reid, 'Bush and father at odds over Iraq strike,' *Times*, 26 August 2002, p. 1; Julian Borger, 'Daggers drawn in the house of Bush', *Guardian*, 28 August 2002, p. 4; Peter Beaumont and Ed Helmore, 'Will Bush go to war against Saddam?', *Observer*, 1 September 2002, p. 17.
2 Michael T. Klare, *Beyond the Vietnam Syndrome: US Interventionism in the 1980s* (Institute for Policy Studies, Washington DC, 1982), pp. 5-7.
3 Matthew Engel, 'Chicken hawks', *Guardian*, 20 August 2002, p. 15.
4 See Chapter X, Reason 8, 'GI Joe Says No'.
5 *Sunday Telegraph*, 18 August 2002, p. 23; 'What they said now and then', *Guardian*, 28 August 2002, p. 4.
6 'Remember Churchill: US hawks cite "lone stand" to justify war on Iraq', *Daily Telegraph*, 29 August 2002, p. 4.
7 *Independent*, 26 August 2002, p. 9; *Guardian*, 31 August 2002, p. 5.
8 Table, 'Attitudes towards the war on terror', *Times*, 6 February 2002, p. 19; Matthew Engel, 'Americans losing faith in Bush on Iraq', *Guardian*, 24 August 2002, p. 17; German Marshall Fund and Chicago Council on Foreign Relations, *A World Transformed: Foreign Policy Attitudes of the US Public After September 11* available at http://www.worldviews.org/key_findings/us_911_report.htm#kf6
9 *Guardian*, 31 August 2002, p. 5; David Rennie, 'American support for attack falls', *Daily Telegraph*, 31 August 2002, p. 21.
10 Julian Borger, 'Can the US go it alone against Saddam?' *Guardian*, 31 August 2002, p. 5.
11 *Daily Mirror*, 30 August 2002, p. 8; *Times*, 30 August 2002, p. 1.

12 *Daily Mirror*, 5 August 2002, p. 5; *Times*, 5 August 2002, p. 1.

13 *Sunday Telegraph*, 7 April 2002, p. 1.

14 *Daily Telegraph*, 27 March 2002, p. 4; *Independent on Sunday*, 7 April 2002, p. 1; *Sunday Telegraph*, 7 April 2002, p. 1; *Independent*, 2 March 2002, p. 2; *Daily Telegraph*, 27 March 2002, p. 4.

15 *Observer*, 24 February 2002, p. 3; *Guardian*, 25 March 2002, p. 1.

16 *Observer*, 24 March 2002, p. 2.

17 *Independent*, 11 April 2002, p. 5; *Times*, 2 April 2002, p. 12; *Daily Telegraph*, 27 March 2002, p. 4.

18 *Financial Times*, 9 April, 2002, p. 2.

19 Article in the *Sunday Mirror* quoted in *Independent*, 18 March 2002, p. 2.

20 *Daily Telegraph*, 27 March 2002, p. 4.

21 *Times*, 2 April 2002, p. 12.

22 *Times*, 2 April 2002, p. 12.

23 *Observer*, 24 March 2002, p. 2; *Guardian*, 4 March 2002, p. 1; *Daily Telegraph*, 11 March 2002, p. 2.

24 *Independent on Sunday*, 7 April 2002, p. 1.

25 *Financial Times*, 25 February 2002, p. 3.

26 On 10 April 2002, when nearly 150 MPs had signed the EDM, 125 of them were Labour MPs. 'Blair faces MPs' anger over Iraq', BBC News Online, 10 April 2002, http://news.bbc.co.uk/hi/english/uk_politics/newsid_1919000/1919606.stm

27 *Independent*, 18 March 2002, p. 4.

28 'Londoner's Diary', *Evening Standard,* 1 May 2002, p. 10.

29 *Daily Telegraph*, 11 April 2002, p. 1.

30 *Times*, 11 April 2002, p. 15.

31 *Daily Telegraph*, 11 April 2002, p. 1.

32 Donald Macintyre, *Independent*, 11 April, p. 18.

33 *Financial Times*, 11 April 2002, p. 2.

34 *Daily Telegraph*, 11 April 2002, p. 1.

35 *Guardian*, 11 April 2002, p. 3.

36 Chris McLaughlin, *The Big Issue*, 8-14 April 2002, p. 6.

37 *Guardian*, 27 February 2002, p. 20.

38 Ben Macintyre, *Times*, 11 April 2002, p. 2.

39 *Guardian*, 16 March 2002, p. 1; *Times*, 8 March 2002, p. 2; London *Evening Standard*, 7 March 2002, p. 2; *Independent*, 8 March 2002, p. 1; *Daily Telegraph*, 8 March 2002, p. 1.

40 London *Evening Standard*, 7 March 2002, p. 2.

41 *Financial Times*, 8 March 2002, p. 1.

42 *Times*, 18 March 2002, p. 4.

43 *Sunday Times*, 10 March 2002, p. 18.

44 *Daily Telegraph*, 12 March 2002, p. 1; *Financial Times*, 12 March 2002, p. 2; *Financial Times*, 18 March 2002, p. 2; *Independent*, 12 March 2002, p. 1.

45 *Independent*, 11 March 2002, p. 1; *Guardian*, 18 March 2002, p. 1; *Financial Times*, 18 March 2002, p. 2; *Independent*, 11 March 2002, p. 1, *Guardian*, 11 March 2002, p. 12; *Guardian*, 3 April 2002, p. 1.

46 Lucy Ward, 'Iraq dossier not pulled, says PM – Brown camp denies split over policy on Saddam', *Guardian*, 22 April 2002.

47 'Delay and danger: More awkward challenges ahead for Blair on Iraq', *Times*, 11 April 2002, p. 23.

48 *Guardian,* 20 June 2002, p. 18.

49 *Sunday Telegraph*, 31 March 2002, p. 25.

50 *Daily Telegraph*, 28 March 2002, p. 27.

51 *Financial Times*, 10 April 2002, p. 4.

52 *Financial Times*, 10 April 2002, p. 4.

53 *Financial Times*, 3 April 2002, p. 6.

54 *Daily Telegraph*, 9 May 2002, p. 8; *Financial Times*, 9 May 2002, p. 3; *Times*, 9 May 2002, p. 14.

55 *Times*, 29 January 2002, p. 4; *Daily Mirror*, 9 August 2002, p. 2. *The Times* states that the Conservative Party was understood to be losing up to £300,000 a month, 'and accountants have said that if the party was a normal business it would not be regarded as a going concern.' *Mirror*, 30 January 2002, p. 4; *Guardian*, 29 January 2002, p. 10. The Conservative Party had 330,000 members, and the Liberal Democrats around 76,000 (rising from 71,000 in 2000 and 74,000 in 2001).

56 See pages 165-170; Times, 30 August 2002, p. 1.

57 *Financial Times*, 9 May 2002, p. 6; *Financial Times*, 3 May 2002, p. 19.

58 See page 163.

CHAPTER II TERROR AND JUST RESPONSE

1 Bush cited by Rich Heffern, *National Catholic Reporter*, Jan. 11, 2002. Reagan, *New York Times*, Oct. 18, 1985. Shultz, U.S. Dept. of State, *Current Policy* No. 589, June 24, 1984; No. 629, Oct. 25, 1984.

2 *US Army Operational Concept for Terrorism Counteraction*, TRADOC Pamphlet No. 525-37, 1984.

3 Res. 42/159, 7 Dec. 1987; Honduras abstaining.

4 Joseba Zulaika and William Douglass, *Terror and Taboo* (New York, London: Routledge, 1996), 12. 1980-88 record, see "Inter-Agency Task Force, Africa Recovery Program/Economic Commission, *South African Destabilization: the Economic Cost of Frontline Resistance to Apartheid*, NY, UN, 1989, 13, cited by Merle Bowen, *Fletcher Forum*, Winter 1991. On expansion of US trade with South Africa after Congress authorized sanctions in 1985 (overriding Reagan's veto), see Gay McDougall, Richard Knight, in Robert Edgar, ed., *Sanctioning Apartheid* (Trenton, NJ: Africa World Press, 1990).

5 For review of unilateral US rejectionism for 30 years, see my introduction to Roane Carey, ed., *The New Intifada* (London, New York: Verso, 2000); see sources cited for more detail.

6 It is, however, never used. On the reasons, see Alexander George, ed., *Western State Terrorism* (Cambridge: Polity-Blackwell, 1991).

7 Strobe Talbott and Nayan Chanda, introduction, *The Age of Terror: America and the World after September 11* (New York: Basic Books and the Yale U. Center for the Study of Globalization, 2001).

8 Abram Sofaer, "The United States and the World Court," U.S. Dept. of State, *Current Policy*, No. 769 (Dec. 1985). The vetoed Security Council resolution called for compliance with the ICJ orders, and, mentioning no one, called on all states "to refrain from carrying out, supporting or promoting political, economic or military actions of any kind against any state of the region." Elaine Sciolino, *New York Times*, July 31, 1986.

9 Shultz, "Moral Principles and Strategic Interests," April 14, 1986, U.S. Dept. of State, *Current Policy* No. 820. Shultz Congressional testimony, see Jack Spence in Thomas Walker, ed., *Reagan versus the Sandinistas* (Boulder, London: Westview, 1987). For review of the undermining of diplomacy and escalation of international state terror, see my *Culture of Terrorism* (Boston: South End, 1988); *Necessary Illusions* (Boston: South End, 1989); *Deterring Democracy* (London, New York: Verso, 1991). On the aftermath, see Thomas Walker and Ariel Armony, eds., *Repression, Resistance, and Democratic Transition in Central America* (Wilmington: Scholarly Resources, 2000). On reparations, see Howard Meyer, *The World Court in Action* (Lanham, MD, Oxford: Rowman & Littlefield, 2002), chap. 14.

10 Edward Price, "The Strategy and Tactics of Revolutionary Terrorism," *Comparative Studies in Society and History 19:1*; cited by Chalmers Johnson, "American Militarism and Blowback," *New Political Science* 24.1, 2002.

11 SOA, 1999, cited by Adam Isacson and Joy Olson, *Just the Facts* (Washington: Latin America Working Group and Center for International Policy, 1999), ix.

12 Greenwood, "International law and the 'war against terrorism'," *International Affairs* 78.2 (2002), appealing to par. 195 of *Nicaragua v. USA*, which the Court did not use to justify its condemnation of US terrorism, but surely is more appropriate to that than to the case that concerns Greenwood. Franck, "Terrorism and the Right of Self-Defense," *American J. of International Law* 95.4 (Oct. 2001).

13 Howard, *Foreign Affairs*, Jan/Feb 2002; talk of Oct. 30, 2001 (Tania Branigan, *Guardian*, Oct. 31). Ignatieff, *Index on Censorship* 2, 2002.

14 *New York Times*, Oct. 1, 2001.

15 Frank Schuller and Thomas Grant, *Current History*, April 2002.

16 Werner Daum, "Universalism and the West," *Harvard International Review*, Summer 2001. On other assessments, and the warnings of Human Rights Watch, see my *9-11* (New York: Seven Stories, 2001), 45ff.

17 Christopher Hitchens, *Nation*, June 10, 2002.

18 Talbott and Chanda, *op. cit.*

19 Martha Crenshaw, Ivo Daalder and James Lindsay, David Rapoport, *Current History, America at War*, Dec. 2001. On interpretations of the first "war on terror" at the time, see George, *op. cit.*

20 *Envío* (UCA Managua), Oct.; Ricardo Stevens (Panama), NACLA *Report on the Americas*, Nov/Dec; Galeano, *La Jornada* (Mexico City), cited by Alain Frachon, *Le Monde*, Nov. 24, 2001.

21 For many sources, see my *Fateful Triangle* (Boston: South End, 1983; updated 1999 edition, on South Lebanon in the 1990s); *Pirates and Emperors* (New York: Claremont, 1986; Pluto, London, forthcoming); *World Orders Old and New*.

22 Bennet, *New York Times*, Jan. 24, 2002.

23 For details, see my essay in George, *op. cit.*

24 Crenshaw, *op. cit.*

25 Chalmers Johnson, *Nation*, Oct. 15, 2001.

26 Ian Williams, *Middle East International*, 21 Dec. 2001, 11 Jan. 2002. John Donnelly, *Boston Globe*, April 25, 2002; the specific reference is to an earlier US veto.

27 Conference of High Contracting Parties, *Report on Israeli Settlement*, Jan.-Feb. 2002 (Foundation for Middle East Peace, Washington). On these matters see Francis Boyle, "Law and Disorder in the Middle East," *The Link* 35.1, Jan.-March 2002.

28 For some details, see my *New Military Humanism* (Monroe ME: Common Courage, 1999), chap. 3, and sources cited. On evasion of the facts in the State Department Human Rights Report, see Lawyers Committee for Human Rights, *Middle East and North Africa* (New York, 1995), 255.

29 Tamar Gabelnick, William Hartung, and Jennifer Washburn, *Arming Repression: U.S. Arms Sales to Turkey During the Clinton Administration* (New York and Washington: World Policy Institute and Federation of Atomic Scientists, October 1999). I exclude Israel-Egypt, a separate category. On state terror in Colombia, now largely farmed out to paramilitaries in standard fashion, see particularly Human Rights Watch, *The Sixth Division* (Sept. 2001) and Colombia Human Rights Certification III, Feb. 2002. Also, among others, Medicos Sin Fronteras, *Desterrados* (Bogota, 2001).

30 For a sample, see *New Military Humanism* and my *A New Generation Draws the Line* (London, NY: Verso, 2000).

31 Judith Miller, *New York Times*, April 30, 2000. Pearson, *Fletcher Forum* 26:1, Winter/Spring 2002.

32 http://www.gallup.international.com/terrorismpoll-figures.htm; data from Sept. 14-17, 2001.

33 John Burns, *New York Times*, Sept. 16, 2001; Samina Amin, *International Security* 26.3, Winter 2001-02). For some earlier warnings, see *9-11*. On the postwar evaluation of international agencies, see Imre Karacs, *Independent on Sunday* (London), Dec. 9, 2001, reporting their warnings that over a million people are "beyond their reach and face death from starvation and disease." For some press reports, see my "Peering into the Abyss of the Future," Lakdawala Memorial Lecture, Institute of Social Sciences, New Delhi, Nov. 2001, updated Feb. 2002.

34 *Ibid.*, for early estimates. Barbara Crossette, *New York Times*, March 26, and Ahmed Rashid, *Wall Street Journal*, June 6, 2002, reporting the assessment of the UN World Food Program and the failure of donors to provide pledged funds. The WFP reports that "wheat stocks are exhausted, and there is no funding" to replenish them (Rashid). The UN had warned of the threat of mass starvation at once because the bombing disrupted planting that provides 80% of the country's grain supplies (AFP, Sept. 28; Edith Lederer, AP, Oct. 18, 2001). Also Andrew Revkin, *New York Times*, Dec. 16, 2001, citing U.S. Department of Agriculture, with no mention of bombing.

35 Patrick Tyler and Elisabeth Bumiller, *New York Times*, Oct. 12, quoting Bush; Michael Gordon, *New York Times*, Oct. 28, 2001, quoting Boyce; both p. 1.

36 Barry Bearak, *New York Times*, Oct. 25; John Thornhill and Farhan Bokhari, *Financial Times*, Oct. 25, Oct. 26; John Burns, *New York Times*, Oct. 26; Indira Laskhmanan, *Boston Globe*, Oct. 25, 26, 2001.

37 Interview, Anatol Lieven, *Guardian*, Nov. 2, 2001.

38 Ann Lesch, *Middle East Policy* IX.2, June 2002. Also Michael Doran, *Foreign Affairs*, Jan.-Feb. 2002; and many others, including several contributors to *Current History*, Dec. 2001.

39 Sumit Ganguly, *Ibid.*

40 For sources and background discussion, see my *World Orders Old and New*, 79, 201f.

41 Peter Waldman et al., *Wall Street Journal*, Sept. 14, 2001; also Waldman and Hugh Pope, *Wall Street Journal*, Sept. 21, 2001.

42 Aldrich, *Guardian*, 22 April, 2002.

CHAPTER III THE SMOKING GUN

1 *Independent on Sunday*, 7 October 2001, p. 7; see ARROW Anti-War Briefing 6 for more details. ARROW Anti-War Briefings are available from www.justicenotvengeance.org

2 *Daily Telegraph*, 4 October 2001, p. 9.

3 *Financial Times*, 20 September 2001, p. 7.

4 *Independent*, 19 September 2001, p. 1; *Times*, 22 September 2001, p. 1, emphasis added. See ARROW Anti-War Briefings for more information on this topic.

5 *Independent*, 1 October 2001, p. 1.

6 *Times*, 8 October 2001, p. 2.

CHAPTER IV DESTROYING UNSCOM

1 Sarah Graham-Brown, *Sanctioning Saddam: The Politics of Intervention in Iraq* (London, 1999), p. 57.

2 Percy Craddock, *In Pursuit of British Interests: Reflections on Foreign Policy under Margaret Thatcher and John Major* (London, 1997), p. 183.

3 There were also three other demands in UNSCR 687, though none of these was explicitly linked to the lifting of economic sanctions. Firstly, the Kuwait/Iraq border was to be defined by a UN Commission; Iraq was to accept the findings of this Commission, and to accept the sovereignty of Kuwait itself; and Iraq was to accept the establishment of a monitored, demilitarised zone between Iraq and Kuwait. These demands were fulfilled with a declaration from the Iraqi parliament in November 1994. Secondly, Kuwaiti and third-party nationals held in Iraq were to be repatriated, and stolen Kuwaiti property returned. On this issue, the Kuwaiti Government continues to accuse Baghdad of holding 600 or so missing Kuwaiti citizens; most state-owned property has been returned, but Kuwaiti military equipment and most pri-

vately-owned assets taken in 1991 appear to remain in Iraqi hands, according to Eric Hoskins. Eric Hoskins, 'The Humanitarian Impacts of Economic Sanctions and War in Iraq', in Thomas G. Weiss, David Cortright, George A. Lopez and Larry Minear eds., *Political Gain and Civilian Pain: Humanitarian Impacts of Economic Sanctions* (Lanham/Oxford, 1997), p. 139. Strictly speaking, paragraph 15 only 'Requests the Secretary-General to report to the Security Council on the steps taken to facilitate the return of all Kuwaiti property seized by Iraq, including a list of any property that Kuwait claims has not been returned or which has not been returned intact'. On the prisoner issue, Paragraph 30 merely required Iraqi cooperation with the Red Cross; it did not demand the return of all missing individuals. Thirdly, Iraq was to renounce international terrorism, and was no longer to allow 'any organization directed towards commission of such acts to operate within its territory'. According to paragraph 33, these were conditions, along with the disarmament provisions, for the declaration of a formal cease-fire. So there were four different sets of conditions required for lifting export sanctions; for lifting import sanctions; for ending the arms embargo; and for a formal end to the war.

4 Dilip Hiro, *Neighbours, Not Friends: Iraq and Iran after the Gulf Wars* (London, Routledge, 2001), p. 80.

5 Sarah Graham-Brown, *Sanctioning Saddam: The Politics of Intervention in Iraq* (London, 1999), p. 78.

6 Sarah Graham-Brown, *Sanctioning Saddam*, p. 79.

7 Cited in Dilip Hiro, *Neighbours, Not Friends*, p. 76.

8 Scott Ritter, *Endgame*, p. 156.

9 Sarah Graham-Brown, *Sanctioning Saddam*, p. 86.

10 *Financial Times*, 12 November 1998.

11 *Financial Times*, 2 November 1998.

12 *Economist*, 7 November 1998.

13 *Independent*, 13 November 1998.

14 Dilip Hiro, *Neighbours, Not Friends*, p. 158.

15 Richard Butler, *Saddam Defiant: The Threat of Weapons of Mass Destruction and the Crisis of Global Security* (Phoenix, London, 2000), p. 206.

16 Dilip Hiro, *Neighbours, Not Friends*, p. 158.

17 'UN Security Council discusses Iraq crisis', BBC News Online, 14 November 1998, http://news.bbc.co.uk/1/hi/world/middle_east/214578.stm ; Richard Butler, *Saddam Defiant*, pp. 206 f.

18 *Guardian*, 3 August 2002, p. 4.

19 Scott Ritter, *Endgame*, p. 141.

20 Richard Butler, *Saddam Defiant: The Threat of Weapons of Mass Destruction and the Crisis of Global Security* (Phoenix, London, 2000), p. 96.

21 Richard Butler, *Saddam Defiant*, pp. 125, 127.

22 Geoff Simons, *Iraq – Primus Inter Pariah: A Crisis Chronology, 1997-98* (Macmillan, Basingstoke, 1999), p. 160. No reference.

23 Richard Butler, *Saddam Defiant*, p. 155.

24 *Daily Telegraph*, 23 December 1998, p. 10.

25 *Sunday Times*, 20 December 1998, p. 1.15.

26 *Times*, 17 December 1998, p. 3.

27 *Mail on Sunday*, 20 December 1998, p. 8.

28 *Financial Times*, 17 December 1998, p. 8.

29 Richard Butler, *Saddam Defiant*, pp. 125, 127.

30 *Guardian*, 16 December 1998, p. 14.

31 Richard Butler, *Saddam Defiant*, pp. 218 f.

32 *Financial Times*, 17 December 1998, p. 8.

33 *Mail on Sunday*, 20 December 1998, p. 8.

34 *Financial Times*, 30 July 2002, p. 7.

35 Scott Ritter, *Endgame*, pp. 20-26. In his memoirs, Richard Butler makes much of the fact that Ritter wrongly claimed that Butler 'met' Albright in Bahrain before ordering the inspection delayed, when in fact he spoke to her 'via telephone'. However, he does not discuss the cancelled inspection that led to Ritter's resignation, or remark on the fact that this same operation turned out to be one of the final confrontations UNSCOM engaged in. Richard Butler, *Saddam Defiant*, p. 193.

36 Scott Ritter, *Endgame*, p. 196.

37 *Independent*, 17 December 1998, p. 4.

38 *Independent*, 23 December 1998, p. 7.

39 *Times*, 22 December 1998, p. 1.

40 AP, 17 December 1998.

41 Richard Butler, *Saddam Defiant*, p. 221.

42 *Independent*, 23 December 1998, p. 7.

43 Richard Butler, *Saddam Defiant*, p. 221.

44 *Mail on Sunday*, 20 December 1998, p. 8.

45 Dilip Hiro, *Neighbours, Not Friends*, p. 161.

46 *Financial Times*, 17 December 1998, p. 8. There were many other charges against the Iraqis, including Iraq's refusal to hand over 11 of 12 requested sets of documents – Iraq said they did not exist, had been destroyed, or were irrelevant. The one document Iraq did offer to show UNSCOM, 'a key document on chemical weapons', would only be displayed in the presence of Prakash Shah, Kofi Annan's special envoy. This condition was 'rejected by Unscom.' *Financial Times*, 17 December 1998, p. 8. Iraqi minders are also said to have 'routinely interrupted' the questioning of biology graduate students at a university where forbidden research is known to have taken place, and to have prompted answers from those being questioned. Iraq also imposed new restrictions, such as the ban on inspections on Friday, the Muslim day of rest (a ban imposed on 11 December). 'Another was a refusal to provide test data from the production of missiles and their engines, as Iraq routinely did in the past.' *Washington Post*, 16 December 1998. There were other problems of this level of seriousness.

47 *Observer*, 20 December 1998, p. 13.

48 *Financial Times*, 17 December 1998, p. 8.

49 Dilip Hiro, *Neighbours, Not Friends*, p. 128.

50 Richard Butler, *Saddam Defiant*, p. 202.

51 Richard Butler, *Saddam Defiant*, p. 224.

52 Dilip Hiro, *Neighbours, Not Friends*, p. 161.

53 Richard Butler, *Saddam Defiant*, p. 226.

54 *Guardian*, 18 December 1998, p. 5.

55 Scott Ritter, *Endgame*, p. 135.

56 Scott Ritter, *Endgame*, pp. 136 f.

57 Scott Ritter, *Endgame*, pp. 144, 143.

58 Scott Ritter, *Endgame*, p. 157.

59 Dilip Hiro, *Neighbours, Not Friends*, p. 134.

60 Dilip Hiro, *Neighbours, Not Friends*, p. 104.

61 Dilip Hiro, *Neighbours, Not Friends*, p. 118.

62 Dilip Hiro, *Neighbours, Not Friends*, p. 118.

63 Scott Ritter, *Endgame*, p. 154.

64 Scott Ritter, *Endgame*, p. 19.

65 Robert Fisk, *Independent*, 6 November 1998, cited in Geoff Simons, *Iraq – Primus Inter Pariah*, p. 180.

66 Dilip Hiro, *Neighbours, Not Friends*, p. 103.

67 William Arkin, *Washington Post*, 17 January 1999, cited in *Sanctioning Saddam*, p. 103 n. 142; *Sunday Times*, 15 November 1998, cited in Dilip Hiro, *Neighbours, Not Friends*, p. 158.

68 See pages 83-84.

69 *Daily Telegraph*, 20 November 1998, p.1

70 Richard Butler, *Saddam Defiant*, p. 228.

CHAPTER V UNDERMINING UNMOVIC

1 See pages 124-126.

2 *Observer*, 17 March 2002, p. 15.

3 *Daily Telegraph*, 17 June 2002, p. 1.

4 *New Yorker*, 24 December 2001, p. 63.

5 *Washington Post*, 11 January 2002, p. A15.

6 *Guardian*, 6 July 2002, p. 16.

7 *Washington Post*, 15 April 2002, p. A01; *Financial Times*, 5 March 2002, p. 10.

8 *Guardian*, 6 May 2002.

9 *Guardian*, 6 May 2002.

10 *Time* magazine, 13 May 2002, p. 38.

11 Anthony H. Cordesman and Abraham R. Wagner, *The Lessons of Modern War Volume IV: The Gulf War* (Westview Press, Colorado, 1996), pp. 884 f.

12 Anthony H. Cordesman and Abraham R. Wagner, *The Lessons of Modern War*, p. 897.

13 Cited in Anthony H. Cordesman and Abraham R. Wagner, *The Lessons of Modern War*, p. 912.

14 Anthony H. Cordesman and Abraham R. Wagner, *The Lessons of Modern War*, p. 913.

15 *Washington Post*, 27 August 1998, cited in Graham-Brown, *Sanctioning Saddam*, p. 103 n. 140.

16 *Washington Post*, 13 January 2000, p. A19.

17 Dilip Hiro, *Observer*, 24 September 2000.
18 *Times*, 8 April 2002, p. 4. The *Times* actually misquoted the Prime Minister as saying 'anyone, any time and place'.
19 *Times*, 16 February 2002, p. 19.
20 *Guardian*, 14 February 2002, p. 1.
21 *Los Angeles Times*, 19 June 2002.
22 *Los Angeles Times*, 19 June, 2002.
23 Eric Schmitt, 'US Plan for Iraq Is Said to Include Attack on 3 Sides', *New York Times*, 5 July 2002.
24 *Independent on Sunday*, 7 July 2002, p. 14.
25 *Washington Post*, 5 July 2002, p. A16.
26 *Financial Times*, 6 July 2002, p. 1.
27 *Financial Times*, 6 July 2002, p. 1.
28 *Daily Telegraph*, 6 July 2002, p. 16.
29 *Financial Times*, 5 July 2002, p. 10.
30 *Financial Times*, 5 July 2002, p. 10.
31 *Financial Times,* 6 July 2002, p. 1.
32 *Financial Times*, 5 July 2002, p. 10.
33 *Guardian*, 16 April 2002, p. 13; *Washington Post*, 15 April 2002.
34 Associated Press report, 1 March 2002; *Independent*, 4 March 2002, p. 2; *Times*, 8 March 2002, p. 23.
35 'Pressure grows on Bush over Iraq attack,' *Times*, 6 August 2002, p. 10.
36 *Financial Times*, 19 March 2002, p. 11.
37 *Financial Times*, 6 July 2002, p. 1.
38 Richard Butler, *Saddam Defiant*, p. 217.

CHAPTER VI INSPECTION IS AN OPTION

1 'Remarks by the President at 2002 Graduation Exercise of the United States Military Academy West Point, New York', 1 June 2002 http://www.whitehouse.gov/news/releases/2002/06/20020601-3.html
2 'Remarks by the President to Troops and Families of the 10th Mountain Division – New York', 19 July, 2002 http://www.whitehouse.gov/news/releases/2002/07/20020719.html
3 James Blitz, 'Blair warns of need for pre-emptive Iraq strike', *Financial Times*, 17 July 2002, p. 5.
4 *Times*, 12 March 2002, p. 5.
5 *Independent*, 13 July 2002, p. 13.
6 *Times*, 18 July 2002, p. 17.
7 *Mirror*, 11 July 2002, p. 2.
8 *Daily Telegraph*, 17 June 2002, p. 1.
9 *Times,* 4 July 2002, p. 16; *Guardian*, 6 July 2002, p. 16.
10 *Observer*, 10 March 2002.
11 *Independent*, 2 March 2002, p. 2.
12 *Financial Times*, 3 June 2002, p. 16.
13 *Guardian*, 6 May 2002.
14 *Times*, 10 July 2002, p. 18.
15 *Daily Telegraph*, 6 July 2002, p. 16.
16 *Time* magazine, 13 May 2002, p. 35.
17 Scott Ritter, 'Redefining Iraq's Obligation: The Case for Qualitative Disarmament of Iraq', *Arms Control Today*, June 2000.
18 UNSCOM Report cited in Scott Ritter, 'Redefining Iraq's Obligation'.
19 Scott Ritter, 'Redefining Iraq's Obligation'.
20 *Guardian*, 15 March 2002, p. 16.
21 UNSCOM paper cited in Scott Ritter, 'Redefining Iraq's Obligation'.
22 Scott Ritter, 'Redefining Iraq's Obligation'.
23 *Guardian*, 5 March 2002, p. 16.
24 Scott Ritter, 'Redefining Iraq's Obligation'.
25 Scott Ritter, 'Redefining Iraq's Obligation'; 'Rumsfeld: Iraq Checks Not Worthwhile', Associated Press, 16 April 2002; Tony Blair, interview with NBC, 4 April 2002, www.number-10.gov.uk
26 *Guardian*, 21 November 2001, p. 7.
27 Dilip Hiro, *Neighbours, Not Friends: Iraq and Iran after the Gulf Wars* (London, Routledge, 2001), p. 61.
28 Dilip Hiro, *Neighbours, Not Friends*, p. 103. The episode is also discussed in Andrew Cockburn and Patrick Cockburn, *Out of the Ashes: The Resurrection of Saddam Hussein* (New York, HarperCollins, 1999), pp. 219–230.

29 This is the view put forward in Dilip Hiro, *Neighbours, Not Friends*, p. 104.

30 Dilip Hiro, *Neighbours, Not Friends*, p. 107.

31 Cited in Jenni Rissanen, 'United States Rejects Protocol', BWC Protocol Bulletin, Acronym Institute, 25 July 2001 http://www.acronym.org.uk/bwc/bwc05.htm

32 Human Rights Watch, 'Arms', World Report 1999 http://www.hrw.org/worldreport99/arms/arms5.html ; 'US fails to block torture convention', *Guardian*, 25 July 2002, p. 13.

33 William Stormont, letter, *Financial Times*, 22 July 2002, p. 20.

34 Anthony Cordesman and Ahmed S. Hashim, *Iraq: Sanctions and Beyond* (New York, Westview Press, 1997), pp. 305, 303.

35 Cordesman and Hashim, *Iraq: Sanctions and Beyond*, p. 336.

36 Richard Butler, *Saddam Defiant: The Threat of Weapons of Mass Destruction and the Crisis of Global Security* (London, Phoenix, 2000), p. 130.

37 Cordesman and Hashim, *Iraq: Sanctions and Beyond*, pp. 336 f.

38 Michael Eisenstadt, 'Curtains for the Ba'ath', *The National Interest*, Number 66, Winter 2001/02, p. 61.

39 Scott Ritter, 'Redefining Iraq's Obligation'.

40 Scott Ritter, 'Redefining Iraq's Obligation'.

41 I have drawn here on the able summary by Dilip Hiro in *Neighbours, Not Friends*, p. 87.

42 Scott Ritter, 'Redefining Iraq's Obligation'.

43 Scott Ritter, 'Redefining Iraq's Obligation'.

44 'Remarks by the President at 2002 Graduation Exercise of the United States Military Academy West Point, New York', 1 June 2002.

CHAPTER VII REGIME STABILISATION, 1991

1 *Sunday Times*, 7 April 2002, p. 28.

2 *Guardian*, 8 April 2002, p. 16; *Independent*, 8 April 2002, p. 4.

3 The first quote comes from the official transcript, see note 5 below; *Sunday Telegraph*, 7 April 2002, p. 21.

4 *Independent*, 8 April 2002, p. 4.

5 'PM meets President Bush for talks', 6 April 2002. The official transcript is available at http://www.number-10.gov.uk/output/page4757.asp

6 'Prime Minister's speech at the George Bush Senior Presidential Library', 7 April 2002, official transcript available at http://www.number-10.gov.uk/output/page4756.asp

7 *Independent*, 8 April 2002, p. 1.

8 'Powell tells Congress there must be regime change in Iraq', AP, 7 February 2002, emphasis added; *Financial Times*, 14 February 2002, p. 18.

9 Andrew and Patrick Cockburn, *Out of the Ashes: The Resurrection of Saddam Hussein* (New York, HarperCollins, 1999), p. 13.

10 Percy Craddock, *In Pursuit of British Interests: Reflections on Foreign Policy under Margaret Thatcher and John Major* (London, John Murray, 1997), p. 179

11 Interview with General Horner for a US documentary; the transcript is at www.pbs.org/wgbh/pages/frontline/gulf/oral/horner/1.html

12 Roger Cohen and Claudio Gatti, *In the Eye of the Storm: The Life of General H. Norman Schwarzkopf* (London, Bloomsbury, 1991), p. 283.

13 Cohen and Gatti, *In the Eye of the Storm*, pp. 292, 294.

14 M.E. Morris, *H. Norman Schwarzkopf: Road to Triumph* (New York, St Martin's Press, 1991), p. 256.

15 Cohen and Gatti, *In the Eye of the Storm*, p. 295.

16 For example, Andrew and Patrick Cockburn in *Out of the Ashes*, p. 22.

17 Cohen and Gatti, *In the Eye of the Storm*, p. 298.

18 Cohen and Gatti, *In the Eye of the Storm*, p. 296.

19 Cohen and Gatti, *In the Eye of the Storm*, p. 297.

20 See Anthony H. Cordesman and Abraham R. Wagner, *The Lessons of Modern War Volume IV: The Gulf War* (Boulder, Westview Press, 1996), pp. 647 f for some useful comments.

21 Cohen and Gatti, *In the Eye of the Storm*, p. 305.

22 Tim Ripley, 'Saddam Next?', *Air Forces Monthly*, May 2002, p. 20.

23 Cohen and Gatti, *In the Eye of the Storm*, p. 306.

24 Andrew and Patrick Cockburn in *Out of the Ashes*, p. 23.

25 Simon Henderson, *Instant Empire: Saddam Hussein's Ambition for Iraq* (San Francisco, Mercury House, 1991), p. 170.

26 Said K. Aburish, *Saddam Hussein: ThePolitics of Revenge* (London, Bloomsbury, 2000), p. 308.

27 See Faleh Abd al-Jabbar, 'Why the Uprisings Failed', *Middle East Report*, May-June 1992, pp. 9, 12-13.

28 *Independent*, 9 March 1991, p. 20.

29 Andrew and Patrick Cockburn in *Out of the Ashes*, p. 39.

30 *New York Times*, 30 October 1994, cited in Said Aburish, *Saddam Hussein*, p. 309.

31 Andrew and Patrick Cockburn in *Out of the Ashes*, p. 36.

32 Andrew and Patrick Cockburn in *Out of the Ashes*, p. 37.

33 Andrew and Patrick Cockburn in *Out of the Ashes*, p. 24.

34 *International Herald Tribune*, 22 April 1991, p. 5.

35 *Financial Times*, 3 May 1991, p. 4.

36 Cited in Stephen Rosskamm Shalom, *Imperial Alibis: Rationalizing US Intervention After the Cold War* (Boston, South End Press, 1993), p. 137.

37 Andrew and Patrick Cockburn in *Out of the Ashes*, p. 37.

38 *Financial Times*, 1 February 2002, Supplement, p. III.

39 *Guardian*, 15 March 2002, p. 17; *Independent*, 18 July 2002, p. 12.

40 *Guardian*, 15 March 2002, p. 17.

41 Andrew and Patrick Cockburn in *Out of the Ashes*, p. 25.

42 Cited in Noam Chomsky, *World Orders, Old and New* (New York, Columbia University Press, 1994), p. 9.

CHAPTER VIII REGIME STABILISATION, 2002

1 *Time* magazine, 13 May 2002, p. 36.

2 *Sunday Times*, 7 April 2002, p. 28.

3 *Guardian*, 6 April 2002, p. 1.

4 *Guardian*, 17 June 2002, p. 15.

5 *Guardian*, 20 February 1991, p. 1.

6 *Times*, 28 September 2001, p. 2, reporting an interview on BBC News 24.

7 *Sunday Times,* 17 February 1991, p. 3.

8 Scott Ritter, *Endgame: Solving the Iraq Problem – Once and for All* (New York, 1999), p. 133.

9 Anthony H. Cordesman and Abraham R. Wagner, *The Lessons of Modern War Volume IV*, p. 499.

10 Cited in Bob Woodward, *The Commanders* (London, Simon & Schuster, 1991), p. 291.

11 Andrew and Patrick Cockburn, *Out of the Ashes* (New York, HarperCollins, 1999), p. 34.

12 *Time* magazine, 13 May 2002, p. 38.

13 Dilip Hiro, *Neighbours, Not Friends: Iraq and Iran after the Gulf Wars* (London, Routledge, 2001), pp. 36 f.

14 Andrew and Patrick Cockburn, *Out of the Ashes*, p. 38.

15 Dilip Hiro, *Neighbours, Not Friends*, pp. 36 f.

16 Andrew and Patrick Cockburn, *Out of the Ashes*, p. 189.

17 Andrew and Patrick Cockburn, *Out of the Ashes*, p. 190.

18 *Daily Telegraph*, 8 March 1999, cited in Dilip Hiro, *Neighbours, Not Friends*, pp. 345, n. 28.

19 *Guardian*, 16 March 2002, p. 5.

20 *Guardian*, 18 March 2002, p. 18.

21 Dilip Hiro, *Neighbours, Not Friends*, p. 102.

22 Andrew and Patrick Cockburn, *Out of the Ashes*, pp. 211 f.

23 Andrew and Patrick Cockburn, *Out of the Ashes*, pp. 213 f.

24 Andrew and Patrick Cockburn, *Out of the Ashes*, pp. 46 f.

25 Charles Tripp, *A History of Iraq* (Cambridge, Cambridge University Press, 2000), p. 31.

26 Charles Tripp, *A History of Iraq*, p. 47.

27 Charles Tripp, *A History of Iraq*, p. 55.

28 Anthony H. Cordesman and Ahmed S. Hashim, *Iraq: Sanctions and Beyond* (Boulder, Westview Press, 1997, pp. 12-13, 21.

29 Anthony H. Cordesman and Ahmed S. Hashim, *Iraq: Sanctions and Beyond*, p. 22.

30 Charles Tripp, *A History of Iraq*, p. 265.

31 Yitzhak Nakash, *The Shi'is of Iraq* (Princeton University Press, 1994), p. 273.

32 Charles Tripp, *A History of Iraq*, p. 277.

33 *Newsweek*, 25 March 2002, p. 18.

34 *Newsweek*, 25 March 2002, p. 19.

35 *Newsweek*, 25 March 2002, p. 19.

36 *Newsweek*, 25 March 2002, p. 20.

37 Andrew and Patrick Cockburn, *Out of the Ashes*, p. 35.

38 *Newsweek*, 25 March 2002, p. 20.

39 *Newsweek*, 25 March 2002, p. 20.

40 *Financial Times*, 3 June 2002, p. 16.

41 *Guardian*, 15 March 2002, p. 17.

42 *Sunday Telegraph*, 17 March 2002, p. 15.

43 *Daily Telegraph*, 13 July 2002, p. 19.

44 Roland Dallas, *King Hussein: A Life on the Edge* (London, Profile Books, 1998), p. 21.

45 *Daily Telegraph*, 13 July 2002, p. 19.

46 *Times*, 13 July 2002, p. 21.

47 *Guardian*, 13 July 2002, p. 2.

48 *Times*, 13 July 2002, p. 21.

49 *Times*, 13 July 2002, p. 21.

50 *Times*, 11 July 2002, p. 15.

51 *Daily Telegraph*, 27 April 2002, p. 19.

52 *Newsweek*, 21 January 2002, p. 22.

53 *Newsweek*, 21 January 2002, p. 22.

54 BBC News Online, 31 Jan. 2002, 02:24 GMT.

55 Seymour Hersh, *New Yorker*, 24 December 2001, p. 62.

56 *Financial Times*, 3 June 2002, p. 16.

57 *Daily Telegraph*, 12 July 2002, p. 27.

58 *Daily Telegraph*, 9 April 2002, p. 27.

59 *The National Interest*, Winter 2001, p. 62.

60 *The National Interest*, Winter 2001, pp. 60, 62.

61 *Foreign Affairs*, March/April 2002, p. 38.

62 *Sunday Times*, 3 February 2002, p. 23.

63 *Observer*, 7 July 2002, p. 17.

64 *New Yorker*, 24 December 2001, p. 63.

65 *Daily Telegraph*, 16 February 2002, p. 12.

66 *Sunday Telegraph*, 7 July 2002, p. 2.

67 *Times*, 11 March 2002, p. 6.

68 *Times*, 18 July 2002, p. 17.

69 *Times*, 11 July 2002, p. 15.

70 *Guardian*, 15 March 2002, p. 17.

71 *Guardian*, 15 March 2002, p. 17.

72 Anthony H. Cordesman and Ahmed S. Hashim, *Iraq: Sanctions and Beyond*, p. 353.

73 Said K. Aburish, *Saddam Hussein: The Politics of Revenge* (London, Bloomsbury, 2000), pp. 55-59.

74 Said K. Aburish, *Saddam Hussein*, p. 59.

CHAPTER IX THE CONTROL OF OIL

1 Altrincham, 'British Policy and Organisation in the Middle East', 2 September 1945, CO 732/88/79338, cited in William Roger Loius, *Imperialism at Bay: The United States and the Decolonization of the British Empire, 1941-1945* (New York, Oxford University Press, 1978), p. 50; Bevin cited in David Dilks, *Retreat from Power* vol. II (Basingstoke, London), p. 27. Document with prefixes CO (Colonial Office) and FO (Foreign Office) can be found in the British Public Record Office in Kew.

2 US Department of State, *Foreign Relations of the United States,* 1945, volume VIII, p. 45, cited in Noam Chomsky, *Towards a New Cold War: Essays on the Current Crisis and How We Got There* (London, Sinclaire Brown, 1982), pp. 310 f.

3 Foreign Office memorandum, 'Sir F. Shepherd's analysis of the Persian situation', 28 January 1952, FO 371/98684, cited in Mark Curtis, *The Ambiguities of Power: British Foreign Policy Since 1945* (London, Zed Books, 1995), p. 91.

4 Mark Curtis, *The Ambiguities of Power*, p. 93.

5 David Dimbleby and David Reynolds, *An Ocean Apart: The Relationship Between Britain and America in the Twentieth Century* (New York, Random House, 1988), p. 212.

6 Telegram no 1979, 19 July 1958, to Prime Minister from Secretary of State, from Washington, FO 371/132 779, cited in Noam Chomsky, *Deterring Democracy* (London, Verso, 1991), p. 183.

7 'Future Policy in the Persian Gulf,' 15 January 1958, FO 371/132 778, cited in Noam Chomsky, *Deterring Democracy* (London, Verso, 1991), p. 184.

8 William Stivers, *America's Confrontation with Revolutionary Change in The Middle East (1948-83)* (Basingstoke, Macmillan), p. 5; evidence of US hostility to the withdrawal can be found in the entry for 12 January 1968 in *The Crossman Diaries*, written by Labour Cabinet Minister Richard Crossman.

9 See Michael Klare, *Beyond the Vietnam Syndrome* (Institute for Policy Studies, 1982), p. 30.

10 Carter cited in Michael Klare, *Beyond the Vietnam Syndrome*, p. 30; Komer cited in William Stivers, *America's Confrontation*, p. 93; Reagan cited in Christopher Paine, On the Beach: the Rapid Deployment Force and the nuclear arms race', in *The Deadly Connection: Nuclear War and US Interventionism* (American Friends Service Committee, 1983), p. 71.

11 Cited in Martha Wenger, 'Getting to the war on time', *MERIP Report*, November/December 1984.

12 *Janes Defence Review*, 31 March 1984, p. 467.

13 Duncan Campbell, 'Secret laws for wartime Britain', and 'If war came close we would have new masters,' *New States-man*, 6 and 13 September 1985. For an apologia for the emergency powers bills, see David Fairhall, 'Why the people must bite the US bullet', *Guardian*, 6 September 1985, p. 15.

14 Christopher Bellamy, *Independent*, 29 November 1991.

CHAPTER X REASON I

1 *Daily Telegraph*, 7 March 2002, p. 1.

2 Interview with NBC, 4 April 2002, available at www.number-10.gov.uk

3 *Sunday Times*, 7 April 2002, p. 28.

4 Cited by Bronwen Maddox, *Times*, 12 March 2002, p. 5.

5 *Guardian*, 12 March 2002, p. 1.

6 *Times*, 12 March 2002, p. 5.

7 *Times*, 12 March 2002, p. 23.

8 *Independent*, 18 March 2002, p. 13.

9 *Time* magazine, 13 May 2002, p. 28.

10 *Time* magazine, 13 May 2002, p. 34.

11 *Economist*, 24 November 2001, p. 45.

12 *Financial Times*, 12 March 2002, p. 2.

13 *Guardian* editorial, 12 March 2002, p. 17; *Observer* editorial, 7 April 2002, p. 26.

14 *Financial Times*, 20 March 2002, p. 11.

15 *Financial Times*, 16 February 2002, p. 6.

16 *Sunday Telegraph*, 24 March 2002, p. 1.

17 *Sunday Telegraph*, 24 March 2002, p. 1.

18 *Daily Telegraph*, 7 March 2002, p. 1.

19 *Financial Times*, 25 March 2002, p. 2.

20 *Financial Times*, 25 March 2002, p. 1.

21 *Daily Telegraph*, 6 April 2002, p. 9.

22 *Daily Telegraph*, 6 April 2002, p. 9.

23 *Financial Times*, 1 April 2002, p. 2.

24 *Financial Times*, 8 April 2002, p. 24.

25 *Financial Times*, 1 April 2002, p. 2.

26 *Observer*, 31 March 2002, p. 13; *Financial Times*, 1 April 2002, p. 2.

27 *Guardian*, 10 April 2002, p. 8.

28 *Observer*, 7 April 2002, p. 27.

29 *Sunday Times*, 10 March 2002, p. 2.

30 *Sunday Times*, 10 March 2002, p. 2.

31 *Sunday Times*, 10 March 2002, p. 2.

32 *Observer*, 31 March 2002, p. 13.

33 *Sunday Times*, 31 March 2002, p. 15.

34 *Guardian*, 1 April 2002, p. 2.

35 *Financial Times*, 20 April 2002, p. 2.

36 *Washington Post*, 7 April 2002, p. A22.

37 *Financial Times*, 1 April 2002, p. 2.

38 *Sunday Telegraph*, 7 July 2002, p. 2.

39 Tun Myat, interviewed by Gabriel Carlyle of **voices in the wilderness uk** and others, 16 May 2002.

40 Paragraph 8 of UN Security Council Resolution 687 refers to 'ballistic missiles with a range *greater* than 150 kilometres.'

41 *Time* magazine, 13 May 2002, p. 35.

42 'Should we go to war against Saddam?', *Observer*, 17 March 2002.

43 *Time* magazine, 13 May 2002, p. 35.

44 Scott Ritter, 'Redefining Iraq's Obligation: The Case for Qualitative Disarmament of Iraq', *Arms Control Today* (June 2000).

45 *Financial Times*, 7 March 2002, p. 20.
46 *Time* magazine, 13 May 2002, p. 34.
47 *New Yorker*, 25 March 2002, p. 75.
48 *Times*, 17 June 2002, p. 15.
49 Daniel Finkelstein, 'Saddam must go', *Times 2*, 29 October 2001.
50 *Time* magazine, 13 May 2002, p. 35.
51 *Times*, 12 March 2002, p. 5.
52 *Times*, 12 March 2002, p. 1.
53 *Times*, 12 March 2002, p. 5.
54 Peter Beaumont, Kamal Ahmed and Edward Helmore in New York, 'Should we go to war against Saddam?', *Observer*, 17 March 2002.
55 *Observer*, 17 March 2002.
56 *Observer*, 17 March 2002.
57 *Observer*, 17 March 2002.
58 *Observer*, 17 March 2002.
59 *Observer*, 17 March 2002.
60 *Observer*, 17 March 2002.
61 *Sunday Times*, 17 March 2002, p. 2.
62 *Times*, 21 December 2001, p. 12.
63 *Observer*, 17 March 2002, p. 15.

CHAPTER X REASON 2

1 *Guardian*, 13 September 2001, p. 1; *Daily Telegraph*, 26 October 2001, p. 13.
2 *Guardian*, 13 September 2001, p. 1; *Daily Telegraph*, 26 October 2001, p. 13.
3 *Time* magazine, 13 May 2002, p. 38.
4 *Daily Telegraph*, 17 September 2001, p. 11.
5 *Guardian*, 20 September 2001, p. 8.
6 *Independent on Sunday*, 7 April 2002, p. 1.
7 *Daily Telegraph*, 20 September 2001, p. 10.
8 *Daily Telegraph*, 20 September, p. 10.
9 *Financial Times*, 7 November 20002, p. 8.
10 *Foreign Affairs*, March/April 2002, p. 170.
11 *Guardian*, 15 February 2002, p. 2.
12 *Guardian*, 19 September 2001, p. 17.
13 *Daily Telegraph*, 24 September 2001, p. 9.
14 *Independent*, 25 September 2001, p. 6.
15 *Guardian*, 10 April 2002, p. 8; *Financial Times*, 8 April 2002, p. 24; *Sunday Times*, 10 March 2002, p. 2.
16 *Guardian*, 13 September 2002, p. 8.
17 *Daily Telegraph*, 19 September 2001, p. 9.
18 *Daily Telegraph*, 19 September 2001, p. 9.
19 *Guardian*, 19 September 2001, p. 2.
20 *Independent*, 20 September 2001, p. 10; *Financial Times*, 20 September 2001, p. 6; *Times*, 20 September 2001, p. 11.
21 *Guardian*, 20 September 2001, pp. 8, 2.
22 'Czechs confirm hijacker meeting', BBC News Online, 26 October, 2001, http://news.bbc.co.uk/hi/english/world/europe/newsid_1622000/1622007.stm
23 *Daily Telegraph*, 1 December 2001, p. 15.
24 *Daily Telegraph*, 18 December 2001, p. 10.
25 *Time* magazine, 13 May 2002, p. 38.
26 'Hijacker "did not meet Iraqi agent"', BBC News Online, 1 May 2002, http://news.bbc.co.uk/hi/english/world/americas/newsid_1961000/1961668.stm
27 *Daily Telegraph*, 17 September 2001, p. 1.
28 *Sunday Times*, 10 March 2002, p. 2.
29 *Guardian*, 10 April 2002, p. 8.
30 *Sunday Telegraph*, 3 March 2002, p. 24.
31 *Daily Telegraph*, 4 January 2002, p. 14.
32 'Mr Blair, point out the real links between Israel, Iraq and al Qa'ida', editorial, *Independent*, 8 April 2002, Review section, p. 3.

33 James Risen, 'Terror Acts by Baghdad Have Waned, U.S. Aides Say', *New York Times*, 6 February 2002.

34 James Risen, 'Terror Acts by Baghdad Have Waned, U.S. Aides Say'.

35 Seymour M. Hersh, 'A Case Not Closed', *New Yorker*, 1 November 1993, whole story pp. 80-92.

36 Captain Mark E. Kosnik, U.S. Navy, 'The Military Response to Terrorism', The Information Warfare Site http://www.iwar.org.uk/cyberterror/resources/mil-response/response.htm

37 'US warned of substantial Iraqi resistance to military attack,' *Financial Times*, 1 August 2002, p. 7.

CHAPTER X REASON 3

1 Anthony H. Cordesman and Ahmed S. Hashim, *Iraq: Sanctions and Beyond* (Boulder, Westview Press, 1997), pp. 352 f.

2 *Guardian*, 15 February 2002, p. 22.

3 *Independent*, 18 July 2002, p. 16.

4 *New Yorker*, 1 April 2002, p. 48.

5 *Financial Times*, 18 July 2002, p. 16.

6 *Financial Times*, 18 July 2002, p. 16.

7 Anthony H. Cordesman and Ahmed S. Hashim, *Iraq: Sanctions and Beyond*, p. 353.

CHAPTER X REASON 4

1 'Report to the Secretary-General on humanitarian needs in Kuwait and Iraq in the immediate post-crisis environment by a mission to the area led by Mr. Martti Ahtisaari, Under-Secretary-General for Administration and Management, dated 20 March 1991', which can be downloaded from the official oil-for-food website at http://www.un.org/Depts/oip/background/chron.html

2 Eric Hoskins, 'The Humanitarian Impacts of Economic Sanctions and War in Iraq', in Thomas G. Weiss, David Cortright, George A. Lopez and Larry Minear eds., *Political Gain and Civilian Pain: Humanitarian Impacts of Economic Sanctions* (Lanham/Oxford, 1997), p. 129. Dilip Hiro cites a lower figure for the Arab Monetary Fund – $190bn – perhaps this excludes private economic assets. Hiro, *Neighbours, Not Friends* (London, Routledge, 2001), p. 34.

3 Hoskins, 'Humanitarian Impacts', p. 129.

4 Hoskins, 'Humanitarian Impacts', p. 106.

5 Michael Gordon, 'US says Gulf raids hit civilian sites harder than planned', *International Herald Tribune*, 24 February 1992, cited in Mark Curtis, *The Ambiguities of Power: British Foreign Policy Since 1945* (London, Zed Books, 1995), p. 190.

6 Anthony H. Cordesman and Abraham R. Wagner, *The Lessons of Modern War, Volume IV: The Gulf War* (Boulder, Westview Press, 1996), p. 502.

7 General Bernard Trainor and Michael R. Gordon, *The Generals' War: The Inside Story of the Conflict in the Gulf* (Little, Brown and Company, 1995), p. 316.

8 Anthony H. Cordesman and Abraham R. Wagner, *The Lessons of Modern War, Volume IV: The Gulf War* (Boulder, Westview Press, 1996), p. 502.

9 Trainor and Gordon, *The Generals' War*, p. 316.

10 Middle East Watch, *Needless Deaths in the Gulf War: Civilian casualties during the air campaign and violations of the laws of war* (New York, Human Rights Watch, 1991), pp. 10, 79, 186.

11 Middle East Watch, *Needless Deaths in the Gulf war: Civilian casualties during the air campaign and violations of the laws of war* (Human Rights Watch, 1991), cited in Mark Curtis, *The Ambiguities of Power*, pp. 192 f.

12 Cordesman and Wagner, *The Lessons of Modern War, Volume IV*, pp. 502 f.

13 Cited in Francis Kelly, 'War Crimes Committed Against the People of Iraq', in Ramsey Clark and others, *War Crimes: A Report on United States War Crimes Against Iraq* (Washington DC, Maisonneuve Press, 1992), p. 54.

14 Robert Fisk, 'The in-try that holds horrors of deprivation', *Independent*, 6 March 1998.

15 Hoskins, 'Humanitarian Impacts', p. 121.

16 *Detroit Free Press*, 27 January 1992, cited in Norman Finkelstein, *The Rise and Fall of Palestine*.

17 Leon Eisenberg, M.D., 'The Sleep of Reason Produces Monsters – Human Costs of Economic Sanctions', *New England Journal of Medicine*, Volume 336(17), 24 April 1997, pp. 1248-1250.

18 Middle East Watch, *Needless Deaths in the Gulf War* (1991), p. 191.

19 Trainor and Gordon, *The Generals' War*, p. 317.

20 Roger Normand, 'Sanctions against Iraq: New Weapon of Mass Destruction', *Covert Action Quarterly* (Spring 1998), p. 5.

21 Cited in Normand, 'Sanctions against Iraq', p. 5.

22 Middle East Watch, *Needless Deaths in the Gulf War* (1991), p. 187.

23 *Report of the Secretary-General Pursuant to Paragraph 7 of Resolution 1143 (1997)*, 1 February 1998.

24 Save the Children UK, 'Iraq advocacy strategy' (London, March 2002), p. 17.

25 'Statement by Save the Children UK on Sanctions against Iraq' (New York, 10 May 2002)

CHAPTER X REASON 5

1 *New Yorker*, 25 March 2002, p. 64.

2 *Guardian*, 19 June 2002, p. 13.

3 *Guardian*, 19 June 2002, p. 13.

4 *Daily Telegraph*, 25 May 2002, p. 16.

5 Michael Howard, 'Dissident blueprint gathers support', *Guardian*, 10 July 2002, p. 4.

6 Julian Borger, 'Rebel groups reject CIA overtures down on the farm', *Guardian*, 10 July 2002, p. 4.

7 *Time* magazine 13 May 2002, p. 37.

8 *New Yorker*, 25 March 2002, p. 64.

9 Kenneth Pollack, 'Next Stop Baghdad?', *Foreign Affairs*, March/April 2002, p. 41.

10 Amberin Zaman, 'Thriving Kurdish enclave fears Saddam strike', *Daily Telegraph*, 25 March 2002, p. 16.

CHAPTER X REASON 6

[1] I am indebted to international lawyer Glen Rangwala for a detailed reading of this chapter, which has led to considerable changes in its structure and content. I have not always followed his advice, however, and he cannot be held responsible for the argument presented below.

[2] *Economist*, 26 January 2002, p. 59.

[3] An html version of the Charter is available at the website of the International Court of Justice (the World Court) at www.icj-cij.org/icjwww/ibasicdocuments.htm

[4] *Times*, 25 March 2002, p. **2.**

[5] Peter Malanczuk, *Akehurst's Modern Introduction to International Law*, p. 314.

[6] The advocacy group PeaceRights has contrasted three differing authorities in a letter to Defence Secretary Hoon, available at www.peacerights.co.uk

[7] Louis Henkin, *How Nations Behave*, pp. 141-2.

[8] *Daily Telegraph*, 21 December 1998.

[9] *Financial Times*, 19 March 2002, p. 24.

[10] *Guardian*, 16 March 2002, p. 1.

[11] Rupert Cornwell, 'The "inside-out" solution to the problem of Saddam', *Independent*, 30 July 2002, p. 11, emphasis in the original article (but not in the Resolution).

[12] All Security Council Resolutions quoted here are available at the UN website at www.un.org/documents/index.html

[13] Noam Chomsky, *Year 501: The Conquest Continues* (Boston, South End Press, 1993), p. 90.

[14] Incidentally, Resolution 678 clearly authorised the use of 'all necessary means' to bring about an Iraqi withdrawal from Kuwait *as a step towards* restoring 'international peace and security in the region'. It would be absurd to suggest that the Resolution authorised military action intended to 'restore international peace and security' *after* an Iraqi withdrawal.

[15] My thanks to Glen Rangwala for bringing this Resolution to my attention. Mr Rangwala comments that Resolution 686 'can be read as limiting the residual authority to use force against Iraq'. (Personal communication, 22 August 2002)

[16] This paragraph is based on part of a draft argument developed by Glen Rangwala (22 August 2002). I am grateful to Mr Rangwala for permission to reproduce these points.

[17] Dominic Evans, 'War on Iraq based on shaky legal ground', Reuters, 28 March 2002, 11:20 AM ET.

[18] *Observer*, 24 March 2002, p. 2.

[19] *Independent*, 11 April 2002, p. 18.

[20] *Sunday Times*, 28 July 2002, p. 1.

[21] *Independent*, 29 July 2002, p. 1. Following these reports, Tam Dalyell MP, the Father of the House of Commons, asked the British Government to place the legal advice it had received on this issue in the House of Commons Library. *Independent*, 30 July 2002, p. 2. While the famous 'dossier' of 'evidence' may one day be published, we may safely assume that these legal opinions will never see the light of day.

[22] *Times*, 9 April 2002, p. 13.

[23] *Times*, 16 March 2002, p. 18; 'Short opens rift on Iraq: Minister hints at resignation over attack', *Guardian*, 18 March 2002; *Daily Telegraph*, 30 July 2002, p. 1; letter, 'Blair's lack of resolution', *Guardian*, 29 July 2002, p. 19; *Guardian*, 31 July 2002, p. 12; *Financial Times*, 19 July 2002, p. 7 *Guardian*, 18 March 2002, p. 13.

[24] 'Kuwait warns US over Iraq action,' *Financial Times*, 19 July 2002, p. 7.

[25] *Guardian*, 27 July 2002, p. 1.

26 *Independent on Sunday*, 7 April 2002, p. 1.

27 *Independent*, 6 April 2002, p. 6.

28 *Guardian*, 10 April 2002, p. 8.

29 *Guardian*, 16 March 2002, p. 1.

30 *Independent on Sunday*, 7 April 2002, p. 1.

31 *Times*, 25 March 2002, p. **2**.

32 *Sunday Telegraph*, 24 March 2002, p. 1.

33 Cited in *New Yorker*, 1 April 2002, p. 46.

34 Cited in Matthew Engel, 'The Iraqi mutiny', *Guardian*, 9 July 2002, p. 15.

35 Dominic Evans, 'War on Iraq based on shaky legal ground'.

36 *Application of the Convention on the Prevention and Punishment of the Crime of Genocide (Bosnia and Herzegovina v. Yugoslavia (Serbia and Montenegro))*, 1993 I.C.J. 325, 440 (Sep. Op. Lauterpacht).

37 'Protocol Additional to the Geneva Convention of 12 Aug. 1949, and Relating to the Protections of Victims of International Armed Conflicts (Protocol I) of June 8, 1977', article 54, cited in CESR, *UNsanctioned suffering* (New York, 1996), p. 38.

CHAPTER X REASON 7

1 *Guardian*, 16 March 2002, p. 4.

2 *Financial Times*, 16 March 2002, p. 10; Thomas L. Friedman, 'An Intriguing Signal From the Saudi Crown Prince', *New York Times*, 17 February 2002; 'Iraq pledges to respect Kuwait', BBC News Online, 28 March 2002, http://news.bbc.co.uk/hi/english/world/middle_east/newsid_1899000/1899048.stm ; 'Saudi Arabia opposes strike against Iraq', BBC News Online, 8 February 1998 http://news.bbc.co.uk/hi/english/world/middle_east/newsid_54000/54571.stm ; *Guardian*, 21 November 2001, p. 7; 'Saudi Arabia and Iraq: anxieties on all fronts', BBC News Online, 19 February 1998 http://news.bbc.co.uk/hi/english/special_report/iraq/newsid_55000/55774.stm

3 *Daily Telegraph*, 12 March 2002, p. 16; *Guardian*, 13 July 2002, p. 15; *Times*, 13 July 2002, p. 21.

4 James Drummond, 'Arabs hold the line on Saudi peace initiative', *Financial Times*, 13/14 July 2002, p. 7; *Independent*, 18 March 2002, p. 13; 'Iraq pledges to respect Kuwait', BBC News Online, 28 March 2002, http://news.bbc.co.uk/hi/english/world/middle_east/newsid_1899000/1899048.stm ; *Times*, 5 July 2002, p. 17; 'Kuwait warns US over Iraq action,' *Financial Times*, 19 July 2002, p. 7.

5 *Independent*, 18 March 2002, p. 13; *Guardian*, 24 July 2002, p. 12.

6 *Guardian*, 11 March 2002, p. 16; *Guardian*, 16 March 2002, p. 4; *Guardian*, 16 March 2002, p. 1; *Financial Times*, 15 July 2002, p. 7; *Times*, 3 July 2002, p. 12; *Financial Times*, 17 July 2002, p. 8.

7 *Guardian*, 9 March 2002, p. 3; *Guardian*, 12 March 2002, p. 4.

8 *Independent*, 18 Mar. 2002, p. 13; *Financial Times*, 20 March 2002, p. 9; *Daily Telegraph*, 14 March 2002, p. 18.

9 *Economist*, 3 August 2002, p. 22; *Financial Times*, 12 March 2002, p. 24; Bruce Anderson, 'Palestine is a lock without a key: so it must now be forced open', *Independent*, 1 July 2002.

10 *Daily Telegraph*, 12 March 2002, p. 16; General Shahak-Lipkin cited in Israel Shahak, *Open Secrets: Israeli Nuclear and Foreign Policies* (London, Pluto, 1997), p. 34.

11 Kofi Annan, *Times*, 26 February 2002, p. 20, and 'UN chief warns against Iraq war', *Independent*, 6 August 2002, p. 1; *Independent on Sunday*, 17 March 2002, p. 2.

12 *Financial Times*, 17 July 2002, p. 18.

CHAPTER X REASON 8

1 Bob Woodward, *The Commanders* (London, Simon & Schuster, 1991), pp. 310, 313.

2 Bob Woodward, *The Commanders*, pp. 299-302, 42.

3 *Washington Post*, 28 January 2002, p. A01.

4 *Sunday Times*, 17 February 2002, s. 5, p. 4.

5 Arthur Schlesinger, *Independent*, 2 November 2001, Review, p. 5.

6 *Guardian*, 15 September 2001, p. 1.

7 *Guardian*, 26 September 2001, p. 4.

8 Bob Woodward, *The Commanders*, p. 299.

9 Seymour Hersh, *New Yorker*, 24 December 2001, p. 60.

10 Seymour Hersh, *New Yorker*, 24 December 2001, p. 59.

11 Seymour Hersh, *New Yorker*, 24 December 2001, p. 62.

12 *Newsweek*, 31 December 2001, p. 16.

13 *Newsweek*, 31 December 2001, p. 16; *Time*, 24 September 2001, p. 53.
14 Seymour Hersh, *New Yorker*, 24 December 2001, p. 62; *Newsweek* , 31 December 2001, p. 16.
15 Seymour Hersh, *New Yorker*, 24 December 2001, p. 62.
16 Seymour Hersh, *New Yorker*, 24 December 2001, p. 63.
17 *Newsweek*, 31 December 2001, p. 16.
18 Roger Cohen and Claudio Gatti, *In the Eye of the Storm: The Life of General H. Norman Schwarzkopf* (London, Bloomsbury, 1991), pp. 231 f.
19 *Financial Times*, 1 February 2002, supplement p. III.
20 *Time* magazine, 13 May 2002, p. 38.
21 *Sunday Times*, 17 February 2002, p. 28.
22 *Financial Times*, 15 March 2002, p. 19.
23 *Observer*, 23 June 2002, p. 17; *Time* magazine, 13 May 2002, p. 37; *Foreign Affairs*, March/April 2002, p. 38.
24 *Foreign Affairs*, March/April 2002, p. 38.
25 *Guardian*, 15 March 2002, p. 17
26 *Financial Times*, 25 March 2002, p. 1.
27 *Daily Telegraph*, 29 June 2002, p. 18.
28 *Air Forces Monthly*, May 2002, p. 21.
29 *Sunday Times*, 17 February 2002, p. 28.
30 Sally Buzbee, 'U.S. Capable of Quick Iraq Strike', Associated Press, 10 July 2002, http://www.washingtonpost.com/wp-dyn/articles/A51522-2002Jul10.html
31 *Observer*, 14 July 2002, p. 3.
32 Sally Buzbee, 'U.S. Capable of Quick Iraq Strike'.
33 *Foreign Affairs*, March/April 2002, p. 41.
34 *Foreign Affairs*, March/April 2002, p. 42.
35 *Financial Times*, 13 March 2002, p. 18.
36 *New Yorker*, 1 April 2002, p. 44.
37 Eric Schmitt, 'U.S. Plan for Iraq Is Said to Include Attack on 3 Sides', *New York Times,* 5 July 2002.
38 *Times*, 11 March 2002, p. 6.
39 *Daily Telegraph*, 7 March 2002, p. 2.
40 *Washingon Post*, 24 May 2002, p. A01.
41 *Guardian*, 15 March 2002, p. 17.
42 *Sunday Telegraph*, 7 July 2002, p. 2.
43 *Guardian*, 15 March 2002, p. 17.
44 *Time* magazine, 13 May 2002, p. 36.
45 *Independent on Sunday*, 24 March 2002, p.21.
46 *Time* magazine, 13 May 2002, p. 37.
47 *Times*, 12 March 2002, p. 5.
48 *Observer*, 17 March 2002, p. 1.
49 *Financial Times*, 12 March 2002, p. 2.
50 *Financial Times*, 8 April 2002, p. 24.
51 *Daily Mirror*, 30 July 2002, p. 2; 5 August 2002, p. 5.
52 *Daily Mirror*, 30 July 2002, p. 2.

CHAPTER X REASON 9

1 *Times*, 15 February 2002, p. 23.
2 *Independent*, 12 March 2002, Review section, p. 3.
3 *Guardian*, 21 March 2002, p. 24.
4 Tony Blair interviewed on NBC, 4 April 2002. The interview can be found at www.number-10.gov.uk
5 *Guardian*, 19 March 2002, p. 1.
6 *Guardian*, 13 July 2002, p. 23.
7 *Time* magazine, 1 April 2002, p. 35; *Daily Telegraph*, 12 August 2002, p. 4.
8 *Sunday Times*, 28 July 2002, p. 1; *Financial Times*, 6 August 2002, p. 2.
9 YouGov, *Sunday Times*, 23 June 2002; other polls *Guardian* 25 June 2002, and *Daily Telegraph*, 27 June 2002.
10 Fox News poll, *Times*, 11 July 2002, p. 15.
11 *Time* magazine, 1 April 2002, p. 35.

12 Ann Scott Tyson, 'Invading Iraq: Would the public go along?', *Christian Science Monitor*, 17 July 2002; 'Poll: Most Americans Back War Against Iraq', Reuters, 12 August 2002, taken from the *New York Times* website, 12 August 2002.
13 Ann Scott Tyson, 'Invading Iraq: Would the public go along?', *Christian Science Monitor,* 17 July 2002.

CHAPTER X REASON 10

1 *Financial Times*, 9 April 2002, p. 1.
2 *Financial Times*, 9 April 2002, p. 6.
3 *Financial Times*, 9 April 2002, p. 34.
4 Edward Morse and James Richard, 'The Battle for Energy Dominance', *Foreign Affairs*, March/April 2002, pp. 18, 19.
5 *Independent*, 9 April 2002, p. 21.
6 *Sunday Telegraph*, 7 April 2002, Business section, p. 4; *Independent*, 16 March 2002, p. 19.
7 *Guardian*, 18 March 2002, p. 23.
8 *Sunday Telegraph*, 7 April 2002, Business section, p. 4.
9 *Financial Times*, 16 March 2002, p. 12.
10 *Financial Times*, 16 March 2002, p. 12.
11 *Times*, 31 July 2002, p. 15.
12 *International Herald Tribune*, 20 March 1991, p. 3.
13 *Independent on Sunday*, 21 July 2002, p.19.
14 *Sunday Mirror*, 11 August 2002, p. 6.

CHAPTER XI SANCTIONS KILL

1 'Report of the second panel established pursuant to the note by the president of the Security Council of 30 January 1999 (S/1999/100), concerning the current humanitarian situation in Iraq, Annex II of S/1999/356, 30 March 1999', available from the chronology at the official oil-for-food website http://www.un.org/Depts/oip/background/chron.html ; Human Rights Watch, 'U.N. Security Council Must Ease Iraq Crisis: Humanitarian Emergency Should be Focus of Friday Debate', 23 March 2000 http://www.hrw.org/press/2000/03/iraq0323.htm
2 John Sweeney, 'How Saddam "staged" fake baby funerals', *Observer*, 23 June 2002.
3 CAFOD press release, 6 February 2001. Julian Filochowski repeated his words in a subsequent statement, 'CAFOD calls for new consensus on sanctions on Iraq', which can be found at http://www.cafod.org.uk/news/iraq20010604.shtml
4 UNICEF press release, 'Iraq surveys show "humanitarian emergency" ', 12 August 1999, (CF/DOC/PR/1999/29) available at http://www.unicef.org/newsline/99pr29.htm - the cumulative mortality estimate is available at http://www.unicef.org/reseval/pdfs/irqu5est.pdf
5 John Sweeney, 'How Saddam "staged" fake baby funerals', *Observer*, 23 June 2002.
6 'UNICEF: Questions and Answers for the Iraq child mortality surveys, BAGHDAD, 16 August 1999'. This internal document was posted for a while on ReliefWeb, www.reliefweb.int/, but now exists in the public domain only on the excellent website of the Cambridge-based Campaign Against Sanctions on Iraq (CASI) www.casi.org
7 Save the Children Fund UK, 'Ten years of sanctions: a silent war against Iraq's children', 25 July 2000, press release.
8 Sarah Graham-Brown, *Sanctioning Saddam: The Politics of Intervention in Iraq* (London, 1999), p. 79.
9 Humanitarian Panel report, paragraph 58. Report available via an entry for 7 April 1991 on http://www.un.org/Depts/oip/background/chron.html The full sentence: 'In presenting the above recommendations to the Security Council, the panel reiterates its understanding that the humanitarian situation in Iraq will continue to be a dire one in the absence of a sustained revival of the Iraqi economy, which in turn cannot be achieved solely through remedial humanitarian efforts.'
10 Human Rights Watch press release, 4 August 2000.
11 Anthony Cordesman and Ahmed Hashim, *Iraq: Sanctions and Beyond* (Boulder, Westview Press, 1997), pp. 141, 144, 127.
12 Richard Garfield, 'Changes in health and well-being in Iraq during the 1990s: what do we know and how do we know it?', in CASI, *Sanctions on Iraq: background, consequences, strategies* (Cambridge, CASI, 2000), p. 47.
13 Centre for Economic and Social Rights, *UNsanctioned Suffering: A Human Rights Assessment of United Nations Sanctions on Iraq* (New York, CESR, May 1996), pp. 37, 36.
14 *Assessment of the Food and Nutrition Situation, Iraq*, FAO, September 2000
15 Rod Nordland, 'Sanctioning Starvation ? An Oil for Food trade program has helped Iraq, but many of the country's children are still going hungry', *Newsweek* Web exclusive, 28 July 2000.
16 International Committee of the Red Cross, *Iraq: A decade of sanctions*, March 2000.
17 Eric Hoskins, 'The Humanitarian Impacts of Economic Sanctions and War in Iraq', in Thomas G. Weiss, David Cortright, George A. Lopez and Larry Minear eds., *Political Gain and Civilian Pain: Humanitarian Impacts of Economic Sanctions*

(Lanham/Oxford, 1997), p. 129. Dilip Hiro cites a lower figure for the Arab Monetary Fund – $190bn – perhaps this excludes private economic assets. Hiro, *Neighbours, Not Friends*, p. 34.

18 Eric Hoskins, 'The Humanitarian Impacts', p. 129.

19 Robert Fisk, 'The in-try that holds horrors of deprivation', *Independent*, 6 March 1998.

20 Eric Hoskins, 'The Humanitarian Impacts', p. 121.

21 UNICEF, *Situation Analysis in South-Centre Iraq* (2000) available at http://www.unicef.org/iraq/situation/sit-sou-cen.htm

22 Cited in Cordesman and Hashim, *Iraq: Sanctions and Beyond*, p. 140.

23 CASI newsletter, July 2002, p. 4.

24 Office of the Iraq Programme, 'Weekly Update (13–19 July 2002)', 23 July 2002.

25 *Economist*, 8 April 2000.

26 *Economist*, 26 May 2001.

27 *Economist*, 24 February 2001.

28 Food and Agriculture Organisation, *Evaluation of food and nutrition in Iraq*, 1995.

29 Humanitarian Panel report, para 58.

30 *Financial Times*, 28 May 2001.

31 Bertrand Russell, *In Praise of Idleness* (London, Unwin Books, 1962, first published 1935), p. 63.

32 Sarah Graham-Brown, *Sanctioning Saddam*, pp. 74 f.

33 Cited in Sarah Graham-Brown, *Sanctioning Saddam*, p. 75.

34 James Fine, 'The Iraq Sanctions Catastrophe', *Middle East Report*, January-February 1992.

35 Sarah Graham-Brown, *Sanctioning Saddam*, p. 77.

36 Sarah Graham-Brown, *Sanctioning Saddam*, p. 81.

37 Peter Boone, Haris Gazdar, Althar Hussain, *Sanctions against Iraq: Costs of Failure* (New York, Centre for Economic and Social Rights, November 1997), p. 38.

38 Dilip Hiro, *Neighbours, Not Friends*, p. 51.

39 James Fine, 'The Iraq Sanctions Catastrophe',

40 James Fine, 'The Iraq Sanctions Catastrophe',

41 Sarah Helms, 'Pressure mounts for flexibility over aid to Iraq', *Independent*, 22 November 1991.

42 *Independent*, 24 July 1991, cited in Graham-Brown, *Sanctioning Saddam*, p. 75.

CHAPTER XII NUKING IRAQ

1 'Hoon's talk of pre-emptive strikes could be catastrophic', *Guardian*, 6 June 2002.

2 Select Committee on Defence, 20 March 2002, available at http://www.parliament.the-stationery-office.co.uk/pa/cm200102/cmselect/cmdfence/644/2032008.htm

3 Richard Norton-Taylor, 'Bush's nuke bandwagon', *Guardian*, 27 Mar. 2002

4 Diane Abbott, oral questions to Geoff Hoon, 29 April 2002, available at http://www.parliament.the-stationery-office.co.uk/pa/cm200102/cmhansrd/cm020429/debtext/20429-05.htm

5 www.un.int/france/documents_anglais/020326_mae_presse_moyenorient_2.htm

6 *Sunday Telegraph*, 10 March 2002, p. 1.

7 Malcolm Rifkind, 'UK Defence Strategy: A Continuing Role for Nuclear Weapons?', 16 November 1993, *Brassey's Defence Yearbook 1994* (London, Brassey's (UK), 1994).

8 David Miller, 'Britain ponders single-warhead role', *International Defense Review*, September 1994. For more about Tactical Trident, see Milan Rai, *Tactical Trident: The Rifkind Doctrine and the Third World* (Drava Papers, 1995); and Paul Rogers, *Losing Control: Global Security in the Twenty-first Century* (Pluto Press, 2000), pp. 49 f.

9 *International Herald Tribune*, 9 August 1990.

10 *Daily Star*, 10 August 1990. This list of threats is taken from a slightly longer list compiled as an appendix in Milan Rai and Declan McHugh, *Nuclear Targeting of the Third World* (London, CND, 1991). Swedish liaison officer Major Johan Persson later claimed to have seen a 200-page document setting out US/UK plans for chemical or nuclear counter-offensives against Iraq in the event of an attack by weapons of mass destruction. Western ships carrying nuclear weapons were also given authorisation to retaliate against 'the worst': 'If exposed to the worst, they would also be allowed to use the worst themselves,' said Major Persson. *Independent*, 26 November 1991.

11 *Bulletin of Atomic Scientists*, November 1990.

12 *Observer*, 30 September 1990.

13 *Daily Mail*, 26 October 1990.

14 *Guardian*, 13 November 1990.

15 *Guardian*, 8 January 1991.

16 McGeorge Bundy, 'Nuclear Weapons and the Gulf', *Foreign Affairs*, Fall 1991, p. 84.
17 Hansard, Prime Minister's Question Time, 15 January 1991, col. 726.
18 *Guardian*, 4 February 1991.
19 *Financial Times*, 4 February 1991.
20 *Financial Times*, 6 February 1991.
21 Cited in Anthony Verrier, *Through the Looking Glass* (London, Jonathan Cape, 1983), p. 171.
22 Andrew Brookes, *The History of Britain's Airborne Deterrent: Force V* (Janes Publishing Company, 1982), p. 114; Dawish and Alexander, *Unholy Babylon: The Secret of Saddam's War* (London, Victor Gollancz, 1991), p. 33.
23 Anthony Verrier, *Through the Looking Glass*, p. 171.

CHAPTER XIII RESISTING THOUGHT CONTROL

1 The following passages are from Edward Herman and Noam Chomsky, *Manufacturing Consent: The Political Economy of the Mass Media* (New York, Pantheon Books, 1988), and Noam Chomsky, *Necessary Illusions* (London, Pluto Press, 1989).
2 Quotes drawn from my own summary in Milan Rai, *Chomsky's Politics* (London, Verso, 1995), pp. 51 f.

CHAPTER XIV TURNING BACK THE WAR

1 Noam Chomsky, *Turning the Tide* (London, Pluto, 1985), p. 252. The passage goes on to warn that 'without a background of popular understanding' civil disobedience 'may be only a form of self-indulgent and possibly quite harmful adventurism.'
2 *Time* magazine, 29 July 1985, pp. 52 f.
3 Richard Nixon, *RN: The Memoirs of Richard Nixon* (New York, Warner Books, 1978), p. 490, cited in Michio Kaku and Daniel Axelrod, *To Win a Nuclear War: The Pentagon's Secret War Plans* (London, Zed Books, 1987), p. 165.
4 Seymour M. Hersh, *The Price of Power: Kissinger in the Nixon White House* (New York, Summit Books, 1983), p. 127, cited in Michio Kaku and Daniel Axelrod, *To Win a Nuclear War*, p. 166.
5 Richard Nixon, *RN: The Memoirs of Richard Nixon*, pp. 497-499, cited in Michio Kaku and Daniel Axelrod, *To Win a Nuclear War*, p. 166.
6 *Daily Telegraph*, 24 November 2001.

CHAPTER XV WAR PLAN IRAQ

1 *Time* magazine, 12 August 2002, p. 24.
2 *Time* magazine, 12 August 2002, p. 24.
3 *Sunday Times*, 28 July 2002, p. 18.
4 *Guardian*, 25 May 2002, p. 1; *Times*, 25 May 2002, p. 19.
5 *Financial Times*, 3 June 2002, p. 16.
6 *Sunday Times*, 28 July 2002, p. 18.
7 *Financial Times*, 1 August 2002, p. 1.
8 *Sunday Times*, 4 August 2002, p. 12.
9 *Daily Telegraph*, 6 August 2002, p. 10.
10 Roland Watson, 'Conflict could soon be nuclear', *Times*, 7 August 2002, p. 15.
11 *Sunday Times*, 28 July 2002, p. 18.
12 *Sunday Times*, 4 August 2002, p. 12.
13 *Daily Telegraph*, 7 August 2002, p. 4.
14 *Daily Telegraph*, 6 August 2002, p. 10.
15 *Time* magazine, 12 August 2002, p. 24.
16 *Times*, 11 July 2002, p. 15.
17 *Guardian*, 2 August 2002, p. 15.
18 *Newsweek*, 12 August 2002, p. 32.
19 *Sunday Telegraph*, 21 July 2002, p. 28.
20 *Time* magazine, 12 August 2002, p. 25.
21 'US plan to invade Iraq raises alarms', *International Herald Tribune*, 23 July 2002, p. 1.
22 'Bush rejects Blair call for Middle East deal before Iraq attack', *Sunday Telegraph*, 4 August 2002, p. 1.
23 *Telegraph*, 19 July 2002, p. 1; *Financial Times*, 12 July 2002, p. 1; *Financial Times*, 12 July 2002, p. 12; *Sunday Times*, 28 July 2002, p. 1; 'Security clampdown heightens war fears', *Daily Mirror*, 6 August 2002, p. 2; *Observer*, 21 July 2002, p. 2, *Telegraph*, 19 July 2002, p. 12.

24 Andy McSmith, 'Slip-up raises Iraq invasion suspicions', *Telegraph*, 25 July 2002, p. 4.

25 *Observer*, 11 July 2002, p. 2.

26 'Come on in: Saddam invites US to search Iraq', *Daily Mirror*, 6 August 2002, p. 2.

27 *Independent*, 18 July 2002, p. 14.

28 *Daily Mirror*, 30 July 2002, p. 2.

29 *Time* magazine, 12 August 2002, p. 25.

30 *Daily Mirror*, 6 August 2002, p. 2.

31 'US strike ended bin Laden feud with Omar', *Times*, 3 August 2002 http://www.timesonline.co.uk/article/0,,3-373034,00.html

32 James Astill, 'Strike one', *Guardian*, 2 October 2001 http://www.guardian.co.uk/g2/story/0,3604,561557,00.html

33 Jonathan Belke, 'Year Later, US Attack on Factory Still Hurts Sudan, *Boston Globe*, 22 August 1999.

34 Mark Huband, *FT*, 8 September 1998, cited in Noam Chomsky, *9-11* (New York, Seven Stories, 2001), p. 51.

Kim Weston-Arnold

NEXT STEPS

TEN POSSIBLE ACTIONS - UK

1 **Keep Informed** Keep track of the ARROW website www.j-n-v.org
2 **Wear An Anti-War Badge** Available from ARROW, Stop The War, **voices uk**.
3 **Write To Your MP** Suggested materials on www.j-n-v.org
4 **Circulate The Stop the War/CND Petition** www.stopwar.org.uk/
5 **Circulate ARROW Anti-War Briefings** www.j-n-v.org or 020 7607 2302.
6 **Form Or Join A Local Anti-War Group** Some ideas at www.j-n-v.org
7 **Join An Email List** See www.casi.org.uk or www.j-n-v.org
8 **Host A voices uk Speaker/Roadshow In Your Town** Phone: 0845 458 2564.
9 **Sign The Pledge of Resistance** www.j-n-v.org
10 **Apply To Join The Iraq Peace Team** www.iraqpeaceteam.org

FURTHER READING

Apart from those books mentioned in the Notes:
Anthony Arnove ed., *Iraq Under Seige: The Deadly Impact Of Sanctions And War*
    (London, Pluto Press/Cambridge, Mass., South End Press, 2000)
Bela Bhatia, Jean Dreze, Kathy Kelly eds., *War and Peace in the Gulf: Testimonies of the
    Gulf Peace Team* (Nottingham, Spokesman, 2001). Also from **voices us / uk**.
Noam Chomsky, *9-11* (New York, Seven Stories, 2001)

CONTACTS - UK

ARROW, c/o NVRN, 162 Holloway Road, London N7 8DQ. Telephone: (0)20 7607
    2302. Email: info@justicenotvengeance.org Web: www.j-n-v.org
CASI, Campaign Against Sanctions on Iraq, c/o CUSU, 11-12 Trumpington Street,
    Cambridge CB2 1QA. Telephone: 0845 330 4520 (local rate); +44 1223 329131
    (international calls). Email: info@casi.org.uk Web: www.casi.org.uk
CND, 162 Holloway Road, London N7 8DQ. Telephone: (0)20 7700 2393. Email:
    cnd@gn.apc.org Web www.cnduk.org
Stop the War Coalition, PO Box 3739, London E5 8EJ. Telephone: (0)7951 235 915.
    Email: office@stopwar.org.uk Web: www.stopwar.org.uk
voices in the wilderness uk, **NEW ADDRESS** 5 Caledonian Road, London N1
    9DX. Telephone: 0845 458 2564 (local rate) +44 1424 428 792 (international calls).
    Email: gabriel@viwuk.freeserve.co.uk Web: www.viwuk.freeserve.co.uk

CONTACTS - US AND BEYOND

Iraq Action Coalition, Email: IAC@leb.net Web: http://iraqaction.org/
voices in the wilderness us, 1460 W Carmen Avenue, Chicago, IL 60640, USA.
    Ph: 773 784 8065. Email: kkelly@igc.org Web: www.nonviolence.org/vitw
Websites apart from those listed so far
Anti-sanctions groups www.notinournames.org and www.uncoverIraq.com

---

Notes   231

CONTRIBUTORS

KIM WESTON-ARNOLD

Kim Weston-Arnold is a professional photographer based in Barcelona. She travelled to Iraq as part of an international delegation in May 2002.

MILAN RAI

Milan Rai was awarded the Frank Cousins Peace Award (Research) by the Transport and General Workers Union in 1993. A founder member of the anti-war group ARROW (see below) he has edited two ARROW publications - *The Rabble Element: Police Interviews with Chris Cole and Milan Rai* (1991), and *ARROW Two Years On* (1993). They are both composed of interviews with ARROW members - some of the interviews were carried out by trained police officers. In 1998, with the support of ARROW, Milan Rai founded **voices in the wilderness uk**, a British branch of the US sanctions-breaking group, and became one of two British citizens to have been arrested for breaking the economic sanctions on Iraq by exporting medical supplies without an export licence.

EMILY JOHNS

Emily Johns is an artist based in Hastings. Her works have appeared in *Peace News*, *Resurgence*, and in a variety of materials produced by **voices in the wilderness uk**. She has contributed images to *Critical Mass: A New Vision of Our Nuclear Legacy*, and *Gene Genie: Making Decisions About Genetic Engineering*, two art/science exhibitions by the 'Critical Mass' group which she co-founded. Emily Johns is a founder member of ARROW (Active Resistance to the Roots of War).

NOAM CHOMSKY

Noam Chomsky is recognised as the dominant figure in modern linguistics. He is also the author of over thirty books of social criticism. His most recent books on US foreign policy include *9-11* (2001), *Rogue States: The Rule of Force in World Affairs* (2000), and *The New Military Humanism: Lessons from Kosovo* (1999).

ARROW

This book is an outgrowth of the work of ARROW (Active Resistance to the Roots of War), a London–based nonviolent direct action affinity group. Formed to oppose the Gulf War in September 1990, the group has held an anti-sanctions/anti-war vigil outside the Foreign Office in Whitehall from 5.30 to 7pm every Monday evening since July 1991. Since September 2001, ARROW has given away thousands of *ARROW Anti-War Briefings* free at mass demonstrations. ARROW welcomes donations to support its work. ARROW c/o NVRN, 162 Holloway Rd, London N7 8DQ. Telephone 020 7607 2302. **www.j-n-v.org**

INDEX